Obreros Unidos

———————————————||||————————————————

OBREROS UNIDOS

The Roots and Legacy of the Farmworkers Movement

———————————————||||————————————————

JESUS SALAS

WISCONSIN HISTORICAL SOCIETY PRESS

Published by the Wisconsin Historical Society Press
Publishers since 1855

The Wisconsin Historical Society helps people connect to the past by collecting, preserving, and sharing stories. Founded in 1846, the Society is one of the nation's finest historical institutions.
Join the Wisconsin Historical Society: wisconsinhistory.org/membership

The front cover was inspired by the artwork *Fighting for Worker's Rights* by Rochelle Weiner Carr. It is part of the permanent art collection at Milwaukee Area Technical College. Front cover art: foreground photo: Jesus Salas at a 1968 Obreros Unidos rally in Wautoma, Wisconsin. Photo courtesy of Jesus Salas. Background photo: members of Obreros Unidos leave Wautoma and walk along Highway 21 to Madison to petition lawmakers to provide better working conditions to migrant workers, August 15, 1966. Photo by David Giffey, WHI IMAGE ID 53386. Interior photographs are from the collection of Jesus Salas unless otherwise noted. The frontispiece photo shows Salas at an Obreros Unidos rally in 1968. The back cover shows migrant workers staging a walkout at Libby's canning company in Hartford, Wisconsin, 1968, in support of cucumber harvesters' union victory the previous year. Obreros Unidos founder Jesus Salas is pictured with a megaphone.

Photographs identified with WHi or WHS are from the Society's collections; address requests to reproduce these photos to the Visual Materials Archivist at the Wisconsin Historical Society, 816 State Street, Madison, WI 53706.

Printed in the United States of America
Cover design by TG Design; Typesetting by Integrated Composition Systems.

27   26   25   24   23   1   2   3   4   5

Library of Congress Cataloging-in-Publication Data
Names: Salas, Jesús, 1944– author.
Title: Obreros Unidos : the roots and legacy of the farmworkers movement / Jesus Salas.
Description: [Madison, WI]: Wisconsin Historical Society Press, [2023] | Includes index.
Identifiers: LCCN 2022049630 (print) | LCCN 2022049631 (ebook) | ISBN 9781976600074 (paperback) | ISBN 9781976600081 (ebook)
Subjects: LCSH: Obreros Unidos. | Agricultural laborers—Labor unions—Wisconsin—History—20th century. | Labor movement—Wisconsin—History—20th century.
Classification: LCC HD6517.W6 S25 2023 (print) | LCC HD6517.W6 (ebook) | DDC 331.88/1309775—dc23/eng/20221031
LC record available at https://lccn.loc.gov/2022049630
LC ebook record available at https://lccn.loc.gov/2022049631

♾ The paper used in this publication meets the minimum requirements of the American National Standard for Information Sciences—Permanence of Paper for Printed Library Materials, ANSI Z39.48–1992.

CONTENTS

FOREWORD

Sergio M. González

Wisconsin is changing. As has been the case in much of the Midwest, the state has witnessed significant shifts in its racial and ethnic makeup, brought on by growing Latino-, Asian-, and African-descent migrant and immigrant communities. The 2020 US census noted that, for the first time in the state's history, Latinos constituted Wisconsin's largest minority and one of its fastest-growing populations. Latino communities now abound in nearly every section of the state, from the traditional environs of Milwaukee, Waukesha, and Madison to quickly growing *colonias* in places like La Crosse, Appleton, and Arcadia.

These transformations have prompted conversations about the future of Wisconsin's social, cultural, economic, and linguistic landscapes. The memoir you're about to read, however, reminds us that while these changes may feel new, Latinos of different national backgrounds, citizenship statuses, and cultural heritages have been making a home in Wisconsin for quite some time. The stories of Jesus Salas's life in fact remind us that this state, and the Midwest as a whole, has been a central destination for Latinos for more than one hundred years.

Like Salas and his family, an overwhelming number of Latinos have been drawn to this region following the same dreams and aspirations that once drove the European immigrants who preceded them—hopes of a better life for themselves and their families. Work has served as a central draw for many. Midwestern farmers first employed Texas-born Mexicans, also known as Tejanos, in the late nineteenth century. As Salas notes, many Tejanos sought an escape from the apartheid-style segregation that plagued much of the US Southwest in the first half of the twentieth century, a system that some scholars have referred to as Juan Crow. The

Midwest offered a potential alternative both economically and socially for families like the Salases. By the early twentieth century, Tejanos were employed in every type of planting, picking, and canning imaginable; in the sugar beet harvest alone, they constituted more than three-quarters of the labor force in states like Wisconsin, Michigan, Minnesota, and Illinois. Throughout the 1950s, when Tejano migration to Wisconsin was at its peak, more than eleven thousand Tejanos traveled to the state annually, accounting for 85 percent of migrants recruited to the state.

Despite being recruited to the Midwest as a vital workforce, Salas shows, Tejano migrants encountered a less than hospitable welcome. Whether it was the cucumber fields of Wautoma or the *barrios* of Milwaukee's near south side, this group of people, part of what the historian Marc Rodriguez has referred to as the Tejano diaspora, grappled with a consistent tension. They were, by all accounts, an economic necessity, an essential workforce that kept Wisconsin's booming agricultural industry running. In nearly every field, town, or city they settled in, however, Tejanos faced discrimination at the worksite and in public life. As Salas recounts in harrowing detail, migrants working in the state often found housing that was substandard (what one state report referred to as "less-than-hovels"), wages that barely covered living expenses, nonexistent educational or health care support, and a general sense of recrimination and lack of respect from employers and receiving communities. With few forms of protective legislation on the books and limited prospects for social or economic advancement, observers often referred to migrants as "children of misfortune" and "the displaced persons of America."

Under such harsh conditions, a reader might assume that migrants had limited power to change their living and working circumstances. The historical record, however, shows us differently. As Salas recounts, Tejano migrants, galvanized by growing civil rights and labor movements around the nation, organized themselves in the mid-1960s and pushed back against these oppressive conditions. Their organizations—labor unions such as Obreros Unidos in Wautoma and student groups on campuses in Milwaukee and Madison—resisted the societal, cultural, and economic marginalization of Latinos and offered alternative visions for what belonging might mean in Wisconsin. They did so by building resilient coalitions that stretched across different Latino identities and racial and class lines, often working alongside other communities that were struggling to find a place in the state. Salas reminds us, then, that the history of migrant work and Latino settlement in Wisconsin is not merely one of dispossession. In vignette after vignette, he presents us with a history of defiance and resistance.

For many Wisconsinites, the histories that Salas presents in this book might be new and perhaps even startling, a troubling challenge to the narrative that Midwesterners are preternaturally hospitable (see: "midwestern nice"). In recounting the story of Tejano settlement and struggle in Wisconsin, Salas unsettles this story line and, in the process, demonstrates the power of personal narrative and the lasting political implications of retrieving and restoring Latino history. It is necessary work that follows in a long literary tradition. Mexican Americans have been writing autobiographies since American colonization began in the mid-nineteenth century in the area that we now know as the US Southwest. Since the end of the Mexican–American War, scholar Genaro Padilla notes, this form of memorialization has served as an "utterance to the threat of social erasure."* Jesus's story fights a similar archival and cultural deletion, showing how memoirs can serve as a form of historical recovery. His book joins a storied history of Tejano memorialization in the Midwest, including works such as Tomás Rivera's . . . y no se lo tragó la tierra, Elva Treviño Hart's *Barefoot Heart*, Maria Elena Lucas's *Forged Under the Sun*, and Saúl Sánchez's *Rows of Memory*. Along with each of these memoirs, Salas reminds us that Latino history is midwestern history.

Memoirs, however, can be a strange model through which to tell a community's history. They are by design reflections on one individual's life. This style of writing can be even more problematic when telling the history of a social movement. An activist's autobiography can tend to accentuate what we might refer to as a hero narrative, where a singular charismatic leader recounts his or her extraordinary ability to create a movement from scratch and galvanize a group of people with pithy speeches and catchy slogans. Any participant of a social movement knows, however, that a movement is only as strong as its members, and that

---

* Genaro T. Padilla, *My History, Not Yours: The Formation of Mexican American Autobiography* (Madison: University of Wisconsin Press, 1993), 4.

movement building is arduous work. In retelling his story, Salas resists that hero narrative, demanding that the reader broaden the frame beyond the singular to look at the communal. Like migrant labor, Salas notes, social movement building was family work. It required the participation of young and old, mother and father, son and daughter. And while agricultural labor unions such as Obreros Unidos may have been new to Wisconsin, Salas acknowledges that the organization was not his own novel invention; instead, he reminds us that Obreros Unidos drew upon a long lineage of mutual aid that stretches back to the Texas-Mexico Borderland. Understood less as a personal history and more as a recounting of an entire community's becoming, Salas's story then serves a form of "collective self-affirmation" for a Latino community searching and demanding citizenship and a full sense of belonging in Wisconsin.*

This memoir and the lessons it offers arrive at an opportune time. As Latino communities begin to grow in new outposts across Wisconsin, many new arrivals find themselves in similar positions as the Tejano migrants who came before them. In struggling farms and rural towns that have witnessed a net population decline over the past few decades, Latino immigrants have been recruited to work in dairy, meatpacking, and agricultural industries. They have become, in a word, essential. Their settlement may offer a lifeline and opportunity for revival for these parts of Wisconsin, not just economically but socially and culturally as well. Many of their neighbors, however, have too often failed to incorporate these more recent immigrants into the fabric of their communities, instead keeping them at arm's length because of their different mother tongue, or their darker skin, or their contingent immigration status.

The history of Tejano migrants and their legacy of struggle in Wisconsin tells us that these divisions can't last. As Salas notes throughout this book, a community's longing for dignity and recognition is much too strong to keep a people subjugated for long. Just as those migrant farmworkers once did in Wautoma in 1966, these "new Wisconsinites" might soon decide to turn to social movements. If they do, they'll be able to draw

---

* Silvio Torres-Saillant, "The Latino Autobiography," in *Latino and Latina Writers. Vol. 1, Introductory Essays*, Ed. Alan West-Duran (New York: Thomson/Gale, 2004), 66.

upon a robust lineage of mutual aid and community organizing, one that has roots in some of the oldest Latino communities in the state. Thanks to the work of Salas—the activist and the historian—Latinos who continue to search for a full sense of belonging in our state will have plenty of history to draw upon.

PROLOGUE

Homesteading along Comanche Creek

B efore the land speculators swarmed into the floodplains where the Nueces River begins to straddle the Rio Grande on its way to the Gulf of Mexico, this was the winter home of the indomitable Comanche. They had earlier separated themselves from the Shoshone and on horseback dominated the territory from north of the Arkansas River to the doorstep of where my grandfather would homestead at the beginning of the twentieth century. The *arroyo* that ran south of my grandfather's homestead would swell with spring rains before the dams at Del Rio and Laredo, Texas, were built. It still bears their name, Comanche Creek. Yearly, the spring rains would fill the sandy loam in this semiarid climate with rich topsoil and minerals from the skirt of the Sierras.

The Comanche had kept the Eastern Apache west of what the Spaniards called the Llano Estacado—the Staked Plains of Texas. They had made peace with the Kiowa on the northeast and with the Eastern Apache tribes to the west, and kept Spanish expansion from linking their Mexican settlements with those at the mouth of the Mississippi and east to the Florida peninsula. Unlike in California, the Comanche had prevented the Catholic mission system from its aim, pacification and conversion. At the time of Mexican independence, in the second decade of the nineteenth century, all that viably remained of the mission system were fragments around present-day San Antonio.

It is common knowledge that the Comanche and Apache raided Mexican settlements across deserts and mountains. Less is known about how the Mexican Native tribes and communal villages, collectively known as Coahuiltecan, collaborated with the Comanche in expanding their presence deep into north central Mexico. Fully one-third of the Comancheria, as their dominion was known in the mid-eighteenth century, was made up of Coahuiltecan Natives from communal lands, Mexican mestizos, and Afro-Mejicas.

In the 1830s the US sent forays led by General William Clark, of Lewis and Clark fame, into the Comancheria. A young artist, George Catlin, had joined the expedition to report on their explorations and in the process drew and painted the most extraordinary images of the Native tribes. Catlin observed the magnificent Comanche cavalry, which included warriors wearing military artifacts from conquests of both Spanish colonial and Mexican soldiers: spears, swords, breastplates, and helmets. At first sight, the Americans thought they had encountered a unit of Mexican cavalry, as the armor shone brightly in the sun. In fact, it was Comanches led by a Mexican warrior, Jesus ("hay-soos").

A few decisive battles led to the defeat of the Comanche nation, which was as weakened by disease as by any cannon. By the time of my grandfather's birth in 1865, Union soldiers had taken control of the new frontier and established a string of forts to defend it. Over the next decades, genocide of the Native peoples continued until the US government enacted its ultimate solution, forcing American Indians onto reservations. The Coahuiltecas from the Comancheria melted back into their native lands south of the Rio Grande to seek cover among the eastern skirt of the Sierra Madre. These now include American Indian tribes from the Midwest, such as the Kickapoo, and some Choctaw and Seminoles from the southeastern United States. With them were people seeking freedom from slavery in the American South they had welcomed and sheltered along the way.

But there was no peace for southern Coahuila during my grandfather's youth. The invasion of the French and their expansion to the top of the southern plateau of Mexico forced my grandfather Teofilo's family from Laguna, a group of lagoons created by draining mountain rivers, to the mining town of Monclova among the Coahuiltecas tribes. Later he established his first family in Nueva Rosita, Coahuila, after President Benito Juarez, who had been exiled to Mexico's northern states, organized a Mexican force to remove the French from the area. Juarez recognized these lands as *autónomas*, distinct from the Mexican government, and advocated for full rights on behalf of the Afro-Mejicas, descendants of formerly enslaved people who had fled the plantation and traveled south with the

My grandmother Rita Rodriguez, on my mother's side, was descended from communities
of formerly enslaved people who found refuge with the Comanche.

Comanche and Kickapoo and now made a permanent home in north central Coahuila, Mexico. Juarez's presence continued long after brothers
Porfirio and Felix Díaz, from his home state of Oaxaca, overthrew him and
undid his reforms to establish their dictatorship.

The Magón brothers, Ricardo and Enrique, and the *mutualista* organizations along the Texas Borderland, under the name el Partido Liber al
Mexicano (PLM; Mexican Liberal Party), organized a resistance to the Díaz
dictatorship. Along the Borderland, they organized mutual aid societies
to oppose the apartheid-style system of the Deep South, resisted the
emerging political power of the Catholic Church, and organized miners
against the US multinational industrial companies that had been welcomed by the Díaz regime. In addition to strikes and uprisings, they led
an armed revolt against the Díazes.

These conditions led my grandfather Teofilo to leave the turmoil of
the mines in the Monclova area. He married Maria Jenobeba Lopez, a
Native Coahuilteca from the village of Musquiz, moved north across the
Rio Grande, and settled in 1906 along Comanche Creek in Crystal City,

My grandmother on my father's side, Maria Jenobeba Lopez Salas

Texas. Crystal City, in the first decade of the twentieth century, as well as neighboring settlements that would later be called the Winter Garden region, were abuzz with the discovery of artesian water. All of the settlements have names that attest to the founding of a reliable source of water and other natural resources: Crystal City, Carrizo Springs, Big Wells. Speculators obtained rights to immense tracts of land such as Catarina, Seven D, and the ninety-six-thousand-acre Cross S ranch in Zavala County. They began to sell the land in both large and small tracts, setting aside ten thousand acres for Crystal City. When the railroad spur came to the area, all that was needed was cheap labor to exploit the fertile region that now, with an abundance of water, could grow crops year-round, especially in the mild winters.

My grandfather and several dozen fellow settlers had been attracted to Crystal City by the fact that they could sharecrop and after several harvests have a chance to own the parcel of land that they were clearing with mule-led teams, crude implements, and few tools. For every acre that they cleared and irrigated, a new family arrived. In a vast, empty area, Zavala County's acreage was nearly eight hundred thousand acres. The total population of the county, according to the 1900 US census, was 792 inhabitants. It would more than double, to 1,882 residents, in the next ten years. The extension of the railroad forty miles from Uvalde and the huge multistory ice plant in the middle of the downtown allowed farmers to fill the refrigerated railcars with fresh vegetables and link the Winter Garden to the rest of the nation. The railroad spur allowed farmers to diversify. In addition to Bermuda onions and spinach, they grew citrus, pecans, leaf crops, cabbage, and melons that could now be shipped on refrigerated rail wagons to markets in the Midwest and far into the Northeast.

The 1910 Mexican Revolution upended this emerging system. As revolutionaries fought to end the dictatorship of Porfirio Díaz and establish Mexico as a constitutional republic, chaos spilled over from the US side of the border. For the only time since their homesteading in the Texas Winter Garden region in 1906, my grandparents became concerned about the safety of their respective families in Nueva Rositas and Monclova and returned to southern Coahuila in 1915. My grandfather Teofilo had a son, Miguel, in Nueva Rositas, and my grandmother Jenobeba had left her family, including a daughter, Sapopa, in Monclova. As war came to my grandfather's former homeland, he now needed a safe conduct, a military pass to travel to visit family. My grandmother spoke of this trip, but her impressions of the one-hundred-mile-plus journey by a two-mule wagon were not what I wanted to hear. She described camping out in the middle of nowhere surrounded by mesquite trees, tall brush, and the ever-present varieties of thorn-bearing cacti, which were a nuisance when traveling at night. She told me about when the mules had not been properly tied and they became spooked during the evening and ran off. My grandparents spent over half a day searching for the mules and bringing them back to the wagon. I wanted to hear about the revolution, the warring parties, and the battles, especially when she remembered that the commanding officer who signed the safe-conduct pass embraced my grandfather. Why? Did they know each other? How? Had they fought together? Either she did not know or she didn't tell me.

When my grandparents returned to Crystal City, the road was filled with fearful travelers fleeing northward to the Borderland already overflowing with an abundance of workers.

—ii—

The original settlement in Crystal City where my grandparents homesteaded was at the low end of the floodplains. Before the dams were built in Del Rio and south of Laredo, the spring rains would fill not only the Frio and Nueces Rivers but also the dry arroyos, including Comanche Creek up the road and Turkey Creek, which would flood to right behind the Salas homestead. Spring floods would bring rainwater gushing to the end of West Holland Street, which began one block south of my grandparents' home in the original settlement, later to be known as the Mexico Grande neighborhood. While settling on higher ground would have avoided these yearly floods, the city was built exactly where the speculators wanted the workers, close to the fertile lands that needed to be cleared, cultivated, and harvested.

The Anglo minority colonists built their segregated commercial center on higher ground, southeast of Mexico Grande. The nonranching Anglos resided primarily on the western side of downtown. When the surge of Mexican refugees arrived after 1910, they settled east of the downtown area, in a barrio that would be called El Avispero, or the Beehive. Unlike the original settlement, where the homes included ample yards for children to play, chicken coops, and an outdoor toilet, homes in the new neighborhood were built extremely close together, like a beehive. At the southeastern side of the segregated commercial center, a new barrio, Mexico Chico, arose to accommodate the final wave that migrated there after World War II.

Most of the families to arrive after 1910 came with few resources. Many constructed mud huts, crudely built adobe structures. Others made makeshift shelters out of a variety of discarded materials to protect themselves from the elements. Most shelters had dirt floors and no sewer system. In the winter, families built large mesquite fires and then placed the hot coals in a tub half-filled with dirt, situated at the center of the house to provide heat, a method that could be toxic for the inhabitants. These conditions continued until midcentury. Living in my grandmother's home during

One of the makeshift shelters made by Mexican settlers in Crystal City in the 1930s

my childhood, I was responsible for taking out the ashes in the winter mornings while my older brothers brought in the live coals from the mesquite fires outside. The Anglo colonists' neighborhood was the first to receive city services such as sewerage and electricity. Our neighborhood, Mexico Grande, remained in the dark throughout my childhood in the 1940s and 1950s.

The railroad that had brought the hope of more jobs for Mexican laborers and more profits for the speculators was built right through the center of town to service the onion- and spinach-processing and packing sheds. It was built right next to Mexico Grande. My grandfather's homestead property was a mere two blocks west of the new railroad line. The massive ice plant built on the other side of the railroad tracks would produce the ice that would fill the refrigerated cars packed with fresh produce for the rest of the nation. The railroad tracks were an iron barrier between the minority Anglo colonists and the Mexican Americans and later-arriving Mexican families.

The Mexican segregated commercial district would emerge immediately west of the railroad tracks. The Anglo institutions—Zavala County

Courthouse, its jail, the City of Crystal City municipal services—would all be located on the south side of the railroad tracks, with the packing sheds acting as a buffer from the exclusively Anglo-owned businesses that became known as the downtown.

Extralegal means were set in place to prevent the majority Mexican American population from participating in the political process. The small Anglo minority, never exceeding 15 percent of the population, maintained control of all political institutions only by keeping the majority of the population uninformed and illiterate, unable to properly understand or design the means to overcome its oppression. Here, the segregated school system was essential, with its separate but unequal educational mission.

Most pernicious were the extralegal means created to deprive the majority population from participating in the political process. As the Deep South had done after Reconstruction, when extralegal means to keep formerly enslaved people from voting were established, the minority Anglo colonists in Texas began to create barriers to voting for those released from slavery, their descendants, and Mexican Americans, some of whom were descendants of the Mexicans who had joined the Texas independence movement. Texas adopted the poll tax as Crystal City was being organized in 1902. It would keep the minority Anglo colonists in power for nearly half a century.

My grandmother kept the receipts for each of the poll taxes paid by my grandfather Teofilo in 1913, 1915, 1917, and 1919. When asked, she didn't know if he paid them other years, if he voted, or for whom he voted. What she did remember is that he singled himself out. The poll tax was enacted to prevent the participation of Mexican Americans in local politics. By registering to vote, by paying the poll tax, my grandfather put himself on the list as opposing "Jim Crow." He encouraged others to do the same.

Becoming a US citizen, paying the poll taxes, and maintaining the documentation of such became essential in the Salas family's ongoing journey to and from central Coahuila, Mexico, where both of my grandparents' extended families continued to reside. Along with the 1915 poll tax receipt, my grandmother Beba kept a receipt of a military pass to travel from the Texas Borderland when she and my grandfather visited their respective families in the interior of Coahuila. These citizen and poll tax documents were essential as the economic recession set in and the deportation activities of the Mexican Repatriation began in the 1930s. In fact, it wasn't a "repatriation." Over half of those being deported had been born in the United States, most of them still children at the time of deportation. Those families that were forcefully removed had nothing to go back to but war and chaos. Some who anticipated they would be forced back to Mexico with their American-born children moved hundreds of miles farther north to avoid the Texas Rangers–led vigilantes now masked as a "deportation force."

My grandmother Beba spoke of widespread fear of deportation by all, even those who had documentation to stay. An overabundance of workers existed before the Depression; there was not enough work for all the new

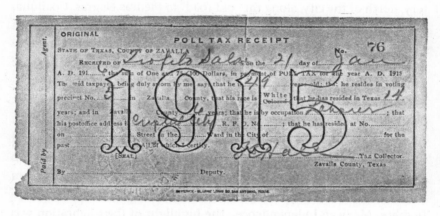

My grandfather Teofilo Salas's poll tax receipts from 1915 and 1919

arrivals. Many just kept going north, after they saw the poor condition of the communities of the once-thriving Winter Garden region.

Those pioneers who continued to be excluded from the county and city political process by extralegal means and were denied basic human services began to organize their own institutions to help themselves. In Crystal City, Texas, in the late 1920s, Mejicanos first organized a *sociedad funeraria* (funeral society) to honor the remains of their loved ones. Even in death Mejicanos would be segregated, as the Anglo colonists maintained a separate burial ground.

The sociedad funeraria was named after the Catholic priest Miguel Hidalgo, father of the 1810 movement for Mexican independence from Spain. The mutualistas acquired a piece of land for the *panteon*, or cemetery, north of the city, along the "old road" to Piedras Negras, Coahuila, Mexico, where some of the first land was cleared for cultivation between the Comanche and Turkey Creeks. They named the segregated cemetery Benito Juarez, after the indigenous Mexican president who had laid the groundwork for land reform and a modern secular government. The naming of the mutual aid society and of the Mexican cemetery should not be overlooked. With the Anglo minority colonists preventing the Mexican American and immigrant communities from participating in US political institutions and organizations, the mutualistas built their own, based on the ideals that were being played out in their home country. Excluded from American Fourth of July events, Mexicans instead celebrated el 16 de Septiembre, Mexican independence. The highlight of the celebration was "El Grito," literally "the yell" for independence. It was a collective expression, a public display for liberty—liberty from oppression then from Spain, now from the minority Anglo colonists and their system of apartheid.

La Sociedad Funeraria Miguel Hidalgo then bought land to construct an office for its meetings in the growing Mexico Chico barrio southeast of the segregated downtown area of Crystal City. In front of the office, they constructed an outdoor plaza for membership meetings and especially for the *fiestas patrias* (national celebrations). The Mexico Chico neighborhood had accommodated most of the recent arrivals between 1910 and 1930. The sociedad initiated the organization of the celebrations, maintained the cemetery El Panteon Benito Juarez, and administered the funerary expenses and the purchase and construction of the plaza for community meetings.

The segregated school my brothers and I attended in Crystal City was housed in a converted World War II family internment center.

The sociedad funeraria spent weeks preparing to celebrate Mexican independence and raised funds through a competition for *reina del 16*, or queen of Mexican independence. The young woman was not selected solely for her beauty, but for how many votes (cents) she could raise for the mutual aid society's coffers. Over the years, the wooden platform stage was removed, one of concrete was built, and the yard was paved.

In the spring, the focus of the celebration was how the ragtag Mexican army, led by President Juarez's most famous general, Ignacio Zaragoza, defeated the French army at the Battle of Puebla, el Cinco de Mayo, May 5, 1863. In the 1930s the mutualistas held mock battles reenacted by children representing the brave troops of General Zaragoza and the defeated French troops. My uncle Julian informed me that none of the children wanted to be French on that day. Later, in the late 1940s, when I attended the one-room neighborhood segregated school run by Ms. Suze Salazar, she taught us to declaim on el Cinco de Mayo and el 16. For weeks we recited the patriotic poems and verses for the el 16 event. We all had to learn and recite verses to "La Patria (The Fatherland)" and "La Bandera (The Flag)." Ms. Suze recommended the best performers to perform on the fiestas patrias. On Mother's Day, we recited the poems for our mothers.

The same bond that brought the impoverished community together to form the sociedad funeraria was evidenced by the establishment and networking of key services and businesses, including butcher shops, *molinos de maize* (corn mills), and grocery or general stores to sell the meat and tortillas. My grandfather Teofilo, along with our neighbor Polina, would herd the steers and goats in the nearby fields into the Mexico Grande barrio to be butchered. Don Amado Coronado, who lived across the street from my grandparents' home, processed and sold the meat to the barrio residents. Next to the Coronados lived Don Jesus and Dona Trine. They barbecued the beef heads from Don Amado in a pit and sold them on weekends. During the week the Coronados and their son Felix made candy with milk from Polina's cows and pumpkin pieces frosted with cane sugar, *dulce de calabaza*. He bought the pumpkins from Ernesto Martinez, who marketed local food products. As a youth my father would accompany Polina to buy goats in auctions in La Pryor, eighteen miles away, and herd them back. During the trip, Polina studied each and every animal. By the time they returned, he knew which goats would be butchered immediately, which would be sold, and which he would keep and breed.

—||—

The population in Zavala County increased from less than two thousand in 1910 to more than ten thousand in 1930, when the Great Depression devastated the four-county Winter Garden region. The land speculators lost their investment and all their obligations to sharecropping settlers like my grandparents. The Depression wiped out the sharecroppers' dreams, the family farms, and most of the small farmers who had emerged over several decades of settlement. The sharecroppers lost the rights to the land that they had worked for more than two decades. When the economy recovered, corporate farming and large-scale ranching was the new face of the economy. For the Mexican American barrios, survival meant fleeing apartheid and a feudal economic structure. Barrio members were forced to look for work outside the area.

The migration outside the region reflected the way we lived in our respective barrios as a community. The work crews were made up of extended family members, friends, and neighbors. My grandparents with their young family would later join these migrations, first to explore for work along the Texas coastal counties and later to the Texas panhandle, where farmers were cultivating large tracts of land. From there, my grandfather showed my father the way north to the Great Lakes region.

In the 1940s, my grandparents' migrations were seasonal, and they never gave any thought to permanent resettlement. The goal was to find work somewhere else so they could stay and survive at home in Crystal City, Texas. They always thought to return, to save the homestead, and to keep the basic structure of businesses and services viable. Before my grandfather passed, he showed my father how to get to the Great Lakes region and Wisconsin from the cotton fields of the Texas panhandle. The journey north was taken in small steps. From the cotton fields in the panhandle, our first trips were east of Oklahoma and later as far as the outskirts of West Memphis to harvest strawberries in the spring. Some of our Crystal City neighbors traveled straight north, to the plains of west Kansas and Nebraska to hoe and thin sugar beets. Before we arrived in the fertile fields west of Wisconsin's Kettle Moraine, we found that the frost thaws earlier in north central Illinois, and we found asparagus sprouting as the earth warmed the soil in Henry, Illinois, our first stop in the migrant cycle.

1

From the Borderland
to the Midwest

Mexican and South Texas workers began migrating seasonally to the Great Lakes region in the 1950s, when the area's agriculture was becoming a national industry leader in food processing for a wide variety of fruits and vegetables. Workers left their homes in early spring, as soon as the frost receded, to begin the planting, cultivating, and harvesting of these crops, returning south when the growing season ended late in the fall.

The pattern of migration followed long-established routes now influenced by the pattern and cycle of the region's growing season. The Borderland migrants' route followed the railway across the Texas panhandle and the lower plains. Some of my family's neighbors would journey to the lower plains states of Nebraska and Kansas in springtime to cultivate sugar beets and then return through the Texas panhandle to pick cotton before returning to the Winter Garden in fall.

Other migrants would leave Texas through Texarkana, cut across Arkansas, and make their way to Michigan and Ohio. Occasionally, migrant workers would follow this road but continue to straddle the Mississippi and then follow Highway 51 to north central Illinois to harvest asparagus, our group's first crop of the cycle. The alternate route was to go straight north across Oklahoma, turn east at Joplin, Missouri, across the Ozarks through St. Louis, and pick up Highway 51 on the other side of the Mississippi.

My parents, Argentina and Manuel Salas, at the Waushara County
Fair in 1958

My father, Manuel Salas, first started migrating as a young man with
a group of bachelor friends, and as they married and had children, the
group grew. During my childhood and teen years, we traveled with a large
crew that expanded from our extended family, friends, and neighbors to
include families from other neighborhoods and, later, neighboring communities. We usually started with the asparagus harvest in Illinois in the
early spring. Some of our hometown neighbors kept going north past
Oklahoma and across Iowa to cultivate sugar beets in the Red River Valley
of eastern North Dakota and western Minnesota, while my family went to
Hartford, Wisconsin, for several weeks of hoeing and thinning sugar beets.
Afterward, we met up for the cucumber harvest in Wisconsin's Central
Sands region. Some of our group would stay in the area for the potato
digging and warehousing, but my family usually moved south of Lake
Michigan to pick tomatoes at that time.

Following my father's lead, the adults fastidiously planned the trip
north each year. We traveled in a caravan to look out for and help each
other, especially for those families who had never made the trip. The
caravan included at least two 2.5-ton, canvas-topped trucks that carried
more than twenty persons each, several pickup trucks with plywood-
constructed cabs that held eight to ten people depending on their age,
and several cars. All the drivers knew before departure where the major
stops would be for refueling, eating, and resting for the three-day, fifteen-
hundred-mile trip.

The trucks rode at the head of the caravan, with my father driving the
front one. Everyone had to follow and stay close to the lead truck because
it contained precious replacement parts, extra tires, and tools to maintain
the vehicles in operation. Inevitably, we had mechanical problems; although my father maintained his vehicles meticulously, not all members
of the caravan did likewise. Over the years, we avoided serious accidents,
but anything else that could have gone wrong, did. Whatever travelers
might think about today's freeway system, those minor inconveniences
pale in comparison to the adventures of traveling two-lane US highways
in the late forties and early fifties.

Crossing the Ozarks going north on US Highway 35 and traveling
northeast across St. Louis was the most challenging because of the mountains and rough terrain. Heading straight on Highway 35 to Minnesota
and getting caught in a late spring snowstorm could be deadly, and the
alternative, driving north through the Mississippi Delta and West Memphis and then Cairo, Illinois, could help you avoid the cold, but the spring
floods could make the route impassable for days at a time. We always had
limited resources and delays on the roads, and costly mechanical problems
could leave us stranded in places where we were unwelcome.

Most of the delays were human errors. We got lost! Vehicles would lose
contact with the main caravan; drivers didn't and sometimes couldn't
follow maps. Unexpected detours and unplanned route changes caused
confusion.

Even on the best of trips, when the weather was good and mechanical
problems absent, it was a difficult journey. The majority of the passengers
were women and children who had to travel in severely crowded, not to

mention unsafe, conditions. Although there were scheduled stops every several hours, human and health needs compelled us to stop more often, especially for the children. Life and death proceeded on their own, and we saw children fall ill, mothers miscarry, women give birth, and old people die on these trips. These families stayed together over a decade, and their numbers grew from several extended families to more than five hundred workers and at least that number of children in nearly half a dozen crews.

Although we children didn't realize it at the time, the early spring departure from Crystal City, Texas, to Henry, Illinois, was due to our dire economic conditions. The harvest of asparagus, which was the first in the chain of cultivating and harvesting seasons in the Great Lakes region, did not begin until the frost receded in May. In 1957–58, my father was making plans for us to depart in mid-April, even though departing so early would mean problems finding housing and steady employment.

The wood-frame barracks that housed us in Henry were not adequate for the cold weather associated with early spring. The housing units were constructed out of two-by-fours covered with non-grooved slats and tar paper. On the corners and by the windows, where the tar paper had worn, wind would whistle through. The only heating was provided by woodstoves located in the kitchen and used for cooking; the bedrooms were unheated. Someone would have to get up early every morning to start the fire for heating and cooking. In the evening, the embers had to be banked to avoid starting the fire over from scratch the following morning. Heat was unnecessary in late June and early July, when the units were so unbearably hot that we sat outside well after sundown. Whether too cold or too hot, a full night's sleep in the barracks was difficult to come by.

Beyond the problems of heating and cooling, the units had no electricity or running water. The field supervisor attempted to alleviate our power needs by providing us with a gasoline engine that powered one electrical line to one room in each of the units. Since we harvested the asparagus crop either early in the morning or late in the afternoon to maintain its freshness, he ran the gas engine only at dawn and dusk. We awoke, washed, and ate breakfast in the dim light of a single bulb, before the break of dawn. Likewise, when we harvested late in the afternoon, we worked until sundown. By the time we got to the camp from the field, it was almost dark. Again, we had to wash, cook, and eat after sundown. That single flickering light bulb, as meager as it might seem, was in fact a godsend, as otherwise we would have been groping in the dark preparing for work or arriving from work and preparing to go to bed in pitch darkness.

The field supervisor addressed the lack of running water by permanently parking a tractor by the water well. Normally water would be extracted from the well by a long-handled, mechanical hand pump that had to be primed. With the tractor turning a belt attached to the pump, large quantities of water could be drawn to supply the more than a dozen families in the camp. The tractor would fill a large open-faced hundred-gallon tub, built over a makeshift shower stall with a pipe running downward to a faucet. As soon as mothers heard the tractor motor, they would send their husbands or one of the older children to draw water for coffee, to wash dishes, to fill the jugs for the field, and more. All other times, families had to pump water by hand.

Washing, bathing, and doing laundry presented the greatest challenges while living in facilities that had no running water or electricity. Water pumped from wells around the Great Lakes region is extremely cold, especially to folks from south central Texas and northern Mexico, where the intense sunlight can warm well water in a short period of time. This was not the case in northern Illinois or central Wisconsin. Exposing the hundred-gallon tank to the sun all day warmed the water somewhat, but for washing, our mothers had to build huge fires and heat cauldrons of water to a boil to wash our soiled work clothes.

—ıı—

Arriving in Illinois a month before the launch of the asparagus harvest meant that we had to look for odd jobs. One major problem was that we were the only Mexican migrants in the area and the authorities in the public school system knew it. While farther south the authorities might have turned a blind eye to truancy, in Henry we children were not allowed to work in the Potter family's plant nursery downtown during school hours. We could work after school and during weekends, which we did, but not during the day while school was in session. Besides nursery work, the other principal job available in springtime was cleaning and pruning yards. The advantage of arriving early to do the pre-asparagus work was that we could fit it in before moving north for the next crop so it didn't affect the rest of the migrant route.

Droughts or extreme rainfall could mean the end of a particular harvest or the hoeing and thinning of a particular crop. We would have to wait several weeks until the beginning of the next harvest. Once we were thrown out of the harvesting cycle by the whims of nature, we lost income and had to spend what money we had to survive instead of sending payments to the homestead in Crystal City. Lost income meant we had to look for additional work after the end of the migrant cycle, which often meant working the tomato harvest.

We picked tomatoes in a number of communities in northeastern Illinois and northwestern Indiana for Libby's Blue Island, Illinois, canning plant. We picked tomatoes until the frost ended the harvest and chased us south, usually in late October. While picking tomatoes, my father broke up the monotony by dividing the family into two groups and organizing a competition to see who could fill the most half-bushel crates. He provided group and individual prizes as an incentive to work harder. The awards included small amounts of money or treats like stopping at a hamburger stand after work, eating all the ice cream we wanted, or taking a trip on a day off.

My older brothers and I were always petitioning our father to allow us to go to downtown Chicago by ourselves. He granted this only if we picked the standard for a field hand, or *mano*. Once he granted our trip, we had to earn spending money by staying after the harvest and loading the tomato-filled crates into immense semitrailers parked at the end of the tomato fields. Our father would pay us one cent for loading them while in the fields and another cent to load them onto the semitrailers, which would take them directly to Libby's processing plant in Blue Island. This meant that after an eight-hour day, we would stay in the field for another two to four hours. Sometimes the semitrailers arrived late, and we had to wait for hours to finish our work, not getting home until midnight.

My father usually tried to avoid keeping us up north longer than five to six months. When the growing season in the north ended, the only harvest available was the picking of cotton, first in the upper Mississippi Delta and later in West Texas. My father usually tried to avoid picking cotton because of the lack of decent housing in both these areas, but sometimes we had no alternative. We were without funds, and outstanding bills kept us from going home.

In Sikeston, Missouri, we were an oddity. Most of the workers were Black Americans. We saw some Anglo workers, who I understood came from Arkansas and Oklahoma, but we didn't come in contact with them. The crew bosses would assign them to particular sections of the vast fields, far from Mexican and Black laborers. While at work, we didn't initially engage with the young Black children. Later we found out that they thought we were American Indian workers from Oklahoma. Some American Indians did migrate from Oklahoma to the upper Mississippi Delta for the cotton harvest, but all the groups were segregated, and we did not interact with them.

When Black children found out we were Mexican and spoke English, they looked for us at the weigh-ins at the end of the day. They wanted to find out more about us, and we of them. They would invite my parents to the dances on payday, and my father and some of the men went. I don't know if they danced, but we learned from the children that they had gambled.

My brothers, especially the oldest, Manuel, preferred to go into town to the movies on weekends. We would invite our new friends, but they wouldn't come. Other than the weigh-ins, they remained on their side of town to avoid exposing themselves to racism. We found ourselves in a similar situation when we picked cotton in Lubbock, Texas, where we were denied service at a hamburger shop and a movie theater. Whereas we had gone to see *War of the Worlds* at the theater in Sikeston, we were turned away from the Lubbock movie theater when we tried to see James Dean in *East of Eden*. After standing in line with the Anglo boys and girls, Manuel wouldn't leave the front of the ticket counter when the cashier informed him that Mexicans weren't allowed. When Manuel's demand to know why caused a commotion, my other brother Carlos and I wanted to leave, but Manuel would have none of it; he demanded to see the manager. The manager threatened to call the police if we continued to make "trouble." We left peacefully, but not before Manuel told him what he thought of the color line.

We came to agree with our father that we should avoid picking cotton, not only because of the racism we experienced in those states, but also because of the poor housing and working conditions. In Missouri, we were assigned a two-room shack for three families, with no water, heat, electricity, or sewers. Although my father always brought his kerosene stove, dried meats, and plenty of canned goods, there was a tremendous burden on my mother to keep us fed and clean. Four of the six children slept in the truck: three of us in the eight-by-fourteen-foot canvas-topped box and Carlos in the front. My father, the other men, and the other families' older children also slept in vehicles outside, while my mother and the two youngest children would sleep in the shack, along with the other women and infants. The rest of us used the shack only to eat and to pick up our clothing. We bathed in the cotton fields by carrying five-gallon buckets of water and a cup to pour over our crouched bodies hidden by the cotton plants.

Like the other couples, our parents seldom had any privacy and would not sleep together. The long days from dusk to dawn in the fields only to return to the chores of feeding, bathing, and bedding us for the next day were not conducive to love. Thus grew an absence of tenderness, and our daily life became hard and empty.

The most vivid impression I have of picking cotton along the Mississippi and in West Texas with Black Americans is of how the working and living conditions consumed our collective spirit. Although we worked in crews, men, women, and children worked at different speeds, some more skillfully than others, so we became spread out across the immense fields. Nowhere was this more evident than in picking cotton in those oceans of treeless white fields.

While other crop harvests allowed for some socializing and competition, cotton fields were not suited for this type of activity. The housing stock was unpainted, just drab, unpainted wood. There were no trees in sight, no bushes lining the properties, and no flowers to be seen. Even though thousands of field hands would descend on the area during the peak of harvesting, the miles upon miles of white fiber would consume all of us, leave us without an identity, and rob us of the human connection of work.

The only voices that could be heard were the gospel-sounding work songs of the Black Americans. To me, at the time, their songs sounded eerie and sad. The way the rest of the workers would act as a chorus to that lone, lamentful sound reminded me of a whole people crying at once. It was so different from how we sang. We sang when we were happy or sad, sober or drunk. Although some of us sang loud enough to be heard while we worked, seldom was there any accompaniment by any other, certainly not all of us singing out loud as one.

2

LAS BARACAS

Although we worked in many states, my family had a strong and long-standing connection to Wisconsin in particular. Going to *el Norte* (the North) meant going to Hartford. My grandfather had shown my father how to get to Chicago in the late 1930s and had told him that he had heard Milwaukee was just as bountiful in work and a better place to live than Chicago.

My father and his friend Panchito Rodriguez, and others, had started migrating to Hartford for work in the late 1930s as bachelors. By the 1940s, both Panchito and my father had married and brought their wives to Wisconsin. My oldest brother, Manuel, was born in Crystal City in 1941, shortly before the attack on Pearl Harbor, and my parents took him to Wisconsin as an infant in 1942. My second oldest brother, Teofilo, whom we called Carlos, was born that October in Hartford. I was born on December 25, 1943, in my grandmother Beba's bed in the home that my grandfather Teofilo had built after his arrival in 1906. My three younger brothers also were born in Crystal City: Rodolfo ("Rudy") in 1946, Francisco in 1948, and Luis in 1950.

Whether because of the cold weather, World War II, or the fact that both of their mothers were still alive and needed their assistance and presence, my parents returned to Crystal City each year, choosing not to relocate permanently to Wisconsin; but they always spoke of it with fondness. During that decade of war and the boom that followed, my father and his boyhood friends would come yearly, send their families money throughout the harvest, and return with an abundance of gifts for

everyone. In 1951 my five brothers
and I, six boys all under the age
of ten, started joining my father
on his trips north. In addition to
the work assignments the three
oldest carried on these trips, my
duties included caring for my
youngest brother, Luis.

My grandfather had cautioned
my father to stay away from
mines and factories as places of
work. Teofilo himself had worked
in the mines at Monclova, Coahuila, Mexico, and never got rid
of his miner's cough. Many of my
father's friends had become en-
amored with the vibrant life of
the Mexican community that was
settling on the south side of Mil-

My father Manuel Salas (center), on Milwaukee's south side in 1942 with friends

waukee along the Menomonee Valley, the heart of its industrial and manufacturing base in those years. However, my father chose to go forty miles
northwest of Milwaukee, where the infrastructure of Wisconsin's vegetable harvesting, processing, and canning was being established. Following
his father's advice and hoping to keep us out of harm's way, he committed
us to working the fields throughout the next decade, harvesting rather
than processing and canning these crops.

My father frequently spoke of his friends being injured and maimed
in the factories. He would tell us that he knew of no meat cutter who hadn't
suffered a severe cut as a result of automated processes that were taking
the place of butchers. He said that he knew of no foundry molder who
hadn't suffered a burn. In the fields, he kept us away from the perils of the
automated processes, the machining of the harvest.

Whereas my father and other young men could find housing in the
early 1940s, Hartford offered no family housing for the hundreds of families migrating there in the 1950s. To ease the housing shortage, Libby's
contracted to use the abandoned World War II hemp mill outside the city.

The cavernous buildings, the longest more than half the length of a football field, had been used to process, hang, dry, and store hemp plants for their fibers to be used for rope during World War II when the United States could no longer import it. After the war, the growers had forsaken their small plots of land for the new cash crops: sugar beets, corn, carrots, and peas. Before herbicides and sophisticated planters were developed, farms brought us workers in for the blocking, thinning, and hoeing of the sugar beets and other vegetables.

Libby's had converted these huge buildings into family housing by subdividing them into twelve-by-twenty-foot plywood units. *Las baracas* (the barracks), as they were called, were overcrowded in a nonsensical way. The subdivisions were constructed along both sides of the length of the building, leaving a massive unused space in the middle that became a promenade for the more than twenty families occupying it at a time. The entire building only had two exits, an inconvenience and a safety hazard.

Large families like ours, which had eight members, needed more than one room, but none of the rooms connected. We had to exit into the wide-open space to enter the next room. Throughout the day and late into the night there was a constant flapping of the four-by-eight plywood doors,

The barracks where migrant workers lived in Hartford. PHOTO BY DAVID GIFFEY; WHI IMAGE ID 93063

as people came in and out of their rooms to cook, to eat, to change, or
simply to meet and talk.

Because my father was a crew chief, and because we had gotten there
when the barracks opened in the spring, he ensured that the ten to twelve
families from Crystal City were all assigned to one building. Additionally,
he secured half a dozen other rooms for families that were to join us later.
All single male workers lived in a separate barrack, which was supposed
to shield families with young unmarried women, although some of these
men objected to not being housed with their other family members. Most
of us had started migrating with family and lifelong neighbors and now
had to get used to working and living with strangers. By a previous arrangement with the Villareal brothers, the crew chiefs from the Texas Valley,
our barrack included another dozen families. We didn't stay strangers
for long.

Children played in the immense area immediately in front of the families' respective units, where there was enough room for them to run and
enjoy themselves. The units had no running water, so there was constant
traffic to the water fountains where families could pick up drinking water
in two-gallon pails. This area was mostly restricted to the women and
young girls who used it to wash their clothes daily. The three oldest in
our family were all in our early teens and when we went to get water, our
mother told us not to address the young girls from the Villareal crew, but
we did.

We also met girls on the way to the communal bathrooms and showers.
These facilities were separated by gender but otherwise had no privacy.
Before Hartford, I had never been naked in front of my brothers, let alone
complete strangers. Here, we would all stand naked in front of one another
and with countless other men and young boys. Nothing in our lives was
private. Living in close quarters, we knew most of what happened in the
other rooms. For instance, my aunt Simona was always leaving her pinto
beans unattended while cooking, and they would burn, stinking up the
whole barracks. Anytime we walked into las baracas and smelled burned
beans, we assumed the stench came from her quarters.

Mrs. Bosquez, a family friend and neighbor, distinguished herself
by having the loudest voice in the barracks. Her young son, Bonifacio, a
gadfly who was always taking us on adventures in the other barracks and

The six Salas brothers, back row from left: Manuel, Teofilo, myself, and Rodolfo, and in the front, Francisco and Luis

surrounding playgrounds, was often absent when she needed him. When she couldn't find him, she wouldn't bother knocking on doors or asking us his whereabouts, but would simply stand outside her door and call out in a booming voice that could be heard to the heavens: "Boniiiiiiiiiiiifaaaaaa-ciooooo!" This way, even if Bony, as he was called, didn't hear her, one of us would and would tell him that his mother was calling.

—⊣⊦—

Most of us were gone from our temporary homes during the day. We worked six days a week and on Sundays spent all day in downtown Hartford. In between, the barracks were full of people and the sounds of music, of children playing, of mothers calling for their children, and of the countless plywood doors slamming. The only time we got a sense of how many people really lived in the barracks was when we all got up to go to work or returned at the same time or were stuck at home when it rained. Then, the barracks seemed unlivable!

On rainy days my older brothers and I would escape to the other barracks, especially the one reserved for single men. Here, we found men talking in small groups, the older ones playing dominos, the younger ones playing card games, some gambling their weekly earnings away. My father did not mind if we gambled; in fact, he taught us how to play most of the common board games, a variety of card games, checkers, and dominos. Teaching us to play was to him as important as learning the art of self-defense. There were many rainy days in a season.

Manuel, my oldest brother, spent his off days differently from the rest of us. Back in Texas, Manuel had taught himself how to read English using American comic books, which he encouraged the Mexican general stores to carry alongside Mexican newspapers, magazines, and other texts. In every town and village where we worked, he always visited the library. He had library cards from three different cities in three different states. I don't know how he got them. I don't recall my father or any of the growers we worked for signing on his behalf. But I know they trusted him with any book that he checked out. He always took care of them and returned them on time. The librarian in Henry, Illinois, had generously taught him how to use the Dewey Decimal System, and over the years he developed a fondness for biographies and historical novels.

Because we stayed for a little over a month at each stop on the migrant cycle, he sometimes had to return books that he had not finished. Manuel would simply wait until we got to the next town and on the first rainy day or Saturday off, he would go directly to the library to a particular section and find the same book! Not yet aware of the system used in the libraries, I found this amazing. So did the numerous librarians we got to know over the years. I don't recall anyone denying us access to books.

In the late forties and early fifties, few of the migrants whom we worked and lived with knew how to read and write. Some could read and write some Spanish, but fewer could in English. Those who couldn't read English often asked Manuel to read documents, letters, and other written materials. He shared those skills with his younger siblings, enabling those of us who learned how to read in English to help our older family members. Rather than make the fifteen-hundred-mile journey in the back of a canvas-covered truck, English-speaking siblings were allowed to ride up front thanks to our ability to read maps and follow signs and directions in the never-ending detours of the 1950s interstate system. But it wasn't just a practical skill. On rainy days, Manuel would keep us, young and old, enthralled with the stories he was reading. Manuel also taught me how to read, not simply the relations of letters to the sounds that they make, not just the learning of written words, but the enjoyment of reading itself, a welcome respite from the difficult work consuming much of our childhood.

3

Harvesting Madness

Our family had picked all types of fruits and vegetables on the ground, in bushes, and even on trees. We had used cans, pails, sacks, and boxes to harvest and crate nature's bounty. But nothing compared to cleaning, blocking, and thinning sugar beets with *el cortito* (a short-handled hoe). Although in our modern age we have a varied mix of weapons of self-destruction, after my Hartford experience I thought the hoe was singularly the instrument that would lead us migrant workers to annihilation. Since humans began to toil on the soil, no other tool has so stunted, warped, and destroyed their body and spirit.

We never completely gave up hoeing. In the days before herbicides were used, hoeing a field was essential. It was part of the process of planting, cultivating, and harvesting the crop. One needed to remove the threats to the plant's growth, such as noxious weeds and water-sucking grasses. Our people had names for all of these: Buffalo grass, Johnson grass, *calio, calitres*.

In the 1950s, before the advances in planting technology and the use of insecticides and herbicides, sugar beets needed to be thinned and weeds and grasses had to be removed by hand. Although long-handled hoes would later be adopted, in the early 1950s most of the crews used el cortito, which had a handle of approximately twelve inches. The obvious difference is that hoeing with the longer handle was done while standing straight up and using the upper part of the body as leverage to drive the hoe into the soil and remove the stunting weeds. The right hand drove the steel head downward while the left hand guided the blade to its mark. Once

Migrant workers hoe and thin cucumber plants in central Wisconsin. PHOTO BY DAVID GIFFEY; WHI IMAGE ID 87205

aimed, both hands would tighten the grip on the handle and drive it to the root of the weeds. The final motion of the long handle was toward one's body, that is, to remove the weeds and grasses away from the row of sugar beets. The roots of the variety of grasses that we chopped were very resilient. They had to be removed from the young beets so as not to reattach themselves to the soft soil. The final motion of the long hoe deposited the broken-up weeds to the middle of the row. If they dared grow back, the tractor-driven cultivator would dig them out once and for all.

El cortito was different. Being smaller, it was especially suited to the women and children who made up the majority of the workforce. Most of us did not have, or had not developed, the upper body strength that made the long-handled hoe so effective as a tool for cultivation. Instead, we were instructed to straddle the rows of sugar beets and swing the short-handled hoe as a club, bringing the arm far back and then leaning into the swing with our young bodies toward the target of weeds and grasses.

Hoeing sugar beets in the diverse soils around the Hartford area was tougher than hoeing cucumbers in the soft sandy soil around the Waushara and Portage County area, appropriately called the Wisconsin Central

Sands. Cucumber plants thrived in the sandy soils of Waushara and Portage Counties. Every strike made to remove the noxious weeds from the young plants drove the steel blade deep into the soil and removed them by their roots.

Sugar beets were planted on the western skirt of Wisconsin's Kettle Moraine. Here, the landscape was varied and hilly. Holy Hill, the largest of the hills, overlooked this magnificent terrain, created by glacial deposit and visible throughout our open-air workplace. Most important for hoeing, the soil here was heavier and rockier than the Central Sands. Some types of grasses grew in clumps, and the worker had to aim the blade to the proper place to dig it out with one swing. The tall weeds had to be chopped first, to avoid damaging the sugar beet plant or hitting rocks with the hoe's blade. Hitting a large rock with a full swing would bounce the hoe back and leave one's arm and shoulder reverberating with a painful, electric-like sensation. Hitting rocks with the hoe would also rapidly dull its blade and make it less effective as a tool.

The most arduous task of using el cortito was swinging the hoe, clubbing the ground while bent at the waist. We could not do this all day without experiencing pain long after the hoeing had stopped.

The strongest worker in the multifamily crew was my aunt Ramona, followed by my mother. Because women and youth were assigned to the inside of the crew, with older males on the outside, I worked closest to both of them, who in my estimation were the best workers, male or female. There was no contest for being the strongest person on the sugar beet fields. I based my assessment on their production. Ramona and my mother were consistently the most productive workers, whether amassing pounds of asparagus or hundred-pound burlap sacks of top-grade cucumbers. It was not about muscles but the combination of strength, technique, and focus. My aunt would attack the tall weeds with her hoe, aiming it like a weapon, striking the ground as if it were an enemy that had to be brought down. In areas of the field that were more heavily filled with weeds, she would dive in, swinging the hoe, and would not rise until all the noxious weeds were lying on the ground. After standing momentarily to catch her breath, she would return and generously help the youngest of the children.

Our parents instructed us that our backs would hurt less if we stayed down. That is, avoid constantly stopping and standing. This didn't make sense! Standing relieved the lower back pain. The problem, they knew, was that the body wanted to keep standing, not to bend down and have the pain begin again. The reality was that standing to rest and relieve the pain was unproductive. We trudged off the sugar beet fields unable to walk properly. At night we couldn't sleep in certain positions without shooting pain from our lower backs consuming other parts of our bodies, our upper backs by the shoulders, down our arms. I would lose sensation in my right hand, the one that gripped that deforming tool. There was to be no lasting relief until the hoeing season ended.

The US government had encouraged and subsidized the growing of beets for the production of sugar since the early twentieth century, including during World War II. In the plains states as well as in the upper Midwest, thousands of migrants did nothing else for months at a time. Even after herbicides were used successfully, the need to do some hoeing remained, especially for the thinning and blocking of beet plants. But hoeing now came with new hazards. Already in the 1950s we were aware of the direct effects of the experimental insecticides and other chemicals they were using in the fields: headaches, nausea, skin discoloration, and worse. What we didn't know was that we didn't have to cultivate the plant, as my two uncles did, to get sick. We would become contaminated by handling the plants that had been sprayed. Only after years had gone by did we become aware that these exposures led to central nervous system disorders, cancers, and birth defects. My father tried to shelter us and keep us away from the factories, the automated food processing, and canning operations that were revolutionizing harvesting because he feared we would suffer serious injury, but as long as we were migrant workers living in primitive conditions and working in factories in the fields, he could not keep us out of harm's way.

Even the sickly, fragile, and young were not spared. During the harvest, only the most elderly and infants would remain in the labor camp. Most of the children, many as young as six or seven years old, would spend the whole day in the fields. They became an integral part of the operations, bringing cool water, warm lunch, and constant messages back and forth between the labor camp and the field. In the field, they would make available the burlap sacks for the cucumbers, as well as move empty boxes near the asparagus harvesters so they could save time when we emptied the crop. On its face, this was cruel, and the children suffered, but we did not know what else to do with them. They could not be left at the camp unattended, and the elders who stayed at the camp were incapable of being further burdened. The young ones' physical and mental condition was considered first, and they were never expected to produce like us, but everyone had to be out in the fields making a contribution. This system was most cruel, not to the weak or the fragile, but to those who were healthy of body and independent of mind and spirit. They had to be molded to toil day in, day out.

—ı⊦—

For three generations, the families of migrant and field workers had bequeathed themselves to the community as workers, harvesters, and producers. There was no other role for us, there were no other choices, and the only variety to our lives was the different crops we harvested. It was as if we had been born to be society's beasts of burden. But anyone who has worked with animals that are bred for toiling knows that while nature may endow them with the physical qualities necessary for work, it doesn't guarantee a predisposition to it. The ox left to itself will not spend the rest of its life looking for fields to plow, nor will the burro languish if people do not load its haunches with objects twice its weight. While the sickly and weak struggled, migrant fieldwork was most oppressive for those of us who had our own mind and desired a different life. The severest forms of discipline were reserved for us. Our parents did not see this as abusive or cruel but rather the opposite. They feared we would grow up without skills and a work ethic, that we would not be able to fend for ourselves, and that we would not be productive members of society if they left us to our own devices.

Not everyone tolerated or accepted these conditions. Two of my first cousins, both girls under fifteen years old, ran away. One of them joined a young man from the Texas Valley whose family had joined our crew; the other left with a near stranger and wasn't heard from again until twenty-five years later. The former was not entirely successful. She had moved from south central Texas to another agricultural region that also exploited migrants, the Texas Valley along the Gulf of Mexico. The latter went to Michigan and ended up working in an automotive-related industry during those twenty-five years.

Our adventurous spirits sometimes led to accidents, and the 1955 season was one of the worst. That is when my younger brother Francisco fell off the top of the cab of the truck and broke his arm. That same year, Rodolfo, the fourth-born brother, whom we called Rudy, was injured while playing with a parked potato digger. He pulled and released the brake and was sent flying. He landed headfirst against stones six feet away. We found him bleeding from a ferocious cut to the top of his head, his collarbone sticking out of his shoulders near his lower neck. Several weeks later our dog, Blackie, the only animal that our father had ever allowed us to keep while migrating, was run over by the neighbor's car. My father thought he should be put down. We begged him to take him to the vet, even though we didn't have the means after paying the doctor's bills for Rudy and Francisco. He relented and Blackie was saved. For a while that summer, all three of them were hobbling along with casts on their limbs.

During this period my mother was in a daze, sleeping little while caring for the wounds of her children at night as well as working from sunrise to sunset. She was never alone during these ordeals. After Rudy broke his collarbone, family friends Viola and Raul would willingly cook for us, make our lunch, and help Mom with the wash. At night, Raul would take the kids out for a root beer in town to let our mother be alone and get some rest. In spite of all the loving assistance from our friends, we could all see that she was beside herself. Our father instructed us to stay away from her.

The following year, while we were in Illinois for the asparagus harvest, she was hospitalized for more than a week with surgery for the removal of gallstones. Again, my father took care of us with support from our aunt, uncles, and friends. They helped out in every way they could, including cooking our lunch and bringing it to the field. Every day my father would drive to the hospital in Peoria, Illinois, to visit our mother. I went only once and could not believe it was her. She was almost unrecognizably pale with her round face now long and a haggard, sad look that mashed her fine features. Unlike my father, whose Indian heritage was painted on his face, my mother was normally *aperlada* (the color of pearls), her eyes soft, her thin lips shaping a delicate smile. Now, she lay in bed covered only by a flimsy nightgown that exposed her thin frame.

I could not stand to look at my mother directly. She seemed undressed, and I did not want to be disrespectful. She asked me to come close, to give her a hug, and I did. But I was afraid to raise my arms for fear of dislodging the IV needles attached to her arms. I was afraid for *us*. I was afraid that her sad sunken eyes, now dazed with drugs from the surgery and surrounded by darkness, would never light our lives again. Although my father drove from Henry to Peoria for several days after the surgery, I never joined him again, and my father kindly never insisted.

When my mother came home supposedly recovered, she could move only with great pain and only very deliberately. She had finally accepted surgery when she could no longer stand the pain, but she seemed to be in as much agony as before. The surgery was supposed to ameliorate the pain, and it hadn't. Again, family and friends were supportive and helped out by bringing food, having us over so she could rest, and seeing that we did not get behind in the harvest. She eventually returned and seemed to have regained her strength, but her face had changed. Her eyes remained sunken long afterward. The darkness in her eyes stayed with her, with permanent half-moons under them.

After her sickness, my mother did not smile as easily, and when she did smile, it did not erase the worry and sadness in her eyes. She was too honest to hide her feelings. She knew that the doctor bills from the injuries to her two young boys the previous year had severely impacted our resources and that her own hospital bills would prevent any gain from the asparagus harvest. She knew that this meant that we had lost a third of our pay for the year, and that we had only the cucumber and tomato harvests to make our money, and that bad weather could affect those harvests. Her eyes reflected the desperation and fear she felt.

I don't remember when my mother's symptoms first appeared. Like the cancer that we suffer from the herbicides and insecticides used in the fields, mental illness takes a long time to manifest and then does not go away easily. It seemed to affect my mother and the other women in our group the most, perhaps due to the dual pressures of labor and motherhood. Women were valued for their production, and thus any measure included all these factors: how many children could she produce, feed, clothe, shelter, and make fit for work so they in turn could serve the process of harvesting and food production? Foremost was this ability to reproduce live, healthy children in an industry that preyed and sustained itself on young, healthy bodies. If by nature she produced unhealthy, sickly, or fragile children, she had to care for these in addition to producing more to feed the added mouths that would not be able to sustain themselves.

I have a lot of difficulty in talking about mental illness because I realize that I am placing modern terms on a culture in the late forties and early fifties that was unaware of the variety of mental and emotional illnesses associated with modern society. In a very profound way, we had no relationship to these terms. But the pain I saw in my mother and others was more than physical and it went beyond the grief of suffering a serious bodily injury or losing a loved one, which we saw fellow migrants experience.

I am not interested in solely recounting aberrant and deviant behavior that I observed or experienced, but we were overcome with confusion and fear in seeing family members inexplicably suffering from it. As children, we didn't know what was going on! The only word we had was *locura* (madness), *loco* and *loca* for male and female, respectively. But we could not speak it or describe any of its various degrees.

When we first saw signs of mental illness, we thought it was temporary, out of character, and that it would soon go away. We were wrong on all counts. We saw the symptoms manifesting in different ways over time, affecting us all. We saw it first in our family, in my mother's difficulties and in my aunt's prolonged *tristeza* (sadness). Whatever its origins, it was what we would call depression today.

My aunt Ramona had always been kind to me, and I felt that she genuinely liked me. I loved her tacos. She made an exquisite plain flour tortilla, thin but large. It would come off the *comal* (flat-iron skillet) freckled with tiny, tasty burns on the outside that would swell with hot air on the inside until placed on its basket to softly deflate, ready to grab and eat. I always felt that I could stop in at my aunt's assigned unit. I simply stood at the door, said hello, and nonchalantly inquired about everyone. She would direct me to step inside, into the kitchen where she was making her delicious tacos. Of course, I would, in the standard perfunctory manner, respond that I had no time, that I was in a hurry, that I was running an errand, or some other unbelievable excuse. My uncle then would again extend the invitation to come in. I would feign an unconvincing reluctance as I made my way to the dining table. Ramona knew that I liked her tortillas, and that pleased her. Occasionally she also had a warm smile for me. Her face, a spider's web of lines that circled her eyes and mouth, would be transformed; a slight half-moon smile would find its way into features that experience had molded for scorn and fear.

One evening after we had returned from the fields, my aunt had an emotional outburst that frightened us all. We were unsure she would work again. To our utter amazement, my aunt returned to the fields the following day, not to work but to bring a hot lunch to her husband and her children, a rare gesture. Normally field workers had *desayuno* (breakfast) in the fields with hot *café con leche* (coffee with warm milk). We snacked on leftovers later in the day to maintain our strength but did not eat another full meal together. To be fed a warm meal in the fields was a treat, in and of itself, on any day and under whatever circumstances. Most other families packed their lunch when they woke in the morning and ate it cold later in the day.

The lunch that she brought to the field on the day following her incapacitation had to be prepared for several hours. That day, the crew was working in the fields immediately next to the labor camp, and we had heard the early sounds that she was making in its preparation: drawing the water with the old, hand-drawn pump, chopping the wood, igniting the fire whose smoke wafted across the asparagus field.

We usually prepared meals at the end of the workday when everyone was home. Under the primitive conditions that we lived in, without gas, running water, or electricity, it took the collaboration of the whole family to facilitate the preparing of supper. On that day, my aunt had undertaken what normally took the whole family, all by herself. We all appreciated what she had done, none more so than her immediate family, who were enjoying her labor.

—||—

To someone from outside our group, all that was evident was so many migrant families harvesting asparagus. In fact, every single one of us had specific roles to play prescribed by our leaders, the elders of the clan. What my aunt had done that morning was out of the ordinary; it was obvious to all of us and most appreciated.

In my family, the roles were changing as we children grew older. My father made the decision to pull my brother Carlos, the second born, from the harvest. His new job would be to grade, count, box, and load the crop. My mother insisted that he do his share of harvest work before he left to undertake his new duties. To be removed from the harvest always meant that he would do less physical work than the rest of us. This was on its face unfair, but my father did not make the decision arbitrarily. Most of the elders who had direct contact with the growers and processors were greatly respected for their wisdom, in addition to their knowledge and skill in harvesting. No one openly quarreled or complained about their decisions and whom they chose to help them.

When my father left his position in the field, Manuel would replace him. Although the eldest, Manuel was not as physically strong as Carlos, but he was tenacious, a steady worker with a propensity to assume leadership roles that required more brains than brawn. Other times, my father would pull Manuel from the harvest for time keeping, recording, and payroll. In the field, Manuel usually occupied the outside position, closer to the single men. He was in his element. Manuel often helped the other young workers with reading, writing, and mailing their letters. He was a good companion in the workplace, as he was the storyteller of the clan, relating stories of his many readings.

With Carlos removed from fieldwork and Manuel taking on new responsibilities, I occupied the place next to my mother and my aunt Ramona. This suited me because of my physical ability and yearning to gain a role of leadership. I would work on the opposite side next to my father, while the younger children were boxed in the middle between our parents. The men on the outside perimeter of workers would shelter the women and children from dangers, real or imagined. Thus, I had spent my first three years of my apprenticeship in the harvest next to or near my aunt, who was the most productive worker in her family, and one of the best of any adult in the field. Besides her immediate family, no one had been closer to her before or after the incident, but we never spoke again of what happened.

My aunt continued to be a valued member of the clan through her contribution and productivity in the harvest. No sooner had she returned than the murmurs began regarding how she had returned to her former "self." The only "self" allowed, the only part of her being that had any value, was in relation to her productivity, to the harvest. In this, she excelled as before. I always thought she was the strongest person in the labor camp, her diminutive size notwithstanding. Now, again, there was no way to measure her strength other than in the harvest. She could easily harvest any crop as well as any of the most productive men.

Whatever fruit or vegetable we harvested at the time, the standard was never strength alone, but skill, endurance, and the ability to maintain a consistent pace over a lengthy period of time. Women exhibited extra-ordinary endurance, equal to or superior to men. In the harvests that were not exclusively based on tonnage, but on skill and quality of the harvest, they were as productive. Here, my aunt had no equal. Our growing group of migrating fieldworkers recognized her as the best.

On her first day back to work, only forty-eight hours after her stay at home, she took her familiar position next to my mother and me. She began work at a horrendous pace, swaying from one row of asparagus to another, her long knife effectively mowing down anything that stuck out of the earth. The twenty-five-pound woven basket that she tied to her waist with a broad canvas belt seemed to fill by itself with green stalks.

Once the basket was filled, she wasted no time in emptying, marking, or stacking the crates, but would simply take another from one of her children and fill it up again. Most of the men refused to work alongside her because she made them all look bad. When she worked like this, no one tried to keep pace with her, but would just let her get ahead and stay in front of the work crew.

In the beet fields, she used el cortito like a club with a sharp edge, swinging it wildly like a pendulum as she straddled the rows of beets, striking the weeds and the grasses that were stunting the growth of the vegetable. Even if men refused to work alongside her, everyone could see her advancing ahead the weed-filled rows of beets faster than any of us.

In the beet fields, even if you were facing down straddling your own row of beets, you could still hear the swinging of el cortito swishing through the top of the weeds and hitting the soil deep into the ground where the root of the noxious weeds lie. If the swing was firm, the steel hoe hitting the ground made a very distinct sound. The "thump" sang out like an earthen bell reverberating to where we stood. She would not straighten herself, but remained bent, never looking up. She would stay down, unleashing the club as if she were throwing herself against the earth, only to swing back in the same pendulum motion and unleash yet another and another strike. Submerged in a sea of weeds and not lifting her head for a gasp of air, she remained working until she had cleared a path where only the red beet plants stood among the fallen dead stalks of weeds and grasses, no longer a threat, laid in the middle of the row, already wilting.

When she momentarily stopped, she slowly became erect to breathe more easily, her chest heaving, gasping as if she had just pulled her head out of water, her face contorted, her eyes bulging, looking blankly at no one, her stare fixated on a spot somewhere across the field.

She unconsciously would tug on her clothes, pulling her shirt from high off her back to cover her exposed backside and pulling her trousers up to her waist without looking, fumbling through the motions repeatedly until she sensed that she was proper.

Her color finally returning, her breathing now regular, her contorted face now back to normal, she began to gaze back and forth between the spot that she had just thinned and hoed and where the rest of us toiled. At that time, she would decide if she should trudge forward or turn back and help the rest of us out of the mire of weeds. This meant helping whomever in her family happened to be farthest behind, usually the youngest members of the family.

Not all parts of the field were the same. Weeds and grasses grew in the most fertile parts of the field just as fruits and vegetables did. That meant some parts of the field were more heavily filled with these noxious plants than others. No one was asked to work in those parts of the field exclusively. My aunt would! When she returned from the front of the crew to help us, she had to navigate through the densest, most difficult part of the field again. I cannot communicate how relieving and encouraging this was. We all regained our strength and, like her, went after these pieces of earth as if we were at war against weeds, scores of steel hoes slamming against the earth, our bodies all swinging in unison.

This is the way we were taught to work. These were our mentors who taught us the process of work as a unit, a group, a team. The organization of work as member of a community of harvesters, each with designated roles.

Although my aunt would work that year and the following with us, after that her family moved on to the potato harvest. I later heard that she had stopped working altogether.

Watching the difficulties of my mother, my aunt, and many others was challenging for all of us. We found that the mental toll of migrant work was not singular; it did not affect only one person or a few. We all suffered its consequences and were pained by it. There was no immunity. It was a communicable disease and long after our seasonal migrant work was over, it would affect us all.

4

CHANGES TO THE MIGRANT CYCLE

We stopped hoeing beets, not because of enduring pains, both mental and physical, but because like the cotton harvest of the Upper Mississippi Delta and West Texas, the housing conditions were deplorable. The dozen-member extended family that had traveled from Crystal City, Texas, to Wisconsin in the early 1950s had grown to scores of families, now joined by crews from the Texas Valley, nearby Laredo, and across the border, from the northern state of Coahuila, Mexico.

We stayed in the former hemp mill for only two years before my father, through a local fellow worker at Libby's, found an old, abandoned farmhouse several miles from the hemp plant. The eight of us occupied the two-story frame building along with Raul and Viola, who were friends from our hometown, and a young married couple. In addition to the main farmhouse, the property had a barn, several utility buildings, and agricultural implements strewn all over the yard as if they had only recently been used. Although we enjoyed the privacy of living in the old farmhouse, it was crowded as the twelve of us attempted to accommodate ourselves in the three bedrooms. We rarely saw the young couple, who stayed in their room when they were not working. Viola would help Mother prepare our meals. Raul would accompany my father searching for sugar beet fields to hoe, and we kids spent the day outside exploring the grounds and surrounding woods.

Although Libby's encouraged migrants to join the canning of peas in early summer and later of sugar beets, my father—following the advice of his father, who had toiled in the mines of Alto Hornos in Coahuila,

Mexico—avoided mines and factories. Factory work could be deadly or injurious to one's health. Some of his friends had earlier moved to Milwaukee's near south side to work in the tanneries and foundries, and others permanently settled in the Hartford area to work in the warehousing and distribution of the vegetables we had nurtured and cultivated. But my father kept our family in the fields, away from these dangers.

In spite of my father's wishes to keep us out of harm's way, the farms in Wisconsin at midcentury were not the ones he had encountered in the late 1930s and early 1940s. They were becoming what investigative journalist Carey McWilliams called "factories in the fields." Wisconsin would become a national leader in the production of fruits and vegetables by undergoing profound technological changes, much as automation was revolutionizing urban factories. The hoeing and thinning of sugar beets and other vegetables was eliminated by the use of herbicides to eradicate noxious weeds and grasses. Technologically advanced agricultural implements, including more effective planters, eliminated the need for thinning by spacing vegetable plants for more effective growth.

Following that final season in Hartford, our migrant cycle was altered. After the asparagus harvest in Illinois, we no longer hoed sugar beets in the Hartford area but moved straight north to the Central Sands region for the cultivation of cucumbers. The move included all of the original several dozen families from the Mexico Grande barrio in Crystal City, most of us related, now joined by families from other neighborhoods. For the first time our crew included families from other communities and across the border. We were now spread out in dozens of small farms between Hancock and Wautoma, Wisconsin. We lived east of Pine Lake and across the road from Fish Lake on the Thompson farm the first year. The following two years we lived at an old spread previously owned by a family by the last name of Hartford, owners of a small farm in the area. The plot included the original home, a general store, and a small two-bedroom home we occupied. In front of the house was a small cucumber grading station.

We hoed and thinned the cucumber plants and arranged the vines so they would grow in a row. For the first picking, we were paid 100 percent of the crop. Thereafter, we would split the graded crop 50 percent, half for the grower, the other half for the pickers. The crop would be graded either in Hancock, if the fields were closer to that station, or across the yard of the Hartford family spread, on the return home. We were paid the best rates for the smaller cucumber sizes, which were graded A, 1, 2, and 3. For grades 4 and 5, the larger sizes, we were paid almost nothing. For that reason, we removed them from the plant and left them lying on the ground.

Cucumbers were picked in five-gallon steel cans. Pickers would be assigned two rows, and we would move between them, picking the cucumbers and depositing them in the can. Most importantly in the early pickings was to avoid stepping on the plant's vines. In the first pickings, it was essential that the vines be arranged to grow in a row. They would not only grow in rows, but so trained, their vines would intertwine and join with each other. At the peak of the harvest, the picker would lift, then pull over the mass of vines, exposing dozens of growing cucumbers. The very smallest would be left to grow; the largest cut and disposed of; while the remaining cucumbers would be picked with both hands.

The cucumber had to be removed from its vine without damaging the plant. It could not be pulled off. It needed to be snapped from its tether. The ideal method was to engulf the cucumber with the palm of the hand, and with the thumb, snap it at the stem on top. Bent at the waist and moving from one row to the other as a pendulum, harvesting the cucumbers with both hands, we removed the cucumber from its vine with a simple twist. Once the best-grade cucumbers were removed, we would neatly lay back the mass of vines so that they would grow north and south.

Once the five-gallon steel can was full of cucumbers, it was emptied into a burlap sack that could hold up to one hundred pounds. The can became a burden to move forward long before it became full, however, so it was usually emptied once three-quarters full. Likewise, the burlap sacks were seldom filled to the brim, as most of us could not lift one hundred pounds onto the truck that would take the product to be graded at the end of the day. Father was constantly gone looking for additional fields for the crew to harvest, and the strongest among the family was my mother and second oldest brother, Carlos. They usually ended up loading the truck after the harvest. To spare our mother, we began to fill the hundred-pound sacks half full. I could lift fifty pounds over my head and onto the truck. Later I learned to load the sacks in one motion, pulling and heaving them rather than lifting the sack. Not all of us learned these skills or adapted.

As with cutting asparagus and hoeing beets with el cortito, the work was back breaking. Not only did cucumbers have to be harvested while we bent, but the steel can full of cucumbers had to be moved forward in that position. Again, as in the earlier work, we were taught that staying bent instead of constantly getting up to rest was the best way to carry out the task. That is, we learned to adapt, to get used to or disregard the constant pain to our lower backs. Rudy never did. He was constantly making excuses to avoid being bent all day. No one relieved himself as much as Rudy.

There were no sanitary facilities in the field. If there were woods near the crop, men and women were assigned different sections of the wooded area to relieve themselves. If there were no woods, cornfields served the same purpose. If the fields were empty, we took turns going behind the trucks or cars that carried us to work. It was humiliating for all of us but especially for the women.

Rudy's trips to the woods became legend. I frequently had to be sent to look for him after long absences. He would disappear and lose himself in the woods. The woods near the kettles, lakes, and wetlands were full of furry animals we had never seen before. One could hear them long before seeing them as they darted along the leaf-covered ground and through the tall grasses in the marsh. I would find Rudy chasing this or that animal. He knew that he would be disciplined, perhaps punished, when he returned, but he didn't seem to care. He was engrossed in his own world. Mother gave up on him. It was useless to take away his privileges when it was clear he wasn't going to adapt to such working conditions. She would try to get as much work out of him as possible and have peace and harmony in the fields. We all learned something from Rudy that summer.

We no longer worked alongside extended family members or even in the same fields with them while working the cucumber harvest. And we did not live in a common labor camp as we had done in the asparagus harvest or in the converted hemp mill in Hartford. The family-owned cucumber plots were small. Each of us was assigned to an individual small farmer who provided converted garages, sheds, or any other type of structure with a roof to house the migrant families. At the Thompson farm, in addition to Crystal City neighbors, we lived with two families from Piedras Negras, Coahuila, Mexico: the young married couple we had met in Hartford and a family of three young women headed by a single mother. Her eldest daughter, Conchita, was in love and waited for letters every day from her boyfriend, Tomas.

At the beginning of the harvest, my father would visit the local post offices in Henry, Illinois, and the Hartford and Hancock post offices in Wisconsin and provide them with a list of the names of the families who were members of our crew. Our address was the post office itself. At the time, our only means of transportation was the 2.5-ton tandem truck, and it only went to the village of Hancock once a day to take the cucumbers to be graded. One of the most delightful times of the day was when Conchita would be overcome by the mail that arrived from her boyfriend, Tomas. Every day Conchita would seek out my father, who was responsible for picking up the mail for all the families, to ask if she had received mail. When she received a letter, she couldn't contain herself with happiness. If the mail came while she was still in the field, the elder women would tease her for demonstrating such an unbridled love for Tomas. Conchita's pearl-colored cheeks would flush red.

We all shared in her happiness, and the women would lovingly plead with her to share what Tomas had written. She would carry Tomas's letter to the fields and read them over and over again throughout the day. She never related what he wrote, but her smile spoke volumes. Later, through her mother, we found out that Tomas planned to visit her upon our return to Crystal City and ask for her hand in marriage. In the monotonous, back-breaking workday, we all found something to be happy about that summer.

—||—

The only time that we got to see family and members of the original crew was at the end of the day at the grading station. Each family was responsible for unloading their harvest from the truck to be graded and to be available for the check, which was drawn each day to the head of the household. Since the truck carried the picking of the whole camp, each family sent a member to the grading station to ensure that their harvest was properly unloaded, graded, and paid for.

At the time, the families of the small farmers who owned the land worked alongside us or planted small plots of cucumbers in their garden areas to be graded and paid for just like migrant families. The Thompson family worked in the same field as we did. Ira Hartford planted our crop and was on-site on almost a daily basis, bringing treats for the youngsters from his sister's general store. When we ended the harvest, he had learned that Carlos had a birthday in October and I on Christmas Day and gave us boxes to be opened on our special day after we left for the tomato harvest. They were full of treats.

We came to know the other members of the Hartford family down the road quite well, and we often walked over to observe the milking of their dairy herd and to help out with their daily chores. We helped the two boys bale hay and fill the corn silos with corn for feeding of the herd during winter. On Sunday afternoons, after our picking and their milking of the cows and other chores, we were invited for Sunday dinner, which was a multi-hour event. Afterward, we all went out to the pasture to bring the dairy herd in for milking. Manuel, Carlos, and I would not return home until nightfall, after the second milking.

The most rewarding treat of all was stopping at one of the more than half dozen freshwater lakes and ponds between Hancock and Wautoma after work. We were warned not to go to the beaches near the supper club, which was along the public landing and where dozens of local youths frolicked and swam. In Crystal City's municipal swimming pool, Mexican American children were not allowed to use the pool except on the day before they changed the water. My father refused to let us go; thus, none of us knew how to swim, and none of us owned swim trunks or even shorts. Still, we ventured across the street from the Thompson farm to Fish Lake to wade along the beach.

Later that year, in Hancock, Wisconsin, my brothers and I attended Hancock Elementary School and would venture into the Halverson's Café for sodas after school, just like the local youth. One of the Halverson girls was our classmate and invited us. We were welcomed by the schoolchildren. We attended school events and shared soft drinks with them at the local teen hangout.

Visiting Wisconsin lakes was the most satisfying on hot days after the cucumber harvest. Marl Lake was between the cucumber fields and our residence at the Hartford family spread. Later, tourists would swarm the countryside buying lakefront plots and building summer cottages, but in the early fifties we had our pick of a handful of lakes, ponds, and streams that were virtually deserted.

On one side of Marl Lake, by the road, there was a farmhouse with several other buildings. The area around the rest of the lake had no other buildings or permanent inhabitants. The reason Marl Lake was so deserted was that visitors had to park several hundred feet from the freshwater lake and walk through brush and shoulder-high grass to reach it. This suited my father's taste and his plan to teach us how to swim in this type of body of water.

Marl Lake had a natural sandy beach, and its shallowness extended over a dozen feet from the shore. It also deepened gradually so as to amply warn nonswimmers like ourselves to go farther at their own risk. My father's first swimming lesson was to teach us how to float, first by standing in water deeper than ourselves, treading with just our face showing. This was difficult because once a person starts to sink, the body reaches toward the top on instinct. But with arms stretched out and slight movement of the hands, the body stops sinking and becomes a buoy. Later he would teach us the same idea on his back as if resting rather than swimming. It worked for me. Rather than moving from one point to another through the water, for me the idea of swimming was about conditioning the body to spend long periods of time in the water. I was always the first to reach Marl Lake and the very last to leave. In fact, I began taking off my shoes and shirt on the way to the lake. I'd jump in as soon as we reached the water's edge and didn't want to come out until we were ready to leave.

In 1954, when we moved to Neshkoro, I learned to swim in the White River, a completely different experience from floating on my back trying to be motionless. The river ran behind the Libby's cucumber grading station and meandered southwest. Local workers at the grading station had told my father where we could access the river. My father went with us only once to show us where to swim safely, as the current was quite strong, although the river was only deep at certain of the bends. Unfortunately, all this ended with the harvest as we moved on to picking tomatoes.

—||—

Picking tomatoes was my favorite work in the whole migrant cycle. The work did not entail bending at the waist for the whole day. We did not arrive for the harvest until after Labor Day, when the tomato plants were in full bloom. The tomato patches were all small, nestled in the remaining farmland between subdivisions, apartment buildings, and strip malls. The fertile soil was less sandy than in central Wisconsin. The landscape was less rocky and hilly than Wisconsin's Kettle Moraine, but the earth was just as productive. What made the work easier was the bountiful crop that required the picker to tend to huge sprawling plants on a raised bed that produced dozens of tomatoes each. The workers could drop to their haunches or even their knees and quickly fill the half-bushel wooden baskets.

An adult worker could pick between eighty and one hundred half bushels per day. Our mother and Carlos were the most productive workers. My father was not in the field with us most of the time. He was the one responsible for having fields to pick for the crew that were scattered over half a dozen sites. When he did join us, he would pick at a rate of one hundred half bushels a day. I picked more than eighty half bushels a day and Manuel at a slightly lower rate. Manuel's contribution to the harvest was not solely based on how many bushels he produced. He served as the bookkeeper for not only our family but also for other groups of families that made up our clan.

We were paid twelve cents per half bushel of tomatoes filled to the brim. Since the earth was so soft, only tractor-pulled trailers could traverse the fields. To not damage the plants that sprawled from the raised beds and down the sides and filled the area in between the rows, we were paid a cent extra to carry the half bushels loaded with tomatoes to a designated thoroughfare about fifteen rows apart. Carlos drove the tractor along the designated road, and a member of each family loaded their bushels onto the trailers. Manuel kept individual family records for the bushels that left the field. Later he would be sent to nearby fields to carry out the same function for other crew members. An extra cent would be paid for each half bushel loaded onto the trucks that would go around to the different fields to be taken to the trailers gathered by the road.

With my father in charge of assigning families to different farms, Carlos and me loading tomatoes with the tractor-trailer, and Manuel keeping the books for the operations, we became separated from our own family members at different times throughout the day. One day, Mother and the younger children were left behind in one of the fields with no way to get into camp. The grower was supposed to bring the families in on one of the empty trailers after the harvest, and he had forgotten ours. My mother's absence was not noted until nightfall, when no lights appeared in our unit and others became concerned and reported it.

On this day, my brothers and I did not get home until late at night due to the loading of tomatoes, and when we arrived, we found my mother packing. My mother, who had spent the last five hours, three of them in the dark, in the field with the three younger children without food or water, had given the grower a piece of her mind. The grower responded by throwing us out of the camp. She was still livid at the grower when we got home, swearing under her breath. She was also concerned about what my father would say.

When my father got home and Mother informed him that we could no longer stay in our unit, he did not get angry as she had feared. He proposed that he would go speak to the grower, but my mother no longer wanted to stay there or work for the grower again. Aside from that day's incident, she was upset that families had been assigned to fields without access to water and sanitary facilities. Unlike when we had been hoeing beets or harvesting cucumbers, there were no wooded areas or cornfields to hide oneself. Here in the tomato fields, there were only busy roads surrounded by residential and commercial units, as the Chicago metropolitan area was consuming all the farmland.

Throughout the conversation between our parents, my older brothers quietly proceeded with the packing that my mother had ordered before my father arrived. He said nothing more, sitting himself down to eat. By daybreak, we were all packed. The bedding and portable kitchen and utensils with a change of clothes for each of us were the last items to be loaded onto the 2.5-ton canvas-covered truck. They would be the first to be unloaded wherever we made camp or worked. Carlos, the twelve-year-old designated driver, was in his costume; he had driven from Wisconsin to Illinois dressed in my father's fedora and suit coat to prevent being stopped for underage driving. He was tall and thick and looked the part of an adult driving his family. Besides, he was an excellent pilot who drove all manner of vehicles.

By midday, my father had found us the oddest housing unit that we experienced during the ten years we spent as migrant workers. We found out that a group of doctors had bought a piece of land to develop a housing project. This was the last year that tomatoes would be grown on the land, and the investors were counting on a return from the cash crop. They offered us temporary housing in the unfinished housing project they were developing.

The thoroughfares between the rows of the proposed units were only partially developed, and we were directed to one of the detached units at the end of the cul-de-sac. The roof and the four walls of these units were up, and the unit had electricity and running water, but little else. The internal division had not been finished, and the drywall was not painted, but everything worked. All the beds that would be moved in at the end of the day were single beds that appeared to be old hospital equipment, as the heads of the beds could be raised or lowered. My mother loved it, and we stayed there until the frost came and ended the tomato harvest.

One of the venues that the tomato harvest provided that no other did was access to Chicago's theaters, small restaurants, and cafés that played the latest rhythm and blues music, none of which was available to us near the Texas Borderland. Manuel, who looked for public libraries wherever we went, would read the entertainment section of the newspaper there to see what movies were playing in the area. He also found a map of the transit system that would take us to these theaters. Driving into downtown Chicago was not an option due to our unfamiliarity with the city and its maddening traffic. Mother was apprehensive about our trips, but Father relented, and we took several daylong trips into the big city. We mapped the city with our feet and later went to see the latest movie, *The Egyptian*. On another occasion, we saw Marlon Brando in Shakespeare's *Julius Caesar*.

On weekdays, when we finished the harvest early or when the weather would not allow us to harvest tomatoes, we would finish the loading early, wash up, and go out for hamburgers and fries at nearby cafés. We loved to play rock and blues songs on the jukeboxes of these restaurants. We were flush with money as we kept the one cent that was paid for loading the tomatoes on semitrailers. These activities had not been available to us

At my eighth-grade graduation in 1957 in Henry, Illinois. I am in the front row, far right.

elsewhere because we were isolated from mainstream society or had been prohibited by apartheid.

In the early 1950s, apartheid and Jim Crow laws were still firmly entrenched in our hometown of Crystal City. Initially, we thought we had to observe those practices in the Great Lakes region as well. On the contrary, we found a more generous acceptance in Henry, Illinois, public schools. I had never sat in a classroom with non-Latinos in my hometown. In 1955, in Henry, we began to attend the public school system. My two brothers and I and Graciela, a fellow worker from the migrant labor camp, attended grade school. We were the only Mexican American children in school.

—╢╟—

The 1954 and 1955 migrant seasons proved to be decisive. First, we bought a new truck. It was a 2.5-ton GMC and, in a first for us, it had an automatic transmission. According to our father, the truck was going to pay for itself through the additional work we could take on. In the asparagus harvest in the spring, it transported young bushes and plants for Potter Nursery in Henry, in addition to the daily transporting of the produce to the canning company thirty miles away in Streator, Illinois. In the cucumber harvest, it not only carried our pickings but also would transport produce from the crews' picking from surrounding small farms to the Libby grading station in the area. In the tomato harvest, south of Chicago straddling the Indiana state border, it carried tomatoes from the remaining fertile farmlands in nearby emerging communities to the canning company in Blue Island, Illinois.

More important, in 1954 my father bought an abandoned 160-acre farm in Neshkoro, Wisconsin. The following year we would pick asparagus as usual but would drive straight from Henry to our own farm, plant our own vegetables, and sell them to Libby's. Not only would we abandon the cotton harvest that fall, but 1954 would also be the last year that we would pick tomatoes in the southern Chicago suburbs.

I do not know the original financial arrangements of the purchase of the farm, how we came to possess it, or what type of funds it took. I know my parents could not have been successful without the assistance of local businesses and growers in the area whom my father had known since he started coming to Wisconsin in the early 1940s. All our work effort was collective, with no individual salaries, and our savings had made it possible. My mother's brother joined us in the early years, making the farm an extended-family affair.

Beginning in 1955, after the asparagus harvest, we moved directly to the 160-acre spread. About one hundred acres were available for cultivation, but only half of them were suitable for cucumbers. In the first years, we also planted and harvested green beans, but Libby's was now machine harvesting them in other areas, so we stopped growing them for hand harvesting. Of the grains, both rye and wheat grew very well and were recommended for crop rotation.

One of the shortfalls of converting an abandoned farm into an effective vegetable-growing operation was the lack of agricultural implements. We did not have the capital to purchase new equipment, so we made do with what we could scrounge together. We bought a tractor with a plow and later a disc, but we lacked a cultivator and had to call Mr. Meyer, our neighbor, to assist us. The used planter we found was ineffective. The used grain thresher was complicated to operate and needed frequent maintenance and repair. Although water was accessible, we did not have the funds to purchase pumps and irrigation equipment. The 160-acre farm had a fresh-water pond, and either well water or water pumped from the pond could have been used for irrigation to maintain the plants during droughts, but again, we lacked the capital or credit to irrigate our crops.

My father experimented with growing other crops that were not common to the area, for which he thought there would be a market, such as pinto beans. We harvested several tons of pinto beans, but the threshing was inadequate and left too much debris and dirt. We didn't get a good price for our effort when we sold them back home, since the beans needed to be graded and washed, and we didn't have the facilities to do it. After our grain was harvested, we shut the farm down and headed home. It was potato-harvesting time, and we loaded the truck with fresh potatoes to sell back home when we returned to Crystal City for the winter.

Libby's was expanding its operation into the Central Sands area and, after 1958, our family stayed into the fall in Wisconsin because of my father's work with Libby's. Both potato and cucumber operations were being expanded into western Waushara and adjoining Portage Counties. Machines had replaced the harvesting of the potato. Previously, workers trekked behind the tractor-pulled diggers filling burlap sacks. Now the produce was dug and placed on a conveyor belt and loaded into trucks to be carried to the huge warehouses being built to wash, grade, store, and distribute them well past the fall.

We enrolled in the Wautoma School District. In 1958, my brothers and I would attend three different high schools in three different states: Crystal City, Texas; Henry, Illinois; and, Wautoma, Wisconsin. A more permanent relocation to Wisconsin to bring some stability to our education became the only realistic option.

5

RETURN TO MIGRANT LABOR CAMPS

After spending nearly ten years as migrant workers, traveling from the Texas Borderland to the Great Lakes region, we officially relocated to Wautoma, Wisconsin, in 1959. My father made the decision to leave the migrant stream and relocate to central Wisconsin much earlier, when he bought the abandoned farm in nearby Neshkoro in Marquette County in 1954. But the purchase of a small restaurant in downtown Wautoma, and not the 160-acre farm, was what led to our successful resettlement. The lack of farm implements as well as the lack of funds to develop an irrigation system provided us with a lot of work but an insufficient, unreliable income. The restaurant provided a more stable income. Although our migration between south central Texas and the Great Lakes region would stop, my parents still drove south to Henry, Illinois, and joined extended family and former neighbors in the harvesting of asparagus until 1961.

After attending three high schools my freshman year as a migrant worker, I joined my two oldest brothers enrolling in Wautoma High School. For the rest of my high school education, we still returned to Henry, Illinois, to harvest asparagus in the spring. What's more, my last semester of high school I was frequently absent as I was working at the restaurant while my parents were in Texas visiting family and harvesting asparagus in Henry.

As a result of my poor attendance, I became disconnected from high school. Although I played football and ran track my junior year, I became injured in a game at Plainfield, Wisconsin, my senior year. I lost consciousness from a blow to the head. That night I was hospitalized, suffering from

My father outside of the restaurant my family opened in Wautoma in 1959

double vision and fainting spells. In 1960, we didn't know much about how to treat concussions.

Although I ran the 880 meters in track my senior year, I was not in good shape and I made the situation worse by skipping school to visit Manuel at Wisconsin State College–Oshkosh forty miles away instead of training in my spare time. After graduating high school in 1961, I enrolled at Oshkosh as well.

We kept in close touch with family and friends with annual trips south. My parents never failed to visit their mothers and siblings in Texas during Christmastime, in spite of operating the restaurant in Wautoma. They would simply close it or allow us to keep it open to eat and have pocket money. Most of the customers during Christmas break were our school peers and classmates. We would open the café to hang out with them, as there was little else to do other than drink in the beer taverns that illegally served eighteen-year-olds in the countryside. That we did also.

My two older brothers and I began to travel to Texas on our own as soon as we obtained our driver's licenses. In 1961, months after I had

graduated from high school at eighteen years old, I left at summer's end
with a migrant family led by our neighbor Lucio Valdez, who was returning
to his family in Crystal City. I joined him because I missed my grandmother Beba and wanted to visit her. I had lived with her for the first
seven years of my life, while the rest of the family moved to operate the
café that my father had bought at the edge of the segregated Tejano commercial area. I also hoped to visit a woman I had met who was a migrant
worker from Laredo. I had visited her in the labor camp and had a tacit
welcome from her parents. I hoped she would consider a relationship, but
she was not interested.

After visits to both Laredo and Crystal City, I returned by hitchhiking
the fifteen-hundred-mile journey to Wautoma by following the major
truck stops en route. Lucio Valdez drove me to the nearest large truck stop
where Highway 57 meets Highway 83. Highway 57 is part of the Pan American Highway and leads deep into central Mexico and beyond. Highway 83
became a major route to both the plains states and farther north to the Red
River Valley of the upper Midwest. Highway 83 would become Interstate
35 and provide a major route for the tens of thousands of migrants who
would seasonally journey to the Midwest and Great Lakes region to seek
work. I was to look for a trucker who was driving straight north.

The first lift back was with a semi going north to the Texas panhandle.
From there, I hitchhiked through Oklahoma's Indian reservations to
Joplin, Missouri. With two more major rides, one to St. Louis, the other
to Madison, I made it to Wautoma on the third night.

My immediate family had relocated in Wisconsin, but the elderly and
many of our extended family that had comprised our clan never abandoned Crystal City. We remained in close touch with our family by visiting
them several times a year. Later, due to the involvement of my father's
brother Julian in the political revolt of the early 1960s, we frequently traveled to help in voter education and registration drives. As migrant workers,
products of our households, and descendants of the Tejano settlers who
challenged apartheid in the second decade of the twentieth century, we
felt compelled to help the efforts of my uncle and others.

The movement helped more Mexican Americans register to vote, pay
the poll tax, and participate in elections. Several organizations joined forces
to form the Political Association of Spanish-Speaking Organizations

(PASSO) with the goal of increasing the political participation and power of Mexican Americans, a continuation of the struggle that first started when Mexican American settlers resisted Jim Crow by paying their poll taxes. We developed organizations that could vie for power, to determine and sustain our livelihood, our community.

Five Mexican Americans, known as Los Cinco, ran for office and won seats on the Crystal City city council in 1963. The jubilation of the electoral victory was short lived. The intimidation and economic reprisals against Los Cinco and their supporters were followed by political defeat two years later. In the counterrevolt of 1965, the Anglo minority enlisted so-called moderate Mexican Americans to retake city power. What was clearly demonstrated was that we had found a way to enhance our political power, but economic power continued in the hands of the minority with devastating effects for those Chicanos who had led the revolt and were now challenging the *vendidos* (sellouts), Mexican Americans who had been coopted by the Anglo minority to regain city government. They identified as Chicanos, a term some Mexican Americans had started to use to embrace their heritage and cultural identity as part of the growing movement for equality.

While visiting Crystal City, I became involved in my uncle Julian's candidacy for Zavala County justice of the peace in Precinct 3. He was the only PASSO candidate who won during the 1965 counterrevolt.

On behalf of my uncle, I rode in Teatro Luna's wagon campaigning for him. The wagon was outfitted with a microphone and a huge loudspeaker strapped to the roof that was used to announce the latest Mexican films at the segregated theater. Now it was used to publicly invite the neighborhood to political rallies at the mutualista plaza in Mexico Chico barrio. Our former living room on Crockett Street became the offices for the political conspirators who were planning the post-counterrevolt activities.

My uncle Julian Salas was a veteran who had served in the Wisconsin Red Arrow Division during World War II.

Uncle Julian's political boundaries included the Mexico Grande neighborhood, the original settlement that my grandparents had homesteaded; the segregated commercial district; and north to the Del Monte canning company. Walking the neighborhood street getting the vote out for my uncle, I knew every household whose door I knocked on between Canela's Bakery at the southern end of the barrio on North Avenue B and four blocks north. I had grown up here. I walked with my brothers to Suze's one-room schoolhouse, from Holland Street to San Jose. Weekly I went north for *pan de dulce* at Canela's. Now neighbors and factory workers from Del Monte, where my aunt Francisca had worked since its opening and had organized into a Teamsters Union, were meeting in our former living room, now Justice of the Peace Salas's chambers.

Uncle Julian would be the only political insurgent to survive and be elected justice of the peace for our local Zavala County precinct. Although he performed marriages, the Anglo-dominated police force would not bring cases that arose in his JP precinct to be adjudicated by his offices. The Anglo minority had regained power through intimidation and economic reprisal. Uncle Julian could not make a living in Crystal City. He, along with most of his neighbors, rejoined the migrant stream to Wisconsin that they had known since childhood. Many of them had been active in the movement to gain the franchise—the right to vote and to participate fully in business, politics, and all aspects of public life. Julian later helped found Ciudadanos Unidos (United Citizens), the precursor to La Raza Unida, an independent political party.

—II—

The success of Mexican American voter drives and political candidates in Crystal City was so unusual that it gained notice in faraway Wisconsin, where UW–Madison professor John Shockley published an account a decade later in his book *Chicano Revolt in a Texas Town*, calling what happened in my hometown in 1963 a "political revolt." Even so, I think Shockley failed to recognize the mutualistas' legacy properly. Some of the first challenges to Jim Crow had been led by the Mexican pioneering families who had migrated from the neighboring state of Coahuila at the turn of the century to clear the semiarid but fertile brushlands of south central Texas. The mutual aid organizations that formed to support Mexican

Americans and assist insurgencies against the Mexican dictatorship had a lasting impact on how Mexicans and Mexican Americans would organize to dismantle apartheid throughout the century.

In Crystal City, the only mutualista allowed to form had to be non-political. While Sociedad Funeraria Miguel Hidalgo maintained the segregated cemetery and held social and cultural events, its organization had long-term political implications. It allowed Tejanos to come together as *socios* (members), a self-designated membership unavailable to white colonists. It was a self-help organization supported by monthly dues and volunteers. My father and others who had been active in the sociedad funeraria led attempts to organize an association of Mexican businessmen. When Del Monte opened a manufacturing plant in Crystal City, the society members came together to establish a union at the plant, which my aunt Francisca joined. Both of my parents paid their poll taxes over multiple decades, and my father continued to be active in the Ignacio Zaragoza Masonic organization. All of these organizational activities were formative in what would later lead to an all–Mexican American city council slate that in 1963 defeated the forty-plus-year domination of the minority Anglo colonists. More personally, this was the context for our relocation to Wautoma in 1959.

—‖—

Although I was enrolled at Oshkosh State for more than two years, I was only a serious student for the first three semesters. To excel, I would need to dedicate more time, more concentration to my studies. Further, I was ill prepared in a number of areas for college. I loved to read and Manuel was constantly supplying me with texts that I dearly enjoyed, but I had not learned to effectively put my thoughts on paper. My academic background was filled with gaps, and it took many years beyond graduation to enhance my basic skills.

For the first two semesters at Oshkosh, in 1961–62, I had little to say about my class schedule. Manuel selected every single class, all of them humanities prerequisites, including the professors who taught them. He helped me get a job in the cafeteria at the Oshkosh Memorial Union, where he and his newfound friends hung out. In my first two years of college, we organized a slate of candidates to run for student government. I was elected freshman class representative and later sophomore class president in

1962–63 with their support. Campus shared-governance policy allowed the student government body to have a voice in the administration of student-funded facilities. We wanted a say in how our funds were being administered in the newly built student union and demanded input in programming. We were not the only ones vying for majority control. Fraternities and sororities, veterans groups, and others were also fielding candidates. Manuel's friends became the core of the emerging student group: David Giffey from the Irish community southeast of Fond du Lac; George Melchior, a transplanted Milwaukeean who grew up in Green Bay; and a number of Wisconsin's Fox River Valley high school graduates. We were also involved in city politics, working with beer distributors and nearby bars to lower the drinking age from twenty-one to eighteen years.

The Oshkosh students who comprised the backbone of the political group that challenged administrators also included a number of artists and actors who were engaged in campus and community theater and the arts. George Melchior, along with Grant "Skip" Killoran and Tom McCain, were outstanding actors and formed the core of a number of plays that were produced by Oshkosh State's Drama Club during that time. They were complemented by female leading actors Patricia Wilson and Bonnie Keough. Skip encouraged me to try out and I was cast in a couple of plays, including as a Chinese guard and a prisoner in one-act play, *Hello out There*. I missed out on a Tennessee Williams Mexican character. I had the accent, some ability, but not the body type. I coached the actor selected in Spanish.

McCain joined Tom Curley and Joey Putzer to form a trio that performed at local clubs. Manuel helped the trio get gigs and then exhorted all of us to attend. Later Joey and Tom would go on the road as a duet and also did stand-up comedy. Curley, after moving to New York, was in a number of early Steve Martin films. These relationships and activities were fun. We looked forward to having a good time onstage or supporting friends designing and painting the sets as well as those who were landing parts and performing onstage. There was a sexual revolution starting, and we wanted to be part of that revolt also.

As Manuel and I were the only Chicano students at Oshkosh, we started to consider questions of our identity. African Americans also had but a token presence of several students out of a student population of more than three thousand. The US census had for the first time used the phrase

"Spanish speaking" in the decennial count of the population in 1960. History and language professors referred to the people south of the Rio Grande as "Latin Americans." Histories of individual "Latin American" nations were not available at the state colleges at the time.

I felt compelled to address the topic on campus by writing a letter to the editor of the student newspaper, *The Advance*. The title of the letter was "What Shall We Be Called?" I argued against the term "Latin" for us and stated that we were Mexicans and should be referred to as Mexican. The editorial carried my byline but reflected Manuel's thoughts as well. At Oshkosh, Manuel had discovered José Vasconcelos's *La Raza Cosmica* and, later, Octavio Paz's *The Labyrinth of Solitude*. Together we studied Justo Sierra's Mexican history as well as novelist and journalist Martín Luis Guzmán's accounts of his border actions during the Mexican Revolution in Spanish, which we bought when we crossed the border into Piedras Negras, Coahuila, Mexico. Manuel happily shared the books with me and urged me to discuss them with our younger brothers as well as anyone else who would listen.

—II—

My college years also launched my involvement with groups assisting migrant workers. While waiting on tables at our restaurant in Wautoma at the end of my senior year in high school, members of an out-of-town group who had just finished their meal of tacos asked if I was a member of the former migrant family who owned the business. When I confirmed I was, they asked if I would be willing to identify migrant labor camps in the Red Granite and Lorhville, Wisconsin, area to recruit children for a six-week child care summer program.

The organizers of the migrant child care program were led by staff members of the former Wisconsin Division of Children and Youth (WDCY), among them the early organizers of the migrant education program, Jenny Lind and Nancy Travis. Through them, I would later find an extensive group of Madison progressives who had lobbied for years in Dane County to improve the working and living conditions of the more than ten thousand workers who were now coming to Wisconsin from the south central Texas Borderland. Among them were members of the local human rights organization Dane County Human Rights Council, which included UW–Madison economics professor Elizabeth Brandeis. Brandeis had long advocated more attention be paid to the deplorable conditions of migrants, especially of women and children. She introduced me to her friend Helen Bruner, wife of Judge Ervin Bruner. Helen would play a key role in support for migrant programs at UW–Extension and UW–Madison.

I don't know what role the organizers of the day care originally saw in me, but it soon went beyond taking them to the labor camps to recruit migrant children. When classes started, I was hired as an aide, the only bilingual staff, and ended up doing everything but drive the bus. The demonstration program took place in the Red Granite Elementary School building, but the migrant children participating were spread out in labor camps over two counties and several villages.

Because the program was situated in Red Granite, the nearest large migrant labor camps were the Marks Brothers labor camp in the village of Lorhville to the south and the Getske Farm farther east toward the city of Berlin. The Getske Farm grew lettuce and Marks Brothers was a

I assist the Wisconsin Division of Children and Youth migrant child care program at Red Granite Elementary School in 1962.

cucumber-growing enterprise. Children occasionally contributed to farm-work in the former, while they were an integral part of the harvest in the latter. Still, most of the migrant families were eager to send their children to *la escuelita*. Occasionally children were absent when their families needed their labor, such as at the peak of the cucumber harvest, but we met the enrollment and attendance goals of the one-room school project.

My days were long. I joined the non-Spanish-speaking driver in Wau-toma at daybreak, drove ten miles to Red Granite, then proceeded to pick up children in the two different areas and small farms in between, an hour-plus endeavor. After spending all day with the children, I would return the children to the labor camps. This took longer as I met and chat-ted with the parents before heading home to Wautoma.

During the school day, I was engaged constantly with the children. The program staff and teacher were very capable and caring but did not speak or understand Spanish, and few of the migrant children knew English. I had to translate all class instruction, including the physical education ac-tivities in the gym and on the playground. The children took a nap right after lunch, for which folding cots were set up in the gym. I had to convince the seven- and eight-year-olds who no longer napped to rest and relax and to help quiet the more apprehensive five-year-olds who initially did not know or trust us enough to fall asleep.

I knew little about curriculum and instruction plans, and there were no bilingual materials. The meetings that the head teacher called were most helpful as I became involved in developing the educational goals of the project. At the end of the six weeks, I was invited to Madison to meet with Wisconsin state staff for a program evaluation and with advocates who were proposing resuming the project in the summer of 1962 and beyond. My trips to Madison to meet with Jenny Lind and Nancy Travis of WDCY also included being introduced to migrant advocates who wanted to expand the migrant education program.

The following year we were able to be more creative with the use of Riverside Elementary School, which had recently been built and was available because it needed little summer maintenance. This was the stan-dard excuse by the local school districts who rejected using local school buildings to provide educational services for migrants—that their facilities needed maintenance and were not available over the summer.

Besides dealing with the maintenance schedule of the school district, two other issues arose during the early days of Wisconsin's migrant education programs. The first had to do with the local teachers wanting to be part of the project. Many teachers worked during the summer, some in the agriculture and food-processing industry that employed migrant families. The problem was that none could speak Spanish. The second major issue was that local school leaders wanted local children to be included in the new summer programs. This was problematic because the majority of the funds were targeted at migrant children. Key to putting the program together was the progressive local administration of the school principal, who organized a summer program that served both local and migrant children and hired some local teachers to complement bilingual aides hired with state funds. But the success from that second summer was never duplicated. The local school district wanted to spend no local funds for summer migrant programs that did not employ local teachers or serve their children, while state funds were targeted for migrant children only and state agencies wanted to maintain that focus.

One other issue that was never satisfactorily resolved locally was the availability of bilingual teachers and academic support staffing for the expanding summer programs. The available teacher core in the area was not bilingual. We had some wonderful teachers, but they could not make themselves understood. Most of the preschool and early education migrant children did not understand English. The option that I suggested was recruiting staff from Crystal City and surrounding communities, where young Chicanos were beginning to attend colleges and universities and choosing teaching as a career. I took it upon myself to recruit teachers and teacher's aides from my hometown as well as in the Texas Valley during my annual family visits to see my grandmothers and to support my uncle Julian and our neighbors in the political revolt.

My initial trips to recruit teachers and academic staff for the summer migrant programs were made during school breaks, primarily around Christmas and Easter. The first trips were unofficial, and I had no authority to offer jobs to anyone. I directed interested parties to contact the program staff in Madison and proceed with their applications.

Of course, my visits to Crystal City in the early sixties were not exclusively about recruiting bilingual staff for the Wisconsin migrant education programs. My trips coincided with the emerging voter education and registration campaigns leading to the 1963 election of Los Cinco.

—⊣⊦—

We paint history with broad strokes. Details remain hidden. César Chávez and Dolores Huerta's efforts to organize farmworkers provided us with the possibility to improve our living and working conditions through collective bargaining. In Crystal City, Texas, with the help of local Teamsters, we were able to organize the workers at Del Monte canning company, but the field laborers, the great majority of the area workforce, continued to work for poverty wages. Few of us thought it was possible to organize a viable workers union to challenge the Anglo minority land speculators and ranchers before Chávez formed the National Farm Workers Association (NFWA). Here in Wisconsin, we proceeded to do so only after developing a close working relationship with the California farmworkers movement and its leadership, including NFWA cofounders Chávez and Huerta and officers Gil Padilla and Antonio Orendain. Padilla and Orendain visited Wisconsin, and we met and worked together during the Rio Grande melon strike later that year. But, for my generation especially, those of us who had been born and raised in the Winter Garden, the attempt to gain the franchise, and not the forming of a farmworkers union, became our primary focus.

This would not be lost on some of us who planned to continue to challenge apartheid. In Wisconsin before we came together as a union, to have a say in our working conditions and to collectively bargain for fair compensation for our work, we began to attempt to curb the abuses, the disregard by the food processors of our working and living conditions.

6

Political Activism in Madison

My summer work with the expanding migrant education program spilled over into the academic year at Oshkosh. I was asked to come for evaluation and planning meetings with state officials and support groups after the summer programs in Madison. Here I met a number of Wisconsin progressives, among them UW–Madison Professor Elizabeth Brandeis, who was most important because she addressed the working and housing conditions that I was running into in my visits to the labor camps. Professor Brandeis taught me the breadth of the work needed to tackle these issues. It had to begin with regulating the industry's unfettered recruitment of Texas Borderland workers. Thousands were arriving with no guarantee of work or adequate housing. A system of work orders that corresponded to the proposed acreage planted would be needed. These work orders had to correspond to the availability of migrant housing. The state needed an enhanced migrant housing code and an inspection process so that the amount of inspected housing available was sufficient for the workers recruited. Housing inspectors needed to be hired to certify the adequacy of the housing and the number of workers and their families that could be housed in those structures. Inspection had to be undertaken when migrants inhabited those structures. Inspectors, we felt, needed to have the power to close migrant camps when there were gross violations. In the mid-1960s more than 40 percent of the units escaped inspections entirely. Once the certified housing units were opened and occupied, many became overcrowded. The overcrowding made the poor living conditions even worse.

My work with Elizabeth Brandeis also made me aware of the litany of progressive worker's rights laws that did not exclude migrant farmworkers, such as workers' compensation, the right to a living wage, and most important to us who wanted to improve our working and living conditions, the right to organize into collective bargaining units. In some cases, as in migrant housing, it meant advocating for the regulation of the Industrial Commission (IC) code. This required us to appear at and testify at a variety of administrative hearings and to advocate for an improved code and to demand enforcement. Professor Brandeis invited me to join her before these Wisconsin agencies and urged me to testify about my experience as a migrant, to report violations of Wisconsin statutes, and to administrate and recommend revision of rules and regulations. The food-processing companies challenged virtually all favorable recommendations for changes to IC rules, further delaying their implementation. The outstanding question was how the rules were to be enforced. IC's migrant housing section couldn't do it with the minimal existing staff. There were no funds available to hire additional inspectors. Here, we demanded that limited-term housing inspectors be hired and trained to enforce the law. To us this meant that inspections be conducted while the migrants were inhabiting the housing.

At the time that our family relocated in Wautoma, more than five thousand out of a population of more than ten thousand seasonal migrants were arriving to cultivate, harvest, and process a large variety of fruits and vegetable in the Central Sands area. Every conceivable structure was converted into migrant housing. Existing housing that met the code barely met the amount of space required, and the units were grossly overcrowded. Sanitary and sewer services, mostly septic tanks, were severely burdened. We advocated for the migrant inspectors to be empowered to declare units uninhabitable for violations and to shut them down. This meant that growers would lose part or all of their workforce during the harvest! These issues took years of advocating to adequately resolve.

Besides adequate, safe, and sanitary housing, wages and working conditions were the most pressing issues for which we advocated. Regarding the minimum wage, this meant proving that the piece rate system, in which migrant workers were paid according to units of work performed, did not equal the minimum wage. Professor Brandeis was sure it did not. According to her, data needed to be collected to prove what she had long suspected. Most important, data was needed to demonstrate what we knew anecdotally—that the piece rate system in two of the major employers of migrants, the cherry harvest in Door County and the cucumber harvest in multicounty central Wisconsin, did not equal the minimum wage. Professor Brandeis was sure that this would lead to court fights, as responsive administrative regulation would be challenged by agribusiness interests.

—||—

Effective regulation of a multitude of state codes meant testifying before the Wisconsin's Industrial Commission committee. At these hearings, paid lobbyist from processor and canning companies, including large growers, challenged our testimony and proposed changes. Professor Brandeis was convinced that the only remedy to create the necessary legislation and effectively impact state regulation was the formation of the Governor's Committee on Migratory Labor that would recommend policy. It would bring together diverse parties to deliberate, design, and recommend policy, administrative regulation, and legislation.

Meanwhile, I regularly traveled to Madison to accompany her to a multitude of hearings, testifying about the migrant condition, policy recommendations, and enforcement. On her recommendation, I was named by Governor John Reynolds to the newly created Governor's Committee on Migratory Labor.

What caused me to leave Oshkosh and move to Madison in the 1964–65 school year went beyond the migrant issues that had so preoccupied me. My friend Susan had transferred from nearby Ripon College to the University of Wisconsin–Madison, and I started to travel there to visit her. UW–Madison in the fall of 1964–65 was a hotbed of political activism. Student volunteers were coming back from the Deep South and reporting on lunch counter sit-ins, voter registration drives, and efforts to dismantle apartheid. Further, I became involved in the antidraft and antiwar movements.

Uncle Julian's participation in the political revolt in Crystal City drew me back to my hometown. During my visits to Texas in the early 1960s

I became more involved in supporting his political candidacy. College became less meaningful, and I began to miss classes as I overstayed my college breaks. The assassination of President Kennedy in the fall of 1963 was devastating and confusing. There was real fear for the future of our country. The following year massive numbers of troops were scheduled to be sent to Vietnam. The last semester I was enrolled at Oshkosh State, I did so not so much for academic advancement but to continue to engage with my fellow students, most of whom were actors and artists associated with the drama club and campus politics.

—||—

After leaving Oshkosh State, I was employed checking IDs at the B&B bar in downtown Oshkosh, cleaning the joint in the early mornings and immensely enjoying socializing with Manuel's friends on campus. George Melchior was managing a hamburger and brat counter in the same establishment I cleaned, and this became our after-school hangout. This too was short lived, as first the Cuban Missile Crisis and later the Vietnam War convulsed our lives. For some of us, the civil rights movement that was playing out in the Deep South, including in my hometown of Crystal City, drew us in the most profound way away from campus. Giffey left first to Vietnam in 1964; my younger brother Rodolfo followed the following year. Manuel volunteered for the army so he could go to Vietnam but ended up at Fort Sherman in Panama. I had stopped going to class and did not take my finals, using the time instead to travel freely in support of the political revolt in Crystal City. Once out of school, I became eligible for the draft and began to resist.

Now living in Madison full time, I got a job as a laborer for Findorff construction company and rented a room at the YMCA, a block west of the State Capitol. After I received my first paychecks, I rented a room down the road in the 500 block of West Mifflin Street, a neighborhood that at the time was heavily populated by student activists. I was ineligible to enroll at UW–Madison due to my academic record at Oshkosh. I would later enroll at UW–Stevens Point and take correspondence courses to be eligible for admittance to UW system campuses.

While in Madison during the winter of 1965–66, I decided to challenge my draft status and take a public stance against the Vietnam War. I had not expressed antiwar sentiments publicly while at Oshkosh the previous years. In the Salas family, in spite of the fact that we stayed abreast of the politics of the southeast Asian conflict, we did not discuss the inequities of the draft that led it to be an army of poor men and minorities.

My uncle Julian served during World War II with the Wisconsin Red Arrow Division in the disarmament of the Japanese army and the initial planning for the occupation. He related how the armed forces were still segregated, and not all Anglo soldiers saluted Black officers, even those who clearly demonstrated by their uniform that they had heroically served in the Pacific Island battles against the Japanese. Still, I never heard him advise any of us not to serve. Certainly, I heard no antiwar sentiments from Manuel, who was convinced that he had to serve, preferably as an officer. Moreover, he did not want to be drafted; rather, he volunteered for the Vietnam War.

My younger brother Rudy delayed going to Vietnam by several days. When I went to drop him off at the airport, we stopped for a beer and he met a kindred spirit and decided to stay an extra weekend. But he never equivocated about his duty to serve, and when he was in Vietnam, he wrote me passionate letters about what he thought of my protesting against the war. Among our peers at Oshkosh, Tom Cavanaugh had served and returned. David Giffey left so suddenly that we were not part of his decision to serve, only aware of the vacuum that his absence left. During the Cuban Missile Crisis, we were glued to the television, concerned more about a nuclear holocaust. I opposed the use of nuclear weapons but at the time did not oppose war or the draft. The discussion among my peers at Oshkosh State did not lead me in that direction. In spite of the fact that I informed my father that I was convinced that the war was unjust and that it was becoming mostly a poor man's war, he insisted that I should serve.

All of the families I knew who had members who served in World War II were affected after their return. The outrageous conduct of Uncle Julian and his war buddies, Macias and Canela, was legend in the barrio. They would go on all weekend, carousing on both sides of the border. Sometimes Uncle Julian was gone for days visiting the border town of Piedras Negras, forty miles away. No one knew of post-traumatic stress disorder. They were expected to self-recover and most of them did . . . but not right away. Uncle Julian finished high school and became a notary public and would later support the Crystal City political revolt of 1963. Canela took over the family bakery, and his delicious pan de dulce would attract people from miles around. Macias opened a bar in the segregated commercial district and organized crews for the local independent growers who planted spinach in the winter and onions in spring.

Of all of these, however, I was most impressed by my uncle Julian's postwar experience. I was living at my grandmother Beba's home when he returned from the war. Behind my grandmother's home lived my aunt Francisca and her husband. In front of the main house, a twelve-by-twenty-foot room was built for Uncle Julian, who lived by himself. I was not allowed to go into his room without my grandmother, and only to pick up his soiled laundry for her to wash. She would not step into his room because she claimed Satan resided there. I was directed first to enter the unit and to put away the adult magazines and pick up empty liquor and beer bottles. Then, I gathered the laundry for my grandmother, who stood by the steps ensuring that I would not linger other than to place clean shirts on a hanger by the door, drop off his clean undergarments, and pick up the dirty clothes from the floor. But as I did this, I glanced at the magazines of naked women on his desk and admired his two samurai swords on his unmade bed that he had sneaked out of Japan in his trunk. On days that my grandmother would enter to sweep and mop the floors, I would go in first and remove and hide all of the above.

On Sundays, my uncle would leave sixty-five cents under a stone by the door for me to purchase menudo and beef barbecue from the neighbor, Don Jesus, across the street. No matter what time he would rise, this was Julian's first Sunday meal. Since he would not arrive until the wee hours of the morning and did not get up until after lunch, he wanted to ensure that Don Jesus's barbecue would not be sold out. As a college student looking back on these childhood memories, I had a sense of the way war could change a person and cause lasting damage to a life, even for those who came home.

My most searing memory of war was not experiencing my uncle's bewildering return from the occupation of Japan, but of Mrs. Longoria pining over her son Johnny's missing in action (MIA) status during the Korean War. The Longoria family had sold my father the café, dining room, and attached home that we occupied on Crockett Street in 1943.

After seven years of living with my grandmother, I joined my parents in the thriving restaurant. All of our foodstuff for the café was to be bought from the Longoria Grocery Store, kitty-corner from my father's restaurant. Only if the item that we needed was not found there were we to go shopping for it somewhere else.

As time went by, Mrs. Longoria's health began to deteriorate. The worry over Johnny's MIA status, of not knowing whether he was alive or dead, broke her down. She no longer served customers. She sat by the doorway to the attached home in a chair while her husband attended to the neighbors who continued to shop there. By then, Mr. Longoria was spending more time caring for his wife than attending the store. Eventually, limited foodstuff was available, but still I was sent there to keep the Longoria business viable and to inquire about the Mrs. Longoria. She no longer sat in the store but stayed in the adjoining house area. When I came in and inquired about his wife, Mr. Longoria would guide me to the living room where she sat, her eyes red and droopy from crying. Here, she was told that it was me in the hope that my visit would lift her spirits, but actually the opposite began to occur. When I came upon her, she would hug me and hold on to me and begin to sob, so that Mr. Longoria had to pry me from her, embarrassed by the whole ordeal. I stopped going to visit, as we all felt worse as a result.

After contemplating these experiences, I decided that not only would I oppose the draft but I would also work to stop the war. I attended workshops held on the UW–Madison campus to discuss methods of protest. We also discussed Thoreau's notion of civil disobedience and how it was being practiced in the dismantling of apartheid and obtaining the franchise in the Deep South. I participated in the 1965 antiwar protest at the UW–Madison Library Mall, where a number of students burned their Selective Service draft cards. I did not burn mine then but did so with a number of protesters at a bar later that night. Going to Canada was never a realistic option; I wanted to challenge the warmongers at home. I also thought claiming conscientious objector status was hypocritical on my part. There was nothing in my background to make that claim. I was encouraged to do so as a tactic rather than based on religious grounds. A friend of mine was doing alternate service at Wisconsin's Mendota Hospital, and he encouraged me to apply. I didn't, but I took his advice and applied to the Children's Treatment Center, a center for emotionally disturbed youth located next to the hospital, one of the most challenging and unforgettable jobs I have ever held.

While in Madison, I proceeded to appeal my Selective Service (SS) status of 1A that made me eligible to be drafted. My argument was based on "national security," as defined in SS as those contributing to the war effort. I felt I had something to offer, advocating and working for migrant workers. I was denied deferment at all SS levels, local, state, and national appeals. I was ordered to report for induction. I didn't, as I continued to mull over my options. I didn't appear to have any, and my mother called me up to inform me that I was being sought at home in Wautoma and that my father insisted I report to SS. I did. Erroneously, I thought I could join protesters from Madison at the Milwaukee induction center, but I was told to report from Wautoma, where I had originally signed up for the draft. I took a bus from Wautoma to Milwaukee and was housed at the downtown YMCA on one of the top floors.

At the Milwaukee Y, US military personnel were all about, and I was directed to a room on a particular floor where other inductees were housed. We were not allowed to socialize, so I did not find out directly why they were at the Y guarded by US soldiers. In the morning, the others and I were driven by bus by US military personnel to the induction center for our physicals. I felt as though I were already in the military.

At the induction center, I looked for young men from Madison but did not recognize any in the sea of draftees. Although in draft resistance trainings we were shown different strategies and tactics we could undertake to disrupt the induction process, I stood in line like all the rest and chose instead to purposefully flunk my aptitude test. I realized that I couldn't fool the test administrators for very long. All my wrong responses wouldn't jibe with the fact that I was a college student. I was informed that if I responded positively to questions relating to "bed wetting," that would signal mental disorders and I would get an interview with a psychiatrist and I could then inform the psychiatrist I would continue to oppose the war in and out of uniform. The other option was to wear pink panties to the physical exam and claim that I was a homosexual. I didn't do either. However, I did get an interview with a captain, who almost lost his cool during my interview due to my obstinance. I didn't have to do much.

But an unanticipated event occurred. I failed my physical examination! I didn't know if it was because of my obstinance at the induction center or an injury to my left eye that happened during elementary school in Crystal City. Conflicts broke out between barrios and a fistfight that started on school grounds spilled over into more fistfights off school grounds. That weekend, several doors down from my father's business, I was showered with stones and mud packs while on my way to my daily errands. One of the projectiles hit me in the left eye. I underwent eye surgery in San Antonio, but my eyesight never returned; I saw only a dim light.

Throughout my youth, my parents raised me not to consider my partial blindness as a handicap. I was taught self-defense with my chin down and my head tilted so my right eye was the center of my body. I boxed in my youth. I played football and ran the half mile in track my junior and senior years at Wautoma High School. I never thought my lack of sight would prevent me from going to Vietnam. After the failed eye exam, I called my mother to tell her that I did not have to join my brothers Manuel and Rodolfo in uniform. I told her that I was returning to Madison. She started crying and praising the Lord.

Thereafter, I received my new SS status; I was now classified 1Y. I also received an invitation to join in a Madison group therapy. I don't know if the invitation had anything to do with my responses on the aptitude test at the induction center. I never reported. I understood the 1Y designation meant that I would not be called unless there was a national emergency. We never declared war against Vietnam and an emergency was never called. Later, due to the clamor about the unfairness of the deferment process that gave college students and other privileged families the ability to avoid serving, the draft ended and a lottery system was established. What was unstated in the deliberations was that Vietnam was a poor man's war. Minority groups served and were killed in greater proportion to their population than whites.

After my change in status, the next of my brothers to be designated 1A was Francisco. Here, my mother called me to see if I would advise him on his status. The news of the war and the fact that minorities and poor whites were bearing the brunt of the combat had changed my father's view on our commitment to serve. Both of my brothers would serve and both would return, Manuel from the Panama jungle, Rodolfo from Cu Chi, Vietnam. The news from our neighbors in Crystal City was not as good. Corporal Melecio Ortiz, age twenty-two, became a casualty of the Vietnam War in May 1967. That same month my father's godson, Rogelio Boca-negra, had stepped on a land mine and had received severe injuries to his left side, leg, and arm. He would later die from his injuries.

In December 1969, after the draft changed to a lottery system, which my youngest brother, Luis, participated in. I continued to oppose the war and participated in demonstrations in Madison and later helped organize the war moratoriums in Milwaukee.

I had returned to Madison in the winter of 1965–66 and resumed my employment at the Children's Treatment Center working with emotion-ally disturbed youth. At the treatment center, because I had worked with migrant children during my summers, I was given the opportunity to join a wonderful team of psychiatrists, nurses, and a very talented staff in an attempt to deal with troubled youth.

But it was the news from Delano, California, in the spring of 1966 that led me to organize migrant workers to protest their working and living

My brothers Rodolfo and Manuel Salas (right) in uniform during the Vietnam era.

conditions. Madison, in addition to being one of the most active antiwar communities in the Midwest, had extensive links with voter registration and other groups who were challenging the system of apartheid. Each week, we met organizers, volunteers, and other youth who were engaged in the Deep South; activists who were traveling from both US coasts would stop in Madison to share their experiences. One of these speakers gave a report of the fact that Dolores Huerta and César Chávez had joined the Filipino Agricultural Workers Organizing Committee (AWOC) strike against Delano, California, grape growers in 1965. The following spring of 1966, California migrants farmworkers were marching from Delano to Sacramento to dramatize their mistreatment and working and living conditions. Inspired by these events, I would return to the migrant labor camps and organize a march demanding improved working and living conditions for Wisconsin migrants.

7

ORGANIZING THE MIGRANT MARCH

My three years working with the migrant youth educational programs and my work with Professor Brandeis broadened my understanding of migrant issues, but it was the march led by César Chávez and Dolores Huerta from Delano to Sacramento that gave the impetus for a Wisconsin march. In the summer of 1966, I returned to Wautoma, not to work for migrant education programs but to organize an eighty-mile protest march from central Wisconsin to Madison.

Setting a distinct tone for migrant programs, Professor Brandeis's preliminary report of the 1965 migrant wage study brought the issue of wages and working conditions to the fore. It documented gross violations of the Wisconsin migrant housing code as well as lack of enforcement of progressive legislation such as worker's compensation. Further, it provided evidence that the piece rate system in cucumbers did not equal the state's minimum wage. Manuel and I were part of a group of UW–Madison graduate students from a variety of fields who had been assigned throughout the state to gather the data. Project leaders presented the report to the recently created Governor's Committee on Migratory Labor. Both Professor Brandeis and I had been appointed by Governor Reynolds to the committee. The committee held hearings to address the issues brought by UW–Madison's Institute for Poverty Summer Project. The committee's work and the release of its findings was an important milestone, but it would mean little if the state did not take action. We wanted to capitalize on this moment by planning a march to draw wider public attention to these issues.

The biggest problem in organizing in the spring of 1966 was that migrant workers were dispersed across scores of grower-owned labor camps over an immense area made up of three counties: Waushara, Marquette, and Portage. There were at least a dozen larger labor camps with more than fifty workers each, but most camps were smaller, made up of several extended families. Although regional and national food-processing companies recruited the Great Lakes region migrants from South Texas and northern Mexico, most migrants lived in housing provided by growers. Moreover, most of the housing units were converted garages, sheds, and outbuildings that were within eyesight of the grower's home. Some of the larger farms had barrack-style multifamily units on grower-owned land, in many cases within eyesight of the grower residence. There was no way that I could go family by family in multiunit, grower-owned structures to recruit workers without the growers' knowledge. When I had visited grower-owned labor camps to recruit children for the migrant education programs between 1961 and 1964, some had not taken too kindly to "do-gooders" crisscrossing their property and encouraging migrant youth to attend school rather than work. We would need a plan to get the word out in other ways.

Since we were calling for collective action by migrant workers, it was imperative that we come together as a group before the protest march, which we had scheduled for the second week of August. Father Michael Garrigan's support was most important in allowing us the use of St. Joseph's unused facilities for our initial small group meetings. A new St. Joseph Catholic Church had been built on the outskirts of Wautoma. Their previous buildings were no longer in use and on several weekends in 1965, the Brandeis Summer Project had held meetings in one of the main buildings.

Father Garrigan was an outstanding athlete and enjoyed organizing and playing touch football with the migrant workers after services along with Green Bay Archdiocese's seminarians. That gave us an idea, and we began to organize softball games after Sunday's church services to get the workers to come together and talk about the union. We would invite the larger labor camps to organize their own softball teams and have one labor camp play another. Because cucumber acreage by Libby's had expanded into Portage County, the softball games were scheduled for the villages of Bancroft and Almond, where the camps were located. Playing for a half barrel of beer during the hot summer months was common practice throughout central Wisconsin's rural areas.

Almost all villages had sandlot baseball diamonds where one bar team played against another. The gatherings after church services and in the sandlots allowed large groups of workers to meet without arousing suspicion that we were planning the protest march and later organizing labor actions. Still, we saw the need to take a public stand as a group before taking action in the form of a strike or picket line.

We saw two reasons why we needed to come together at a mass meeting before the march. The first and most important was that we wanted to galvanize support for improvement of migrant worker wages and working conditions. After the UW–Madison's Poverty Institute wage study report, processors and growers challenged the findings, alleging that migrants were happy with their working conditions. We wanted workers to be on the same page about what we wanted to counter in these claims.

Further, we were no longer called "do-gooders," as we had been when we began the migrant education programs in 1962. Now we were provoking and inciting workers. Ambrosio Melendrez, one of the Crystal City teachers I had recruited for the summer migrant education program in central Wisconsin, was a veteran of the voter and education programs during the political revolt in our hometown, where we had once gone to school together. By nature, he was deliberate and cautious. At our planning meetings organizing the rally and eighty-mile march, he expressed concern about grower retaliation, citing the extralegal actions undertaken by the Anglo colonists in the Crystal City counterrevolt of 1965. Mindful of the economic reprisals and retributions that our compatriots had suffered in Crystal City, we did not want to put workers in danger of losing their jobs for joining the protest. Thus, we would call for a mass meeting to demonstrate support for the march, but we would only allow one member per family and one family per camp to participate in the march. In Crystal City the political revolt leaders risked losing their jobs and livelihoods. Added to these risks, migrants were not living in their own homes. They lived in housing provided by processor and growers. They would be thrown out of the migrant labor camps, losing both their jobs and their homes overnight.

In addition to the generosity of Father Garrigan and the experienced advice of my old friend Ambrosio Melendrez, we had many allies in pulling off the march. However, no one was more helpful in organizing the rally and preparing for the march than my oldest brother, Manuel. Manuel had volunteered and was in the US Army Infantry, but he spent a couple of weeks in Wautoma before being shipped to the Panama jungle at Fort Sherman. It was Manuel, during his short visit before he was shipped out, who was responsible for the rally calling for the migrants to come together and volunteer for the march.

First of all, Manuel and I agreed we should call César Chávez in Delano, California, to express support for the grape strike and request the use of the Aztec thunderbird symbol, which would become a national symbol of the movement, from the National Farm Workers Association (NFWA) banner. I had never met Chávez, so I called him from a pay phone at Salas Café.

After introductions, I told him of my plans to march from Wautoma to Madison, as he had done from Delano to Sacramento in California. Chávez agreed to allow the Wisconsin farmworkers the use of the banner, and he, in turn, asked us for support of the grape boycott. Chávez explained that the 1935 Wagner Act that had created the National Labor Relations Board excluded farmworkers. The grape growers shut out and replaced striking farmworkers with scabs.

The NFWA and the Filipino-led Agricultural Workers Organizing Committee (AWOC) grape strikers had no recourse but to force the growers back to the negotiating table by carrying out a national consumer boycott. Wisconsin was crucial in the national boycott. Besides grapes, large amounts of wine and especially brandy were popular products in Wisconsin. Although the law had never been tested, as there had never been a sustained attempt to organize farmworkers, Wisconsin's labor law did not exclude farmworkers. We agreed to initiate statewide support for the California grape boycott.

Manuel immediately began to design a huge banner that would hang between the concrete pillars on the doorsteps of the Waushara County Courthouse, where he foresaw the speakers standing at the planned rally. We agreed that it was insufficient to organize the rally solely by personal contact. We needed to announce it publicly. The farmworkers, we felt, needed to take a public stance in support of the eighty-mile march. The rally should be a call for volunteers, individual farmworkers publicly volunteering to march. Where Manuel again prevailed was in the content of the posters we agreed to put up. I was of the opinion that it should simply state the date, place, and time. Manuel thought the rally as well as the poster should challenge migrants to voice their support of the union. It should provoke a dialogue for us to engage them. His poster designs provoked the workers to action:

Juntarnos para ser Oidos (Come together to be recognized)

Hablar para ser Oidos (Speak to be heard)

La Raza Tiene Causa (Our people have cause)

We decided not to designate the site, date, or time of the rally on the poster. We were concerned about retribution by the processors and growers. The organizing for the meeting and the details would be communicated personally.

As Manuel explained, Chávez was using the pre-Columbian thunderbird symbol on a black-and-red background to announce the strike, to get workers to join the farmworkers union, and to call for all to support the farmworkers' cause. The banners were black and red because these were the colors the Texas Borderland mutualistas used to announce labor actions. In Crystal City, the only mass organization allowed under apartheid was the mutual aid society, Sociedad Funeraria Miguel Hidalgo. Across the border, the Magón brothers' mutualistas were organizing Alto Horno mines, where my grandfather Teofilo had worked. Public demonstrations and in some cases picketing were restricted if not outright prohibited. The mutualistas announced strikes, walkouts, and boycotts by showing the black-and-red banners for labor action in the mining regions and

The posters designed by my brother Manuel were a call to action.

related industries in which my grandfather had toiled. During my youth in Crystal City, I had been sent to represent the family at *quinceañeras*, birthdays, and other events of the Salas family members still living across the border in Nueva Rositas, Coahuila, Mexico, my grandfather Teofilo's former residence. His granddaughter, Aunt Dolores ("Lola"), had married a miner who worked for the Altos Hornos mines. Strikes and walkouts in protest of dangerous working conditions were lengthy. They reached out for us for economic assistance during these times.

Many in the Native population on both sides of the border recognized that the black and red colors belonged to the pre-Columbian priestly scribes who wrote of community values. We decided to use the same colors to promote the march. Further, both Manuel and I were fascinated with what the NFWA's thunderbird symbolized. On its face it was Mexican; it was an image of ourselves that was pre-Columbian, of a heritage that was distinct from how we were presently viewed. The qualities of a historian that had been evident in Manuel while he was a student at Oshkosh were now being carried into banners, posters, and leaflets that were becoming known to the Mexican and Mexican American seasonal migrant workers who harvested cucumbers in central Wisconsin.

The question of our identity was not solely academic and did not occur only in deliberations at Oshkosh State. In 1963, I was approached by the editor of the local newspaper, the *Waushara Argus*, to help create a migrant-focused summer shopper. Local newspapers published special summer editions, or "shoppers," directed at the tourists. Local businesses supported these shoppers, welcoming the large tourist population that frequented the area lakes and rivers. In addition to the nearly five thousand seasonal migrant workers, thousands of tourists would descend from Chicago and Milwaukee to frolic in our freshwaters and streams. The summer publication in Waupaca, thirty miles away, in addition to the ads, always included photos of vacationing young women enjoying the beaches in the area.

The paper hired high school graduate Jim Johnson to sell subscriptions and to help design the ads for the shopper, to be called *Semanario Español* (*Spanish Weekly*). I only worked for the summer publication one year. In 1964, Johnson and I developed a different publication, a migrant-focused newspaper called *La Voz Mexicana*. Again, the question of identity was at the forefront, this time as a front-page header. But it went beyond head-lines. The news from *La Voz* spread by word of mouth up and down neigh-borhood streets, similar to a vocero or town crier in colonial times. It included bits of news from the Borderland cities of migrants, the south central Texas area, and the Texas Valley. For the young migrant we printed the top ten music hits. Rather than tourists, the pictures on its pages were migrants, working and enjoying their weekends in downtown Wautoma. In the summer of 1966, when I returned to Wautoma to organize the march, Johnson and Mark Erenburg were publishing a new edition of *La Voz*. Their publication was not used as a tool to organize in the summer of 1966 activities, but they both supported the march, and their last pub-lication had many photos of the event.

—||—

In organizing the rally and eighty-mile march, I found many families I had worked alongside during my ten years of migrating, as well as families I knew from Crystal City. Now I looked for them after work in the labor camps, joined them at the regional grading stations, or met them on week-ends when they came into town for shopping and to attend church services. I also knew many families from my three summers recruiting their children for the migrant education programs. When I began to organize farmwork-ers, former students would rush to greet me when I visited those labor camps. Still, I was concerned that if the growers knew the purpose of my visiting the camps, the workers would get thrown out of their homes. On weekends, I did not have to leave town to look for migrants to organize. Most of the workers came to town to shop and for church on Sunday at St. Joseph Catholic Church. I would spend the afternoon by the downtown Wautoma Mill Pond parking lot, where families gathered before and after shopping, and after mass on Sundays. I spent the two weekends before the rally in the Wautoma Mill Pond area, greeting workers and inviting them to the rally at the Waushara County Courthouse steps. Rainy days were like an extra weekend day. Workers and their families poured into town. The sidewalks and park became my office.

The banner designed by Manuel called for a large public meeting to take place on Sunday, March 14, to propose the march and call for volun-teers to begin planning the following day. The banner listed no host organization. The call to action in the posters was by and for *La Raza*, the people. Manuel found a printer in Oshkosh that printed in color because we wanted the thunderbird symbol to appear with its natural plumage against the red-and-black background. Like the Wautoma residents later, the printer workers were struck by the colorful poster but could not read the Spanish words. Manuel and I peppered the city with the posters several days before the rally. The poster had its desired effects. It provoked a reaction from both the migrant workers and the growers and local townsfolk who wondered what was going on. It provoked dialogue among workers: Where were we going to hold a rally before the march? What was the course of action? Throughout the spring and summer, we continued to meet at the former St. Joseph parish hall to plan. The main discussion was to develop the list of demands.

The final organizational effort on the day of the rally took place on St. Joseph Catholic Church grounds and later at the Wautoma Mill Pond. We urged the parishioners to attend the rally, now identified in a handout to be at the county courthouse at a specified time. We used the term *Raza* to designate who we were as a people and that we had *causa*, a reason to meet and protest our condition. Vasconcelos, at the turn of the century, had used the term in his famous essay *La Raza Cosmica* on the search for a definition of the Mexican people. It was the translation of *raza* as "race" that we wanted to avoid. We decided not to translate it and to use it as it was commonly used among the Crystal City youths, as a means of self-identification, as a people. The workers related to this. However, the reaction to the migrant protest by the community at large, beyond the Central Sands, concerned me.

All of us were mindful of the Black American demands for the franchise in the Deep South and how violently their constitutional rights had been denied. In Milwaukee, the nonviolent open housing marches had been met by heavily armed riot police and later the National Guard, who had orders to shoot. Some protesters rioted, as in much of urban America in the late sixties, some rioters set fires and looted local businesses. We had seen on television the violence that had been showered on the protesters in Mississippi and Alabama. The issues, challenging apartheid's legal segregation of races by ethnic groups, by ordinances, as well as real estate instruments, were lost by the media reporting on the "lawlessness" of the demonstrators. We also were acutely aware of the reprisals faced by Los Cinco and their supporters in Crystal City.

Before the march, I called David Giffey, my former classmate from Oshkosh, to meet me at Lorenzo's restaurant in Madison, where I was organizing the reception of the eighty-mile march on the steps of Wisconsin's State Capitol. I needed his advice on how to deal with the press. Giffey had just returned from Vietnam and was working for a Fox River Valley newspaper. It was great to see him. I informed him of our activities and asked how he thought the press would respond to our message. I pointed to the negative reaction from town folks and growers to the posters.

Giffey assured me that the march would be one of the top Wisconsin stories of the summer. He asked me for exclusive rights to the story on the rally that would take place on the day before the march. He would cover the rally and take photos and put them on the Associated Press wire. This was a tremendous opportunity; we planned to lay out our goals at the rally, and we would be able to more effectively communicate our message and prevent future misunderstanding through Giffey's coverage.

The rally on August 14, 1966, was a huge success. We had targeted about ten large labor camps and most of those that were closest to Wautoma, and we had arranged for crew leaders and family heads to bring the families in their tandem trucks and pickups. Previously, we had asked the workers to be in downtown Wautoma for a rally without specifying the location, to avoid tipping our hand. We were afraid that we would be denied the right to gather a large number of workers in a public place.

We decided to meet next door to the Waushara County Courthouse. It would be closed on the Sunday of the rally, so we wouldn't be interfering with operations. The sheriff's office and jail were on the same grounds; we wanted a peaceful gathering, and the first to realize it, we thought, should be local law enforcement. When Manuel hung the red banner with the black Aztec thunderbird between the roman pillars at the entrance to the courthouse, more questions arose from the neighboring non-Mexican residents. Soon they would melt into the background.

Giffey's coverage of the plans for the rally and march caught the attention of Wisconsin state officials who were responsible for enforcing Wisconsin's progressive legislation. Industrial Commission chairman Joseph Fagan began to question the need for a march. State agencies responsible for enforcing the statutes and administrative law covering migrant workers were willing to come to Wautoma to meet and hear our complaints, so there was no need to march to Madison, they claimed. However, Governor Knowles's office informed us that he would not be able to meet with us, as he was scheduled to be someplace else.

Further, IC chairman Fagan informed us that he was organizing a hearing for which top Wisconsin state officials were traveling to Wautoma on Monday—the same day we were to begin the march—to meet with us and hear our demands. I faced two challenges. First, I had to get word back to more than a dozen labor camps to deliberate on the offer to stop or delay the march until after the evening meeting. Second, we had to show up before the hastily called meeting to state our case publicly. There was no time to contact all the leaders of the labor camps, so I concentrated on reaching out to those camps that were sending marchers. None of the workers I contacted wanted to stop the march. We agreed to meet with the politicians, but we would not commit to stop the march. We would march as planned after mass at St. Joseph, walking from the outskirts of Wautoma, along Highway 21, to the neighboring village of Coloma. There, we would make camp for the marchers to rest and sleep at the public wayside at the outskirts of the village. I would return for the scheduled meeting at the Waushara County Courthouse and meet with state officials that night.

—‖—

Hundreds of migrant workers and their families had shown up for the rally. Lucio Valdez, my old neighbor from Crystal City, worked for the Green Bay Food Company and was instrumental in bringing people to the event. Most of the crews were from our hometown. Lucio had married one of the Coronado girls who lived across the street from my grandparents' homestead, where we had been longtime neighbors. Salvador Sanchez, a Texas Valley crew leader who was working with my father for Libby's, organized several labor camps in the Bancroft-Almond area and brought families to the rally by the truckload. Other community leaders who helped bring workers to the demonstration were Gil Perez, Conrado Lopez, and Jose Garcia. Garcia would later follow me as a member on the Governor's Committee on Migratory Labor. Mr. Hinojosa, Salvador's neighbor from Pharr, Texas, along with Mrs. Ortega's sons, attended our rallies, community meetings, and the march that summer. In the downtown area, Perfecto Villareal took it upon himself to walk up and down Wautoma's three commercial and retail blocks of Main Street and personally invite workers to the rally.

At the rally, we presented to the attendees the demands that we had developed at the midweek planning meetings. It was to be a "March for Respectability." When the workers spoke during planning meetings, they put *respect* at the top of the list. I knew what that meant, but I didn't know how "respect" could be translated as a demand. It was a distinct working relationship with our employers that we sought. The list of more formal demands included the enforcement of Wisconsin statutes regarding wages, housing, and working conditions. At the time, none of the demands called for new legislation. To bolster our demands during these early years of the movement, we relied on the support and research of Mark Erenburg. Erenburg had been on the migrant wage study headed by Professor Brandeis the previous year, and as a PhD candidate in economics his research focus was Wisconsin migrants. He had the data at his fingertips to argue against the growers' claims on wages and working conditions. Any notion that Fagan had about his rapidly organized meeting at Waushara County Courthouse halting the march was quickly dispelled by our testimony.

We wanted enforcement of Wisconsin's social and progressive legislation, minimum wage, worker's compensation, and enforcement of Wisconsin's migrant housing code. We refrained from listing the overcrowded and unsanitary housing facilities in the demands. We didn't know how to address these most important issues. What was harder to communicate was the demand for respect. The idea of respect as a demand, I think, had to do with migrant workers wanting their work to be valued, to be appreciated. They wanted their contribution to the harvest to be recognized, for being responsible for nurturing, cultivating, and harvesting the crop. This dialogue arose again whenever we discussed how we should identify ourselves.

Father Garrigan and Reverend Barry Shaw representing the Migrant Ministry initiated the rally with a benediction and a call for a peaceful demonstration. I then proceeded to lay out the problems migrant families were facing and how we needed to demand that they be addressed. Years of migrant education programs had not addressed the basic condition of the worker, how they lived, what they earned. We needed to protest this by marching to Madison. I called for volunteers for the protest march to begin the following day, August 15, after mass at St. Joseph. Some of the crew leaders had asked to speak to defend company policies and one of them, a man from the Chicago Pickle Company, actually got up on stage to address the crowd, but I delayed giving him the microphone. When I called for volunteers for the march to join me at the courthouse steps, he exited the stage without speaking.

Concerned over mass firings of whole families, we asked that only one member of a family, and no more than one worker per labor camp, volunteer to march. We would be marching more than fifteen miles a day, so I asked that only physically fit persons volunteer. For safety reasons, as a group we had decided that only men would be allowed to march. I thought it was a mistake not to call for women to march, especially since in the harvest many women were as productive if not more so than men. This was visible as we worked in multifamily crews, and who was more effective at harvesting was known by who filled the most five-gallon pails or hundred-pound burlap sacks of cucumbers. Women and children made up the majority of the family-based workforce. However, we were concerned about not having any sanitary facilities for the women to use, and no plan of where we were to sleep other than on the ground at wayside parks en route to the State Capitol. In spite of organizers' requests, entire families joined us throughout and at the end of the march.

As for media coverage, Giffey had been correct! His stories and pictures made the news statewide. A Green Bay film crew and Madison reporters showed up to mass on Monday, August 15. The *Capital Times* publisher sent James Maranis and photographer Skip Heine to cover the event, including following up after the march with some extensive features. Charlie House, a *Milwaukee Journal* outdoor writer, met us on the march and wrote a piece on our lack of marching shoes and appropriate garb. Giffey had been right, people throughout Wisconsin were extremely interested in our story and surprised at the poor wages, the deplorable housing conditions, and the gross violation of child labor laws.

As families dropped off the marchers on Monday morning at St. Joseph for mass, we invited them to join us at the meeting with state officials after work. Throughout the first day of the march, we continued to organize for the meeting and to plan for the next five days on the road.

I had made a pledge to the two dozen protesters who had volunteered to march that I would march with them every step of the way. We would stay together throughout the week. Everyone was pleased, but this immediately challenged my being present in activities outside of the march. Since I would be marching during the day, I could not organize the workers for the Wisconsin Industrial Commission meeting Monday evening. I counted on Lucio Valdez and Salvador Sanchez again to help me organize the migrant turnout for the meeting. I also sent word to Perfecto Villareal, who lived in Wautoma, to make sure he attended and brought fellow workers. What I would most miss was my brother Manuel's advice and company. He had finished basic training and was ordered to report to the jungles of Panama at Fort Sherman. I would not see him for another year.

—||—

It quickly became apparent that our fears regarding employer retribution were coming true. As anticipated, once marchers' faces started appearing on television and in newspapers, several were fired for not showing up to work. This meant their families would also lose their housing. We hurried to accommodate them in the homes of families in other labor camps who were sympathetic to the march. This had to be done without the growers' knowledge. We also sought legal advice and publicly stated that we would sue growers responsible for violation of workers' labor and civil rights. Further, at the start of the march we faced some hostilities from townsfolk, with oncoming cars appearing to want to drive us off the side of the road. After that, we kept a vehicle nearby in case of emergencies and to respond to or witness any incidents. Upon hearing this, my father sent a school bus for shelter and as an alternative to sleeping out in the open and being subject to harassment. To assure the safety of the marchers, I asked Father Garrigan to call ahead to see if we could camp out at Catholic parishes on the way to Madison instead of sleeping at waysides.

I can't overstate the help that my family provided before, during, and after the march. The Salas restaurant became our offices. My younger brothers, who were the restaurant's waiters, took messages from the pay phone in the side dining room and communicated them to me. On the first day of the march, my father woke and instructed my younger brother Francisco to stay beside me throughout that first day. Francisco was supposed to alternate with my other younger brother, Luis, but Luis was unable to join the march, and Francisco stayed with us the entire time. Francisco must have been the one who informed my father of the need for a backup vehicle. My father, initially without my knowledge, followed up our phone calls with interviews with my brother, who now never left my side. Later, my father would simply ask me to pass the public phone to whichever of my brothers was with me. If Salvador was around, he would simply demand to discuss whatever was going on with him. When my older brother Carlos dropped off the bus for us to sleep that first night, it included tacos for all the marchers, from my mother.

Since most of the marchers were healthy, young, and in good physical shape, we were very much up to the task of marching the scheduled fifteen-plus miles per day. But we were poorly dressed for the endeavor. The biggest problem was inappropriate shoes. Marchers started getting blisters on their feet before the first day was out. Clothing was another problem, with many marchers experiencing chafing around the groin. Later, we would call for changes of socks, petroleum jelly to alleviate chafing, and antiseptics and bandages for the blistered feet. One of the marchers needed medical attention after the fourth day. Finally, we underestimated entirely the large quantities of water we needed to consume during the hot days. We also needed toilet paper, soap, and towels to be brought along with the meals, as without mobile sanitary facilities, we ignominiously relieved ourselves along the road.

Through Father Garrigan, we were able to obtain permission to sleep at church and parish meeting rooms on the second and third nights. This allowed the marchers the opportunity to relax safely on the grounds. In fact, the third night, the facilities were near a baseball diamond, and the young men played ball until dark.

On the fourth day, on the outskirts of Madison, we were fêted with a potluck by well-wishers who drove from Madison to treat us and to plan for the next day's activities at the State Capitol. Everyone ate heartily, and our spirits were lifted. That night the workers watched 8 mm Abbot and Costello and Charlie Chaplin movies that the Madison volunteers had brought.

Migrant workers begin the march on Highway 21 between Wautoma and Madison on August 15, 1966. I am pictured at the front of the group (left), next to Obreros Unidos organizer Salvador Sanchez. PHOTO BY DAVID GIFFEY; WHI IMAGE ID 92280

I was driven to Madison, where I met with the support group that was making the final arrangements for the rally at the State Capitol on Friday, August 19. Although state officials had informed us that Governor Knowles would not meet with us, our support group in Madison kept up the pressure. Fagan responded, some claimed for the publicity, by coordinating the Monday meeting the first day of the march as well as a reception at the Wisconsin State Capitol's governor's meeting room after the rally on Friday. Arrangements to eat and sleep at St. Vincent de Paul after the rally were also being made.

During the last days of the march, the City of Madison police released a statement to the press that I would be arrested once I stepped inside city limits on Friday. I owed outstanding parking tickets from my stay the previous winter. But an anonymous Good Samaritan paid the tickets and defused the issue. The local press out of Wautoma, the *Waushara Argus*, began to discredit the march as being led by college students (my brothers, Mark Erenburg, and I), high school dropouts (my brothers), and outsiders (our Madison-based supporters). Thereafter, the *Argus* coverage attempted to demonstrate that only several dozen people had marched, that we did not represent the workers, and that most migrants were happy here in Wisconsin. They also gave vent to local members of the John Birch Society, who attacked us by claiming the farmworkers movement was part of a communist-led national movement. As a result, future farmworkers' rallies and grape boycott pickets drew counterpickets and "pinko" taunts suggesting farmworkers were communist sympathizers.

—II—

We reached Madison on the fifth day, tired and dirty. We had accomplished a lot in a short amount of time. Yet, my speech at the rally at the State Capitol steps that afternoon did not go well.

At the beginning of the march, I had pledged that I would march every step of the way. I did, in addition to organizing migrant turnout for the IC-called meeting in Wautoma and later traveling to Madison to organize support for the rally there. Besides developing the program for the Madison rally, I had to find a way to feed the marchers afterward and find a place for those who would be spending the night in Madison. Whenever the five-day march was interrupted, the marchers would rest while I met with individual supporters and press. After I was done, the march would resume. I was exhausted, and I felt it when it came time for me to stand before the microphone and state the migrant case. I lacked the energy at that point to present our case as well as I had hoped. The press covered the meeting with state officials after the rally, and that went better. The news reports were positive.

That afternoon, a great celebration with tons of food was held at Madison's St. Vincent de Paul center. It was a great facility to use at the end of the march, as not only did it have a kitchen, but it also had a meeting area and even a dormitory. I was the first to turn in to sleep. It was still before dark. I did not wake until the following day.

We had achieved what we had set out to do. I would not at this time publicly state my views regarding the forming of an organization, but it was clear when I spoke to workers that we had to move in that direction. To come together as a union was the only way to improve our working and living conditions. Chávez had sent a grape boycott union volunteer to observe the protest march. After she reported to Chávez, I spoke to him by phone again, and we discussed meeting soon.

I returned to Wautoma after spending the night in Madison. The cucumber season was fading, and workers and their families would soon move to food processing in nearby towns as well as the local potato processing and warehousing in the Bancroft/Almond area. Sadly, others would depart to the tomato harvesting in the lower Great Lakes region of Michigan, Ohio, and Indiana. Still others made plans to return to the Winter Garden district and my hometown of Crystal City, which was in turmoil as the Chicano revolt was followed by economic reprisals and retributions that were still being felt by our community leaders. I told those who were moving on and the new friends and supporters that came from the Texas Valley that I would see them that winter when I visited my dear grandmothers and my uncle Julian, who had recently been elected justice of the peace. These were fond, heartfelt farewells, filled with pride at what we had accomplished. But we all knew that the main tasks remained.

The purported goal of the march was to get the Wisconsin state agencies to enforce Wisconsin's social and progressive legislation. The Office of the Governor responded affirmatively, and Fagan orchestrated immediate initiatives responding to our demands. The agricultural industry

unanimously condemned our claims that they underpaid workers with
the piece rate system in the cucumber harvest, among other crops. Neither
the growers nor the food processors wanted to go on record as being the
migrant workers' employers, each trying to pass off the responsibility to
the other. Both argued that migrant workers were independent contrac-
tors. Further, growers that were responsible for maintaining migrant
housing to code on their land testified that they did not have the resources
to build new housing units, nor did they enjoy long-term commitments
from the food processors for which they grew.

The most important reaction to the march, however, came from the
migrants themselves, hundreds of whom attended the Waushara County
Courthouse rally. They filled meetings called by the Wisconsin Industrial
Commission, and they participated and supported the march to Wisconsin's State Capitol.

We gathered under the image of the thunderbird and called ourselves
Obreros Unidos (Workers United). Chicano migrants were not *campesinos*
as the California migrant farmworkers called themselves, even naming one
of the important venues to organize El Teatro Campesino. Campesinos is
an old term for farmworkers with a lot of baggage. The Wisconsin agricultural industry had attempted to adopt the *capataz* (foreman) system,
an old vestige of the Spanish colonial patron–peon system, remnants of
which had not disappeared along the Texas Borderland. There the capataz
was the buffer between the land barons, the *patrónes*, and the campesinos,
as was the crew leader, the crew boss, the link between the cucumber harvesters and the processors and growers in Wisconsin.

But Wisconsin was too far from the Texas Borderland to sustain a
patron–peon system. More than one hundred thousand Texas Borderland
migrant seasonal farmworkers were coming yearly to the Great Lakes region in the early 1960s. With the labor of more than fifteen thousand seasonal migrants yearly, the Wisconsin agricultural industry was
transforming from small farms to agribusiness. By the 1960s Wisconsin
was becoming a national leader in the processing and canning of a wide
variety of vegetables, including peas and corn. Although farmworkers
were at the whims of nature as well as the emerging multinational food
processors, we were no one's peons. Migrant workers were not tied to the
Mexican hacienda as were the peons of Spanish colonialism or bonded

to the Southern plantation as Black Americans. There were no patrónes in the cucumber harvest in Wisconsin in the mid-1960s.

Instead, the crew leaders were clan leaders, heads of extended multi-generational families fleeing apartheid as much as seeking employment. We were thousands of miles from where feudalism had taken root. Although we worked in the *campo*, we were not campesinos. This term did not denote the relationship the Tejano, the Chicano/Mejicano migrants had with their employers. We worked and labored, and thus we were *trabajadores* (workers), but we were also the cultivators. We nurtured cucumbers from a seed to a vegetable-producing plant. We harvested this bounty that was feeding the growing metropolitan areas along the Great Lakes and beyond. To us, this meant that we produced an *obra*; we made it come to be, to appear, as a craftsman produces an object or an artist, a work of art. We were Obreros Unidos. In English, *obreros* would be translated as "workers," but in Spanish, *obreros* are not *trabajadores*.

The poster inviting the migrants to publicly state their grievances and propose a plan at the Waushara County Courthouse read "*La Raza tiene Causa*." The migrant families responded; la Raza stood, spoke, and were heard, just as the poster that called them to the mass meeting urged.

8

Striking and Organizing for Recognition

As the cucumber season ended, the fall food processing began. I say fall processing because the pea harvest, which at the time was almost entirely automated, actually preceded the labor-intensive cucumber harvest in Wisconsin. The major vegetable crop to be harvested and canned in the fall was sweet corn, but most of it was somewhat south of the cucumber-growing area, where the main fall vegetable was potatoes. Potatoes were once harvested by hand, but by this time mechanical potato diggers did the job. Potatoes were no longer bagged in the field and then lifted onto trucks to be washed and graded. The mechanical diggers loaded them into dump trucks by a belt-driven loader. Then, the massive trucks drove them to the processing plant and dumped them in bins. Most of the processing work was washing, grading, and bagging the potatoes. Potato growers have adapted other technologies, most importantly in warehousing, with automated controls for the temperature and humidity of the storage space to maintain the crop's freshness. Bagging was also evolving. Over time potatoes were marketed in a wide variety of bags: plastic, cotton-and-plastic cord bags, and the traditional burlap sack. More attention was paid to the washing process, including maintaining uniformity of size in the smaller bags.

The eighty-mile march to Madison had created excitement in the fall processing industry. To some, it was a call to arms. Large numbers of Crystal City residents worked at the Hartford-area canning operations.

Some of them came to see me about lending assistance in addressing plant issues. We had no specific plans to continue organizing in the fall, but if we did, it had to be around the Waushara County area, close to home. This was determined by my state of being. I was broke and living hand to mouth. I had not worked all summer and had no income. I had to live at home. I ate at my family restaurant, and my mother cooked for me and the organizers and supporters that helped out for the summer events. As with all my brothers, I had to work for my keep. I could no longer work as a waiter, which had been my main job before organizing the farmworkers union. My father didn't think it was practical. At a minimum, it cost too much consternation with customers trying to provoke an argument about the farmworkers joining a union. In the summer when thousands of migrants would flood the street of downtown Wautoma and patronize our restaurant, the most welcoming of all the area eating places, there was no mistake that Salas Café was a Mexican restaurant that catered to Mexican migrant workers and their families. But, as soon as the harvest was done, the face of downtown would revert to its original self. Many tourists, thinking that the café was still run by Bea Keitzer, would walk in and be surprised by the handsome Native American face of my father. They would ask to see the owner, thinking that my father was a waiter or a maintenance person. My father had a ready response for these customers, which I can't repeat here. I can say that when the dining room was built, he would offer the reluctant customers who appeared not to want to sit by the Mexican workers a place that was reserved, he would say, for Nazis. They were welcome to sit there by themselves. Upon hearing this, they would run out the door. After the march, some local customers who were antagonistic to our cause would come in to utter their "disappointment" in me and what I had done to the town. To avoid further tension, I was no longer asked to wait on tables. Mom and Dad usually worked in the kitchen. Now Mom and I worked in the kitchen and Dad waited tables. This wasn't the best arrangement, as Dad still could not speak English well and, according to Mom, he used to cost us sales as he chased away customers that came to argue against my union activities. Business usually would slow considerably in the fall, and most of the steady customers were our peers. Now there was a boycott of the restaurant due to my union activities.

I decided to stay in Wautoma and enrolled part-time in nearby Stevens Point State College several days a week. This would take me on a daily basis past the potato-processing operation, and I considered whether this would be our first organizing target. Certainly, the conditions called for it.

Two people were instrumental in getting me involved with worker grievances: Perfecto Villareal, who lived in town but daily drove to work at the James Burns potato-processing plant in nearby Almond, and Frutoso Rodriguez, my mother's older brother, whose whole family also worked at Burns. The Jesus Ramirez family would also commit to and support the union early on. Once I agreed to help, Perfecto and Frutoso would bring coworkers to the restaurant to meet with me. We would discuss the poor working conditions at the plant and what to do about them. Chicano farmworkers were assigned the hardest jobs: the unloading, the bagging, and the loading and shelving of the washed potatoes. Chicanas did the dirtiest jobs: the grading and the washing of potatoes going through the belt line. White, local workers undertook all the mechanized jobs: harvesting and trucking the potatoes from the field to the plant. Inside the plant, all mechanized tasks and maintenance were undertaken by non-Mexican workers, including operating the carts and forklifts.

From the Wautoma restaurant, we would schedule meetings with the workers in the villages of Bancroft and Almond, in labor camps, and at individual homes. I began to make stops on my way back from Stevens Point State. Unlike during the summer, I was mostly alone visiting families in the late afternoon and evenings. Many times, I drove back late at night. Organizing was a lonely endeavor at the time. I wasn't sure how to handle the workers' grievances. I continued to reach out to the Madison network that we had developed over the years for advice and support.

The food-processing industry was local and scattered throughout Wisconsin's small south central communities. They depended on primarily small to medium-size family farms to supply them with a variety of fruits and vegetables. The canning operations were in the center of these fertile fields and, with the help of part-time farmers, homemakers, students, and migrant seasonal workers, propelled Wisconsin to be a national leader in the production of sweet corn, peas, carrots, and sauerkraut. Some of these enterprises began as family operations that grew to integrate not only field cultivation and harvesting, but also processing and warehousing. James Burns potato operations and several others in the Central Sands area shared other, less desirable characteristics: sexism, job discrimination, preferential treatment, and wage inequities.

The food-processing industry, in businesses large and small, privileged local white men over the women and students who made up the majority of the seasonal workforce besides the migrant workers in the summer and fall months. They were paid the highest wages in the machining aspect of the harvest and received preferential treatment in the assignment of maintenance and shipping jobs in the off season. The Chicano migrant worker was the lowest paid of all.

Food processors and large growers used to accuse Obreros Unidos of threatening the industry with demands that they could not meet, thus ushering in automation. In fact, automation in harvesting fruits and vegetables was rapidly advancing before the emergence of the union.

At the time of our march, the corn and pea industries were nearly completely automated, with the exception of the disposal of the pea vines that used to be dumped outside the plants, creating huge mounds of the smelly mulch. The cherry industry would eventually perfect a tree shaker that caused minimum damage to the tree. The harvesting and maintenance of the potato would greatly advance as thermostatically controlled warehousing would keep the product fresher longer. Eventually, the industry would expand and include freeze packing. But at that time, the potato-harvesting and related equipment were crude.

Unlike the cucumber industry, where most of the workers stayed in labor camps on growers' property, some of the potato workers lived in abandoned farmhouses and even in units in nearby villages and towns. This facilitated our meeting with the workers without provoking the growers and processors who owned housing. Further, members of the same extended family worked in different potato-processing plants, so my organizing went beyond the Burns plant. Once we had a core of workers committed to doing something about their grievances, we became more open about our meetings, gathering after work at one of the several camps owned by Burns near the plant. I knew very little about how to form a union or how a union gets recognized. The only thing I knew for sure was that it had to be supported by the great majority of the workers.

Because the industry was so segregated, Chicano migrants, both men
and women, occupied key aspects of potato processing in the whole area.
I felt that I could count on at least two-thirds of the workers at Burns in
Almond to begin the process of union recognition, either by signing
cards or by voting in an election once we got the Wisconsin Employment
Relations Board, which later became the Wisconsin Employment Relations
Council, to order one. The only other plant where I could count on more
than 50 percent of workers' support was Central Sands in Plainfield. But
because the processing was so stratified, Chicanos played a key role in the
process, the grading, the cleaning, and the bagging of the potato. We didn't
need to represent the whole industry to shut the plant down. Although
mostly white male workers dug the potatoes and trucked them to the processing plant, Chicanos did the majority of the work inside the warehouses. The trucking out of the clean, graded, and bagged potatoes was
done externally by over-the-road truckers, some of whom belonged to
the Teamsters. I expected fellow union truckers to not cross the picket line.
Some of them were from the area, and I would begin to approach them
when it came time. I would soon learn I should have done this earlier.

Organizing is about seizing moments. During the organizing of the
Burns plant workers, we extended our efforts into other local potato-
processing plants: Frontier, Paramount, Central Sands, and others. Although the target was Burns, one way to prevent any collusion among the
processors, especially that of using workers from other plants to break our
initiative at Burns, was to strike them all at once. I concentrated on Burns,
but I made sure that workers at Central Sands and the other plants knew
that it was in our best interest to take common action. We didn't want
any of the seasonal workers from other plants involved if Burns workers
went on strike.

—❙❙—

In a relatively short period of time, from organizing the march to Madison beginning in early June to the first week of October, and with few
resources, we had effectively established a foothold in central Wisconsin's agricultural industry, primarily among cucumber cultivators and
potato-processing seasonal workers. This was not a reflection of my organizational ability, but because of the large number of worker grievances

and complaints and the preexisting relationships I had with workers. After nearly ten years as a migrant worker, I had labored alongside many of the crews in the cucumber industry. For the last several years I had visited migrant families encouraging them to allow their children to enroll in the migrant education programs. Everywhere I went I saw overcrowded, unsanitary housing facilities and heard complaints of violations of Wisconsin minimum wage laws. We felt it personally, as members of our extended family still worked as migrant workers. In fact, former neighbors and relatives were employed by Burns.

But the actual process of obtaining union recognition in order to resolve these issues collectively, I learned as I came along the process of organizing the workers into Obreros Unidos. I was informed at my meetings with supporters in Madison that one of the first steps in getting union recognition was to demonstrate that we had signed up the majority of the workers in a particular plant. Signing up workers was a challenge among the suspicious migrants, who saw signing anything as perilous. Organizers discussed many times what union elections and membership organizations meant and what the workers would be doing by voting for a union and signing up as members. We also had to explain that sustaining a union meant paying dues and electing representatives to carry out different tasks.

Most of the migrants had never belonged to any organization, including a workers union. Such organizations were prohibited all along the Texas Borderland. But unlike the rest of the Winter Garden and the Texas Valley agricultural industry, Crystal City workers at the Del Monte canning company were represented by the Teamsters Union. The Teamsters had been instrumental in supporting voter education and registration initiatives that led to the Chicano revolt of 1963. Some of the Burns workers from Crystal City, including my extended family members, belonged to the Teamsters. Through the efforts of Perfecto, the Ramirez family, and my uncle Frutoso, we could count on the majority of workers at the Central Sands plant and nearly two-thirds of those at Burns to sign up with Obreros Unidos. We had to accelerate our initiative because it had become common knowledge that the Burns plant was our target. Retaliation would soon follow, as it had after Crystal City's political revolt in 1963 and the march earlier in the year. We had to take the offensive.

The great majority of the seasonal workers at Burns chose Obreros Unidos as their representative in the negotiation of wages and working conditions. Workers did so by agreeing to become a signed member of the union, allowing us to demonstrate support for the union. If the Wisconsin Employment Relations Commission (WERC) would have conducted a union election in the potato-processing industry the first week of October 1966, Obreros Unidos would have won union recognition at Central Sands with a majority of the workers and with nearly two-thirds of the workers at the Burns plant voting affirmatively. A simple card check would have shown the same results. As we had the majority of those workers signed as members of the union, the potato processors would have been obliged by law to negotiate working conditions and wages.

Although the 1935 Wagner Act did not allow farmworkers to organize or bargain for wages and working conditions, in 1937 Wisconsin established WERC as its own labor law and board covering a broader group of workers that included distinct legal protections for farmworkers' rights. We did not have to organize a national boycott to get a response from our employers. Besides union recognition of Obreros Unidos, the demands we made at James Burns Potato Company were modest: slight wage increases and time-and-a-half pay for overtime with worker approval. It was the proposed changes in the working conditions that provoked the most negative reaction from the potato processor. Burns wanted to maintain its wage inequalities and preferential hiring of white men. The hiring and wage differential discriminated against local and migrant seasonal workers. They were paid less than local Anglo workers. Obreros Unidos exposed the authoritarian and paternalistic system that Chicano migrant men and women worked and lived under. It was unlawful.

On the day that we informed the Burns plant that Obreros Unidos represented the majority of its workers and wanted to meet and negotiate wages and working conditions, the owner, James Burns, retaliated by harassing and threatening the workers. He began to force Chicano workers that he suspected of being members of Obreros Unidos to sign affidavits stating they did not belong to the union. Some of the workers admitted they were union members and were summarily fired and locked out of company-owned homes. We officially called a strike, and sixty-five of the ninety packing shed workers walked out. Even though union members who lived in company housing were up to date in their rental payments through paycheck deductions, they were prohibited by a Portage County sheriff's deputy from entering their homes. We immediately appealed the lockout to his boss, the county sheriff, and impressed upon him that what Burns was doing was against Wisconsin law. We argued that migrants needed to be given thirty days to vacate the premises. The Portage County sheriff saved the day! He refused to evict the workers without giving them proper notice. He allowed the workers into their homes, but he warned us that as soon as their advance rent was exhausted, more than a dozen families would be out in the cold.

The picketing lasted as long as we could keep the workers housed, which was about three weeks. The involvement of the sheriff early in the strike proved crucial in maintaining a peaceful process. We got to meet him before the picketing grew intense. In the first week, some strikers were being more aggressive at the picket line in hopes of stopping the trucks from entering and leaving the site. Again, clear heads prevailed, and we were able to maintain a peaceful picket line, thanks to the discipline of the workers and to the sheriff. Both of us wanted a nonviolent strike. In the local beer joints, fights broke out between striking and nonstriking workers, but we immediately put a stop to that.

As anticipated, Burns was able to maintain operations at a low level as he scuttled for workers around the area. Although we also represented the Central Sands workers, whose processing plant was in the

A young worker joins the picket line at the James Burns plant in 1966.

neighboring community, we planned no labor action there. In fact, we
didn't have the capacity to carry out any other labor action. With Burns
firing workers and preventing them from entering the rental homes he
owned, we had our hands full the first several days of the strike. Nonetheless, Central Sands increased wages for packing shed workers in response
to our organizing.

In a surprise move, Teamsters crossed the picket line and picked up
the few potatoes that Burns was able to process for delivery. The drivers
appeared to have some sympathy for our strike but told us that because
we were unaffiliated, they didn't have to honor our picket line. I hadn't
thought through the liabilities of not being affiliated with a national
union. Later, the leaders of Obreros Unidos thoroughly discussed the decision to remain unaffiliated and resolved that we, as a body, would remain
independent.

Obreros Unidos as an organization established a means of making col-
laborative decisions on whether we should continue to be unaffiliated. The
issue came to the fore when the National Farm Workers Association
(NFWA), which had joined the Filipino-led AWOC in the initial grape strike
in 1965, later joined the national labor movement and reorganized itself
as the United Farmworkers Organizing Committee AFL-CIO. Although
we were never formally invited to become a member of the new union, we
agreed to continue to be unaffiliated, even allowing volunteers who were
assisting us in the grape boycott picket line in Madison to participate in
the decision.

Two main considerations were always before us when we deliberated
affiliation with either NFWA or other AFL-CIO locals. One was the Vietnam War, which we wanted to continue to oppose as an organization.
Chávez generally wanted to keep the war out of his organizing. He was a
navy veteran, but he did not promote military service, and later we found
out that he resented the mistreatment of Black and Mexican soldiers that
he witnessed and suffered. Further, he realized that a high percentage of
Mexican migrant workers had children who were serving. Military service
had always been one of the ways out of the barrio, but the draft, he realized,
was taking a high toll among Black American, Mexican American, and
poor white families. Chávez wanted to be supportive of families that had
children in the war. He would later publicly speak about these feelings, but

Cesar Chavez (right) and me at our first meeting in Chicago in 1966 .

his reluctance to involve the union gave us pause. Two, as a product of the Chicano political revolt in our hometown, we wanted to continue to conduct voter education and registration activities while we organized during the winter months. We considered the role of Obreros Unidos in supporting the Texas political revolt in the four-county Winter Garden, as well as workers' attempts to form collective bargaining units in the Texas Valley. We thought they were one and the same. We could only carry this out by remaining independent.

I failed to anticipate the demands of the strike on myself, as in addition to my time supporting workers on the picket line, I had to spend time meeting with lawyers, union leaders, and supporters and raising funds for the strikers. Weeks following the first strike at Burns, I met Chávez in person for the first time in Chicago and found his words of caution appropriate: "You can't organize and strike at the same time."

In addition to the time commitment, I think he was referring to the bond of union members, that workers must come together and become union brothers and sisters before sharing the hardships of the strike. Most had never belonged to formal organizations outside of church or the mutual aid societies in the Borderland, such as the sociedad funeraria in Crystal City. Before they faced the demands of a strike, they had to know each other, work with each other, and find that they were striving for the same goals.

For those of us who came from the semiarid lands at the foot of the Sierra Madre Oriental, the basic structure was not the family, but the clan, the complex relationships among extended families, neighbors, and friends. Clans were made up of generational, filial, and communal relationships that went back since time immemorial. Members of the labor organization valued one another distinctly from family, extended or not. The union structure proposed by Obreros Unidos did not relegate women to a subservient status, as many Mexican families did. In the harvest, men and women toiled alongside each other and women endured the brutal hardship of fieldwork alongside men. Working the harvest was a question of not only strength, but also guile and endurance. Many women were as productive as men and some more so. Obreros Unidos demanded a restructuring of work assignments in the food-processing industry, which at that time relegated Mexican women to the worst working conditions and lowest pay. The Wisconsin farmworkers' movement and the changes that we called for challenged not only the role of women in the workplace but also in our families. Because not everyone supported these family-level changes, the union had the potential not only to unite us as workers, but also to divide us as families.

Although our immediate family had relocated in Wisconsin in 1959, we still had many family members on both my mother's and father's side who were seasonal migrants. Although my mother's brother, Frutoso Rodriguez, assumed a leadership role in the strike, not all the Rodriguezes or a single member of the Garza family, who were distant relatives of my grandmother Rita, supported the strike. Their support would have meant ten more striking workers whom Burns would have had to replace to keep operating during the labor stoppage. Later, I would hear young, inexperienced Chicano organizers expound their cultural identity with slogans such as "Mi Familia Primero" (My Family First). Familia and union solidarity are not always synonymous, I found very early on in organizing.

The union was greatly assisted by the leadership of Uncle Frutoso's daughter Carolina Reyes and the Ramirez family. The Ramirez women would all continue to advance issues that arose during the Burns strike, among them the role of women in society as well as in the workplace. All

were ardent supporters. They
stayed until the end, suffering
extreme hardship months
after the strike to provide testimony for the WERC hearings
on Burns's unfair labor practices. Even after we had ended
the strike, they along with Perfecto Villareal, who had originally helped me organize the
Burns employees, refused to
leave and return to Texas or
look for work in the factories in
the Milwaukee area. We would
all remain in Wisconsin with
the plan to continue what we
had started.

John Schmitt, president of the AFL-CIO, and I in
1967. PHOTO BY DAVID GIFFEY; WHI IMAGE ID 92052

One of the most decisive events for the migrant workers' strike, immediately and in the long run, was my being invited to the Wisconsin State
AFL-CIO annual meeting in nearby Madison in 1966. John Schmitt, the
Brewery Local #9 leader, was elected state AFL-CIO president. He allowed
me to address the union convention. While at the podium, he called for a
donation for the strikers, and we collected more than $2,000. He promised
to make available legal and technical assistance. We began the formal process for recognition with the assistance of a Milwaukee labor lawyer. At
Schmitt's direction, the staff of the UW–Extension School for Workers,
especially faculty member Frank Lyons, assisted me. I developed excellent
relationships with United Automobile Workers national and local leaders
in Milwaukee. I reached out to other state-affiliated unions to develop
support for Obreros Unidos. After I joined Chávez in support of the California farmworkers' grape boycott, I visited the majority of local labor
councils requesting their support.

—⊣⊢—

What I think Chávez meant about not organizing and striking at the same
time is that workers must first effectively come together as a union, a unit,

a sustainable entity before undertaking such a challenging endeavor. Chávez would also say that if farmworkers wanted a union, they had to pay for it, and if they couldn't pay, they had to work for it.

Having been raised in families that belonged to the mutualista movement, Chávez and Huerta saw the purpose of a farmworkers' union not just as obtaining higher wages and better working conditions, but as providing a wide range of services for its members. Chávez saw unions as mutual aid societies, self-help organizations like the ones that had swept across both sides of the Borderland by the Partido Liberal Mexicano before and long after the Mexican Revolution. His family had belonged to them in the 1940s in California around the same time my father had belonged to and had actively supported the sociedad funeraria.

We in Wisconsin had underestimated the need for workers to come together and experience the sense of unity and solidarity that is produced by an effective organization. This is essential in sustaining a labor action such as a strike. Chávez and Huerta realized this and over several years built and strengthened their organization, providing essential services as the mutualistas had done before them. They went as far as naming the workers organization a national association of workers. The name of the California farmworkers that would gain the first union contracts in farmworker history did not have the word *union* in it. In California, *union* meant "strike," and strikes meant hardship, leading to failure in developing a sustainable organization. Huerta and Chávez wanted to make sure that the grape workers saw themselves as joining together to help themselves and to organize and provide essential services for a sustainable community. The original NFWA had established a health clinic, a credit union, and legal services in addition to publishing its own newspaper before it joined the AWOC grape strike and formed the UFWOC-AFL-CIO. Along with the Filipino workers, they established a network of California community organizations in the Mexican American barrios and fields that they had developed with Fred Ross and other community service organization volunteers and supporters. Their new organization saw itself as an organizing committee, a term that foretold its approach.

In central Wisconsin, part of the problem in bringing workers together was how dispersed they were. As inadequate as housing was for cucumber workers, these same housing units were almost uninhabitable for those who stayed in the fall for the potato harvest, when temperatures dropped to near freezing in late September and lower in October. The migrant units were simply one-inch board wooden frame structures covered by tar paper. They lacked indoor plumbing, and unheated outhouses were the norm. Few of the camps had adequate hot-water units, and migrants bathed in what seemed like the coldest waters in the Northern Hemisphere. The migrants would huddle in the most adequate of these buildings spread out over several counties. A few lived overcrowded in rental units in the surrounding unincorporated villages.

We had no place to meet during the Burns strike, especially after the union families were thrown out of their units. My father's restaurant was always available, but it was sixteen miles away from the nearest migrant camp and nearly twenty miles from the potato-processing plant. Worse, we had not made adequate plans to consistently feed ourselves. Although families volunteered to prepare food for the picket line, what we needed was a soup kitchen—a central location where we prepared food collectively. Worst of all, we were unable to sustain families who were fired from their jobs and thrown out from grower-owned housing. In most cases, workers moved away rather than break the strike.

—||—

Obreros Unidos could not obtain an immediate response from the Wisconsin labor board during the Burns strike. WERC would not hear our petition of unfair labor practices until December, even though workers had been evicted from their housing in October, at the end of the thirty days. Obreros Unidos could not house or sustain the striking workers through those three months.

Further, WERC would not issue a ruling until the following spring. At that time, it found James Burns guilty of unfair labor practices and ordered him to cease and desist anti-union activities. In the meantime, however, we could not sustain the strike until the hearing date, let alone the date of their final decision almost half a year down the road. Clearly, the law didn't favor unaffiliated unions, especially not unaffiliated farmworkers unions with few resources.

Central Sands migrant workers depended on processors and growers for their work and housing. I had underestimated Burns's harassment and intimidation of workers and overestimated the role WERC would play in providing quick relief. Once we realized this, we pulled the picket line. The workers began to disperse, most leaving the area. Fortunately, at a great hardship, the Villareal family, the Ramirez family, and my uncle Frutoso Rodriguez, who had suffered Burns's unfair labor practices, stayed with us through the effort, so that they could testify on behalf of the union several months later. Without their sacrifice, there would not have been a labor case.

We had a tremendous advantage that the California farmworkers didn't enjoy in that Wisconsin's labor board did not exclude farmworkers, but we found that the slow process was ill suited for agricultural workers, in particular seasonal migrant workers who cultivated perishable crops. We knew we had to strategize around that reality. We needed to learn to use the WERC process more effectively and to exercise our right to organize without endangering workers' livelihoods. We knew we needed to organize so that we always had the right to contribute our labor or to cease to offer it, to strike or not. We had to use the work stoppage more strategically. Our next labor action, at Libby's the following year, would be a walkout. We would strike, stop work, but we would return to our posts the following day, retaining the right to walk out again. For short-term relief for striking workers, we had to develop our right to strike more intelligently to avoid mass dislocation, with fired workers being thrown out of grower-owned migrant housing.

9

TARGETING THE MULTINATIONALS

After the August 1966 migrant march, the cucumber harvest ended and many workers began leaving, some to the tomato harvest around the Great Lakes region, others on the way to the early cotton harvest, still others returning directly to their home bases in Texas and northern Mexico. Before they left, we began to select an organizational target for the following season. We had identified several contenders from the bevy of food processors: the Chicago Pickle Company (formerly Red Granite Pickle Co.), Green Bay Food Company (later Dean's Foods), and Libby's.

The Chicago Pickle Company had been the most recently expanded operation in the industry, with the largest crews coming from the Laredo area. Being more recent, these crews had the fewest permanent ties to the growers. Green Bay Foods had stable crews from Del Rio and Crystal City and the strongest ties locally. Its labor camps were closest to Wautoma, including one labor camp right in the city limits, with a small grading station in the same area. Green Bay Foods also had large grower operations nearby, where cucumber grading took place on-site. Chief among them was the Spees farm, where mostly families from Del Rio, Texas, lived and worked. I had gone to school with one of the Spees boys. I became friends with members of the crew before I started to organize and had visited them in Del Rio. Green Bay also had crews headed by my dear friend Lucio Valdez, who had been instrumental in bringing people to the migrant rally at the Waushara County Courthouse in 1966. Libby's crews originally came from Crystal City, but their expansion had been through crews mostly from the Texas Valley. Since some of the Libby's workers came from my hometown, I was able to introduce myself. They knew me from my family, especially my father, who had first come to Wisconsin in the early 1940s and had helped many Texas Borderland migrants find work in the Kettle Moraine area. Although all three companies gave us valid reasons for a walkout, we chose Libby's for the 1967 labor action.

There were several major reasons we chose Libby's. First, we didn't want to organize the union on a grower-by-grower basis. I thought we could win some victories and get established earlier by concentrating on grower-processors, such as those that were emerging in Wisconsin's Central Sands area in the potato industry. With more than five thousand migrant seasonal workers who cultivated and harvested cucumbers, the question that needed to be immediately resolved was, who was their primary employer? We thought it was the major processors, not the growers.

Although they were more formidable to organize, in the end I thought we could get a larger foot in the door and prevail by targeting the major processors. The valley crews headed by Salvador Sanchez, Gil Perez, and Conrado Lopez had been among the most supportive during the formative period of Obreros Unidos the previous summer. Further, Libby's operated several processing plants in the state where we could vertically integrate union organizational efforts from the harvest to the food-processing and canning companies. Importantly, my father had worked for Libby's since the time we were migrants. I was afraid if I chose any other target that I would be accused of favoritism. Our second choice was Green Bay Foods. This target was tempting, as it included large family units from the Crystal City area and open support from some of the chief crew leaders and family clan leaders. A number of Obreros Unidos organizers were Green Bay Foods employees. We decided to start with Libby's and later expanded our plans to Green Bay Foods as well.

One of the most challenging aspects of targeting Libby's was that it included a large number of crews from the Texas Valley, not the four-county Winter Garden region in south central Texas where I was most familiar with the crews and clans. The valley was a couple hundred miles on a road that meandered toward the Gulf of Mexico along the Rio Grande. I had been to the Texas Valley only in passing. I recalled vividly how the communities, one after another, straddle old Highway 83. Highway 83 was the most direct and common route from the Texas Valley through the Winter Garden to the plains states of Nebraska and Kansas and the sugar beet fields there. The highway ran north to the Red River Valley at the Minnesota border, where sugar beets were widely planted after the Dingley Act of 1898 subsidized their cultivation. Tens of thousands of migrants had traveled this road for decades.

I knew I would have no trouble finding the migrant families who worked for Libby's, though. I was encouraged by the relationships I had developed with the valley workers and by their assistance before and during the march. I traveled to the Texas Valley during the offseason to begin organizing. When I arrived, everyone was welcoming and generous. Most of the days, I was overfed, as everywhere I went, I had to eat. I couldn't stay at a hotel as I had no funds other than for gas and snacks, but I didn't need to worry. At each home, everyone wanted me to stay with them. I ended up staying with Salvador Sanchez's family home, which was several blocks from his father's in Pharr, Texas. Salvador's wife, Berta, stayed with her parents during this time so that their home was temporarily made available for my stay. I didn't realize it then, but this was done to accommodate my organizing. Salvador's brother Juan and his two sisters lived with their father. We ate most of our meals with them. Salvador's sister Maria had worked for the migrant education programs in 1964 and had volunteered to help in translating for *La Voz Mexicana* before it became a union newspaper.

Juan was very well read and he, Salvador, and I discussed extensively the forthcoming union organizing in central Wisconsin, as well as the Chicano political manifestations in our hometown and the Texas Valley. Like Crystal City, their hometown of Pharr also enjoyed a numerical majority of Mexican Americans.

The most exciting local news in this regard was of Eugene Nelson, who had been sent to Texas by César Chávez to organize the grape boycott. While organizing the grape boycott in May 1966, Chávez became involved with La Casita Farms farmworkers strike in nearby Rio Grande City. Later, Gil Padilla, vice president of the National Farm Workers Association (NFWA), was sent from Delano, California, to help with the La Casita melon strike. Unfortunately, the legacy of the Bracero Act, which had brought hundreds of thousands of workers to the US while our men were engaged in World War II, was still alive. Mexican nationals, scab laborers who legally crossed the border as day laborers with green cards, broke the strike.

In order to dramatize the plight of Texas Valley farmworkers, Nelson set out on a several-hundred-mile protest march to the State Capitol in Austin in June. As in Wisconsin, Governor John Connally refused to meet with the protesters, although he did travel to New Braunfels during the march and informed them that he did not agree with their demands. In September Chávez sent Antonio Orendain, secretary-treasurer of the farmworkers union, to replace Nelson in handling the La Casita Farms strike. Obreros Unidos would later develop a special relationship with the Texas farmworkers, including sending experienced organizers in support of their efforts. David Giffey, who went on to publish Obreros Unidos's union newspaper, as well as my brother Manuel, both Vietnam-era veterans, would move to help the Texas Valley farmworkers organize.

I found it impossible to organize migrant farmworkers who journeyed yearly to the Great Lakes region and not get involved in NFWA's early assistance of the Texas melon strike at La Casita Farm. I stopped to meet Padilla and later Orendain and leaders of the Texas Farmworkers Union before I met with Libby's workers deeper in the heart of the Texas Valley. During one of my first trips to organize Libby's workers in the Texas Valley, I came upon the melon strike with workers picketing La Casita Farms. Melon strikers were just coming from the picket line and were meeting at a former Mexican movie theater that was serving as union offices. I introduced myself to Padilla, and he introduced me to the striking workers and asked me to speak about Wisconsin union organizing and the Texas Valley. I was unprepared to say anything, but I got up and was warmly greeted.

That's the way it went the rest of the week. I was drafted! Before I left for Pharr, Padilla invited me to a meeting he was organizing in the middle of the week, where he again directed me to address the workers. That night, he stayed over at Salvador Sanchez's home, where I was staying. We would meet again a couple of years later in Wisconsin when he was working for the California grape boycott.

—||—

Setting off a target in Wisconsin before the workers returned to their home base was important. Organizing drives had to be planned while the workers were still in Texas because the two-month growing season for cucumbers was too short to organize nearly seven hundred workers to risk everything and walk out on their jobs. It had become obvious during the organizing for the rally, the march, and the potato strike the previous year that the harvesting season was so short that effective organizing had to be done during the winter months in the workers' home base in Texas.

I had other reasons for returning to Texas, of course. Our family was now resettled in Wisconsin, but we visited our grandmothers and aunts and uncles yearly. It was a real treat to be with my extended family again, especially with my grandmother, Mama Beba.

My trips to Texas were seldom taken alone. Truthfully, I had meager resources and depended on our extended family for support while in Texas. My initial trips were with my parents in our personal vehicles during the holidays. Later, we pooled our resources to get there and back. One winter, we drove Mark Erenburg's new Chevy Malibu and made the fifteen-hundred-mile trip in twenty-four hours. I had worked with Mark on Professor Brandeis's 1965 Migrant Wage and Working Conditions Study. Joining us for this trip was Bill Smith, a graduate student studying history at UW–Madison. We had earlier met working at Findorff's construction company. He had introduced me to the student activists and organizations that were volunteering to dismantle apartheid in the Deep South, as well as those that opposed the Vietnam War. We attended, after work, Students for a Democratic Society's sponsored meetings on campus, where I was first introduced to attorney Lloyd Barbee, the future Wisconsin legislator who would lead the dismantling of the segregated Milwaukee Public School System. Bill was a key Madison supporter during the early years of Obreros Unidos and would later join Obreros Unidos full time.

On this trip to Crystal City, Bill attended an organizing meeting for the Political Association of Spanish-Speaking Organizations (PASSO), at Uncle Julian's Justice of the Peace Office. PASSO asked both of us to address the forthcoming rally in support of Crystal City's City Council candidates. At the PASSO rally we shared the platform with other guests, including Bexar County commissioner Albert Peña from San Antonio, who was an early supporter of the Crystal City revolt. We spoke not only in support of

PASSO candidates at the Mexico Chico's Sociedad Funeraria Placita, but of migrant worker rights in Wisconsin. The audience was thrilled to hear Bill Smith, a Black American who spoke to them in English.

On one of those early trips, Helen Bruner from UW–Extension accompanied us recruiting teachers and staff for summer migrant education programs. She generously paid for most of the expenses throughout the trip. I had first met Helen through Professor Brandeis's participation in a Dane County human rights group. Traveling with Helen, who was older than us, was a delight. Traveling with three adult men during that week was an extraordinary adventure for Helen as well. Back on campus, Helen would engage other UW–Extension staff to support and advocate for migrants and ex-migrants. This would prove crucial later, after United Migrant Opportunity Services (UMOS) was funded, and we demanded that migrant and former migrant workers be added to its board of directors.

During the 1966–67 winter months in Texas, I began to plan a model for the union. It was to be a membership organization with dues. It would also be a service organization, and members would have access to the most pressing need besides child care that I saw as I returned to the camp: legal services. In addition to complaints over wages, nearly half of the migrant labor camps went uninspected and contained gross violations of Wisconsin's housing code. We desperately needed legal assistance. At the reception for migrants after the march at the State Capitol, I had become further acquainted with Wisconsin state assemblyman Lloyd Barbee, and later Fred Kessler, the youngest legislator ever elected to the Wisconsin Assembly. Barbee, who was also active in the civil rights movement, would join the grape boycott picket line in Madison and help organize support among NAACP supporters in Madison. Later he would invite Bill and me to his home in Milwaukee, which was filled with families giving depositions for the court filings that would challenge the segregated Milwaukee Public School System.

Kessler recognized immediately the need for legal assistance and helped in organizing a fundraising party at Someplace Else, a pub on Wisconsin Avenue in Milwaukee, to recruit volunteer lawyers to assist migrants in central Wisconsin and to raise funds for legal expenses and filing fees. As mentioned earlier, Wisconsin progressive legislation did not exclude farmworkers, so the problem was enforcement. But there had never been a wage case, a workers' compensation case, or farmworkers filing for recognition from WERC until we came along. Every case became a test case.

Looming on the horizon was the most challenging question: the legality of the piece rate system in the cucumber, cherry, and other harvests that the processors and growers claimed equaled the minimum wage. I wanted to follow up on Professor Brandeis's finding in the 1965 UW–Madison's Institute for Poverty study, which documented that the piece rate did not equal Wisconsin's minimum wage. Also related was determining who was the migrant's employer. Who would be responsible for funding and keeping the bookkeeping system that effectively guarantees the minimum wage? Here, Professor Brandeis would testify in Wisconsin state administrative agency hearings and later in court with the data and first-hand testimony of her years-long study of migrant wages under Wisconsin's piece rate system. To effectuate a living wage in Wisconsin, the piece rate system had to include a guarantee of a minimum wage. The processors, such as Libby's and Dean Foods, had the responsibility to keep records showing that wages earned divided by hours worked equaled Wisconsin's minimum wage. This would begin with testimony before the Industrial Commission's respective hearings on wages and responsibility for housing standards. After the hearings, recommendations would go to the commission itself, but migrant issues were seldom enforced at the IC level.

They eventually would be resolved by the courts as processors fought the Wisconsin administrative law changes that we were recommending in the courts. These decisions were crucial, not only to determine who was the employer for more than half of the ten thousand migrants who came to Wisconsin and harvested crops under the piece rate system, but also for union recognition of Obreros Unidos. Without an employer, there were no legally-binding employer-employee relationships; we were back to the lawlessness of late-nineteenth-century modes of unregulated labor.

10

La Voz Mexicana

O breros Unidos's message would be made public through *La Voz Mexicana*. We did away with commercial ads, knowing that no local business would support our union activities. The local Wautoma newspaper, the *Waushara Argus*, had previously lambasted the 1965 Brandeis wage study, personally attacking the union leadership as outsiders and claiming that migrants were happy. We sold *La Voz Mexicana* throughout the state, offering our supporters subscription rates for the summer copies in the hope that they would pay us in advance so that we could have funds to publish it. The copies were also sold on the street for ten cents: five cents for the paperboys and papergirls who peddled it in downtown Wautoma and five cents for the union. The Villareal boys and girls, children of the lead organizer for the Almond potato strike, did a tremendous job in disseminating the union newspaper on weekends. They anxiously awaited the newspaper for the weekend sale when the majority of the migrants came into town.

The only business we approached to sublet property was our neighbor, the shoe shop next door to the family restaurant in downtown Wautoma. The owner, whose last name was Wrase, was an independent-minded first-generation German immigrant who treated workers fairly and even allowed them to lay away items purchased on credit. The union rented office space on top of his shoe store. Daily we ran up and down the stairs to and from my father's café to eat, use the public phone, and gather. Mr. Wrase and his wife spoke with heavy accents, much like my parents, but they were great neighbors. During the winter, we helped Mr. Wrase shovel the sidewalk that ran half a block to the alley. Occasionally, the family would call us after snowstorms to go dig them out of their personal home several blocks down the street so they could come open the store.

In addition to space to produce the newspaper, the office allowed us to have a centralized place where the workers, union supporters, and volunteers could meet, something that had been absent and quite detrimental during the first strike. It was most important for the workers to meet with each other. The Libby strike involved more than five hundred workers spread over a three-county area in labor camps large and small from a wide variety of Texas and Mexican cities. The office space allowed them to meet and engage with one another. Now, I seldom traveled alone to visit the workers in the labor camps as I had done during the Burns potato organizing effort. I would always pick up workers from one camp to accompany me to visit other camps. This way they could become acquainted with one another. When the Milwaukee lawyers came to assist the members, the office space was an excellent facility to take testimony for the upcoming test cases.

After David Giffey returned from Vietnam and got married, he and his new bride, Missy, quit their jobs to come to Wautoma to publish *La Voz Mexicana* for the 1967 summer. David laid out the newspaper in the union office. Not only did they do an outstanding job, but David was willing to undertake any responsibility to advance the cause of the Obreros Unidos. The Giffeys were good companions with whom I enjoyed working and sharing large amounts of time. David was a hard worker and a trusted friend, while Missy, who had just gotten back from a school year abroad in France, was a delight to be around. Both were levelheaded persons with a great sense of humor, two qualities that were much needed in our line of work. It was a treat to return from long days of organizing in the labor camps to the Giffeys' household. Their apartment became the social center of organizers and volunteers who would come from Madison and throughout Wisconsin's Fox River Valley to help.

The publishers of the National Farm Workers Association union publication *El Malcriado* had allowed us to use the hand-drawn illustrations depicting El Teatro Campesino, Luis Valdez's guerrilla theater troupe whose performances rallied farmworkers who were attempting to unionize. It complemented the organizing of farmworkers by bringing alive the characters

involved in the struggle, such as *el patron* (the boss), *el huelgista* (the striking farmworker), and *el esquirol* (the scab worker). Just as El Teatro Campesino brought to life the issues of the strike, *El Malcriado* wonderfully
drew these characters to tell of the struggle. Using his newspaper experience and his photojournalist skills, Giffey creatively used *El Malcriado*'s
drawings along with his photos and writing skills to develop an educational organizing tool throughout the 1967 Libby's campaign. Besides the
sale of *La Voz*, we promoted the union message among our allies, who
included labor, human rights, religious, and student groups. Alternative
newspaper networks informed us of ongoing civil rights and antiwar activities all over the country. We all shared our copies and news as well as
our art. Giffey's pencil profile of Mexican revolutionary Emiliano Zapata
was published throughout this network without citing its authorship.

—||—

The best time of day to visit labor camps was in the afternoon. In the mornings, the Giffeys, the Salas family, and volunteers would meet at my father's
restaurant for coffee. We chatted and anxiously awaited the mail that became available at 9 a.m. when the local post office opened. Sometimes the
mail determined the day. We depended on a daily basis on the contributions
from union members, supporters, and subscribers to the union newspaper,
in addition to honoraria I had begun to receive for speaking engagements.
We also depended on being fed at my parents' café. For this, we all did small
chores, ran errands, cleared tables, and in my case, washed dishes. I no
longer waited on tables, but since the union office was next door, I would
be called to help my mother in the kitchen during rush hour. For this
work I would always be handed several dollars. At the time, one could
get almost three gallons of gas for a dollar. The Giffey's Volkswagon and
my old DeSoto were on the road on a daily basis. The VW ran on fumes,
while the DeSoto was more expensive to run. If it rained, I got out to the
labor camps after the mail to speak with workers returning from the fields.

None of this would have been possible without the leadership and
assistance of John Schmitt, the recently elected Wisconsin State AFL-CIO
president whom I had met the previous fall. Not only did he make state
resources available to us, but he also set up a fund for us at his former union,
Brewery Workers Local #9 in Milwaukee, to help with the publishing of

La Voz. He encouraged affiliated unions to invite me to their union meetings so that I could address them, and inevitably they reached deep into their pockets and contributed to Obreros Unidos. This laid the groundwork for labor's support and assistance that we would initiate later during the grape boycott. In the last two weeks before the Libby's strike, Schmitt sent union organizers to help me get from one camp to the other as my old DeSoto had died. The drivers he sent did not speak Spanish, but they were both experienced organizers who were most helpful with their advice and insights, and they had reliable cars. Although I was hesitant to pull into labor camps with late-model vehicles, there was no alternative. Mine had conked out in the early days of the summer campaign.

The most interesting character from the unions who helped out that summer was Charlie Heymans. Schmitt had directed me to visit the United Auto Workers (UAW) International Union offices in Milwaukee at the end of North Street and Prospect on the near east side and meet its leader, Harvey Kitzman. Both Kitzman and Heymans were legends in state union organizations. They were veterans of the Kohler strikes that had lasted for years in the 1950s. Heymans was a renowned orator who would speak of union organizing for whatever time was allotted, the longer the better. The only thing that appeared to hold him from speaking all day was the timepiece that he kept at the podium. The night before the Libby's strike, I invited him to the labor camp that we had designated for the kickoff rally, and even though some of the workers were not proficient in English, we all enjoyed his enthusiastic support.

Schmitt also called the executive committee of the Wisconsin State AFL-CIO to meet in Wautoma two weeks before the Libby's strike. I had asked him to gather in Wautoma for their summer meeting to demonstrate that Obreros Unidos enjoyed statewide union support. I wanted to send a message to Libby's and other processors and growers that we were not alone in the labor action that we were taking against Libby's. This was a message that I wanted Obreros Unidos organizers and supporters to hear also. The Salas Café dining room where Schmitt and fellow union leaders met was filled with union leaders and migrant worker supporters.

Schmitt put me in contact with the UW–Madison Extension's School for Workers program, which was most helpful in structuring the union. I developed a strong relationship with both Frank Lyons and Norris Tibbits, two experienced organizers who were at the Madison campus training workers. Schmitt also invited me to address Wisconsin State AFL-CIO/ School for Workers summer training sessions of local union leaders. Lyons gave me the schedule for the sessions, and I tried to meet and address all of the worker training sessions that he recommended. Lyons wanted me to relate the challenges of organizing migrant seasonal farmworkers to the mostly industrial union workers represented in the audience. In fact, it was I who was the student. I met with local plant union leaders and learned how industrial and craft workers were structured and affiliated as well as how they used time study, a study of how much time it takes to complete various job tasks, to review how to set wages and pay rates. Before each training session Lyons would briefly relate the presenter's history. After each of my presentations, he would prompt someone from the crowd to make a motion to pass the hat in support of our work. We made new friends, more supporters who would be crucial in the later grape boycott, and the dollars that we collected kept the operations going.

As a Vietnam veteran, Lyons was active in the local Veterans for Peace antiwar movement that I had participated in before the march of 1966. Together we witnessed one of the most horrific acts of police brutality of the antiwar years: the demonstrations on Bascom Hill at UW–Madison campus against Dow Chemical Company. Dow was on campus recruiting, and the demonstration's purpose was to discourage students from applying for work at the principal maker of napalm, which was being used as an antipersonnel weapon against combatants and noncombatants. Many gruesome narratives were coming out of Vietnam of whole villages being sprayed with napalm, women and children being burned alive. Seared in our minds were the videos of villagers, of noncombatants, their faces contorted in pain, clothes along with pieces of burning flesh dragging from their bodies, alongside women, the ever-present children, an infant in her arms, now a mass of flesh. Along with these pictures, for Frank Lyons and me and others who witnessed that day, are engraved the images of Madison's riot-dressed police officers mercilessly beating sitting, nonviolent protesters and dispersing assembled pickets and chasing peaceful protesters with swinging clubs. I would do everything in my power to prevent the same kind of violence in the strikes and walkouts that I organized in the summer of 1967 and beyond.

—ıı—

The most challenging aspect of organizing the 1967 Libby's strike was the distance between the labor camps. Libby's had begun its cucumber operation in the southwestern part of Waushara County near Marquette County line in Neshkoro, Wisconsin, a small unincorporated community. It had both a grading station and a pickling operation. Rows of huge wooden barrels made from plank board would keep the cucumbers in salt, brine, ample amounts of dill, and little else over the winter. In the spring, they would be removed and hauled to processing plants to be jarred and sold as dill pickles. The barrels would be dried, cleaned, and ready for another summer harvesting season.

Libby's had expanded its presence from Hancock farther north and west along the Portage County region known as the Central Sands. The Salas family's first several years of harvesting cucumbers in the early 1950s had been nearby at the Thompson farm and later at the Hartford family homestead halfway to Wautoma from Hancock. Later, Libby's expanded into the Central Sands area with grading and brine operations in Bancroft, Wisconsin. The farms in this region were much larger than the farms in the Hancock or Neshkoro area. Following the main roads, the distance between the two areas was more than thirty miles.

The other major issue impeding our organizational attempt was bringing the workers together. They not only were spread throughout three counties, but they also came from distinct areas, from the Winter Garden region to the Texas Valley. During the previous labor action against James Burns, although all worked at the same site, union members worked in different aspects of the potato processing and warehousing. At the end of the day, each went their own way. We now had an office where we could meet in small groups, but we needed other activities, including mass meetings and, if possible, a major rally before the strike. The office in Wautoma was nearly half an hour's drive from the main cucumber acreage and labor camps. The only time the workers came into Wautoma was on weekends, to purchase food and other goods on Saturdays and to attend mass on Sundays. We had to plan our organizational activities around their leisure time.

First of all, the union newspaper had to be published and available for the paperboys and papergirls by Friday night so they could sell it in the downtown area over the weekend. Worker complaints had to be scheduled on weekends because that was when the volunteer lawyers drove from Milwaukee to meet with migrant workers who had wage and other claims.

Two years before, we had attempted to provide a dance for migrant youth at the Waushara County Fairgrounds facilities. The Green Bay Archdiocese nuns had agreed to help promote it and assured the migrant families that they would chaperone the event, but two things went wrong, and their effects would be lasting.

One, the nuns didn't like the music. I had befriended a group of migrant workers who had come together and formed a band. They called themselves the Savages and not only played Tejano or Rancheras Norteñas music but also rock and roll. They played a rendition of Otis Redding's "Satisfaction" that had been popularized by the Rolling Stones, and the migrant youth took to the floor en masse to dance. The nuns were scandalized.

Two, beer bottles were found in the parking lot the next morning. Evidently, some of the adults had stayed in their cars after the dance and consumed beer and had not disposed of the bottles properly. I took responsibility for not being on the grounds early enough to clean the rented premises before county employees appeared for work. No beer had been brought into the dance, nor were there any incidents. But the nuns were adamant, they would not be part of any future events that played rock and roll. The Savages were the only group I knew that played gratis. Besides, they were my friends. Adam, the drummer and lead singer, was extremely talented and later redrew by hand the masthead for *La Voz Mexicana*.

The village leaders on the county board would not rent to the union, and the nuns were unwilling to sponsor dances on the county grounds for us as a front for union activities. St. Joseph Catholic Church on Sundays continued to be the site of the largest gathering of migrant families in the three-county area, and we had to access them there. Father Garrigan continued to be supportive and allowed us to approach congregants on church grounds. We couldn't pass up the opportunity to talk to them and to pass out leaflets informing them of who we were and what we stood for.

We also continued to host softball games, providing another opportunity to talk to workers about improving our living and working conditions and to hear their ideas about how to go about it. This helped to keep our union organizing away from the labor camps where our presence would threaten the migrants, as it had done the previous fall at the James Burns potato strike. These gatherings would later be extended to the softball diamonds in the villages of Bancroft and Almond during the week, where we could have access to the workers in those areas after work. We did this by pitting one labor camp against another. Huge crowds would gather for the games. But none of these gatherings compared to the one that came together to participate in the Teatro Campesino performance at the downtown theater.

When Chávez and I met in Chicago over the winter of 1966, I had invited him to come to Milwaukee. I arranged for him to be hosted by the Archdiocese-funded Centro Hispano that was headed by Father John Maurice. We kept in touch after the Milwaukee meeting, and he later called to inform me that El Teatro Campesino was on a national tour promoting the grape boycott and raising funds for the union. He asked if Obreros Unidos could accommodate them with a fundraising performance in Wisconsin. I thought of two things. One, the best venue for Teatro Campesino's performance was Memorial Union's Great Hall at UW–Madison. We had the community and student network to support such an event. Not only would it accommodate an audience of several hundred students and supporters, but the stage was uniquely suited for Teatro's live performances. It also occurred to me that this would be a great audience to promote the California grape boycott to. But I had another idea as well. I agreed to book El Teatro Campesino at UW–Madison, but only if they would also come to Wautoma to perform for Obreros Unidos before an audience of principally migrant workers. César agreed.

A special treat for the Obreros Unidos organizers was spending time with Luis Valdez and the Teatro Campesino theater company as we drove them the eighty miles between Wautoma and Madison for the two performances. Since we had few resources, they ate with us at my father's restaurant down the street from the local theater in downtown Wautoma where they performed. We had no money to put them up in hotels, so they stayed at the Salas family farm, which presently grew no crops and where the farmhouse and buildings were used for union organizing in the summer of 1967.

   As anticipated, the Teatro's performance at UW–Madison was a great
success, but the lasting impact that the troupe made for the Chicano
farmworkers and union supporters in Wautoma among the migrant
youth was immeasurable. With no stage or costumes, the characters came
alive with a simple cardboard tag hanging from their necks indicating their
character: "El Ranchero," "El Campesino," "El Esquirol," "La Iglesia," and
so on. The workers had a hilarious night. The migrant youth then took the
roles to the labor camps and reenacted the conflict between the growers
and the workers. Teatro Campesino skits spread from the labor camps to
the urban barrios and became a staple of how we communicated our message through music and skits. Later, in organizing barrio youth in urban
areas, we seldom held a rally without live music and performances and
long speeches. In multiple ways, across generations, our message was
spreading and gaining momentum.

11

FIGHTING FOR RECOGNITION

The organizing plan for the Libby's walkout included a rally before the labor action, preferably in one of the migrant labor camps that were spread out across three counties, Marquette, Waushara, and Portage. We chose the Salvador Sanchez family labor camp in the northwestern part of Waushara County, near Portage County and the Central Sands, to host the rally. The Sanchez camp was home to many of the Texas Valley workers who supported Obreros Unidos. I had spent several weeks during the previous winter in the Texas Valley in the City of Pharr and had gotten to visit a number of the families in their homes. Organizers agreed that on the day of the walkout we would rally at Libby's Bancroft grading station, as this was closer to the largest growers in Wisconsin's Central Sands area and where the majority of the seven hundred workers resided.

The prestrike rally was scheduled to kick off late in the afternoon to give enough time for the neighboring labor camps and the crews to attend. Earlier we had avoided mass meetings at the labor camps, fearing reprisals against the workers. The Sanchez labor camp was not by the grower's home, however, and since we were striking the following day, we decided to risk showing our hand the night before.

Technically, the labor action was a walkout; we were not going to keep the workers out as we had done in the potato strike the previous year. We would shut the operations for a day, but we would return to work the following day until further notice. Walking out instead of going on strike was a way to salvage the crop and protect the workers. We didn't want any labor action to be prolonged and threaten the crop. The harvesting was at its peak and if the cucumbers weren't harvested for more than several days, it would affect the product's value, which was based on small and midsized cucumbers for jarring. Further, we didn't want any of the workers to be thrown out of grower- or processor-owned housing as had happened the year before during the potato strike.

The rally at the Sanchez camp lasted well into the evening. We had to wait until late in the afternoon before starting to make sure that all the neighboring labor camps had sent representatives. It was important to the families present that the labor action be well attended. Anything less would affect the morale of the crowd and perhaps the walkout planned for midmorning the next day.

The highlight of the rally was the speech by Charles Heymans, international representative from the United Auto Workers office in Milwaukee. John Schmitt, Wisconsin State AFL-CIO president, had introduced me to state UAW leadership. At the time, it was led by Harvey Kitzman and Heymans, two giant labor leaders. I had earlier appealed for help from Kitzman and had heard Heymans speak at one of the labor meetings in Milwaukee. Heymans was present when Chávez visited Milwaukee earlier in the spring, and I asked that Heymans keynote our rally before the labor action against Libby's. Kitzman agreed. Heymans was an extraordinary orator who could speak about organizing and striking one of the most challenging work sites in the state, the Kohler plant in Sheboygan.

Before we retired, exhilarated by the forthcoming events and Heymans's speech, we made arrangements for the next day's action. Half a dozen cars would be spread out over the three-county area's major labor camps and cucumber fields. The drivers would give the signal to begin the walkout by honking their horns as they traveled from field to field. Following the signal, all workers were to cease work and drive to Libby's processing plant in Bancroft, where we would present our written demands for union recognition and show Libby's management that their workers supported Obreros Unidos.

It was obvious the following day, as the morning progressed and the caravan of 2.5-ton canvas-top trucks, pickups, and cars made their way into Libby's cucumber-processing yard, that the walkout had been successful. All of the workers from fields around Bancroft were coming in, and as each crew appeared, there was cheering and applause from those of us waiting.

Salvador and I got on top of one of Libby's supervisor's cars and congratulated the delighted crowd. Every time a crew from a particular camp came in, we would be interrupted as the workers welcomed arriving fellow strikers.

The biggest cheer went up when the Jamaican workers joined us. We always suspected that they had been brought on board at Libby's to break the strike and keep Libby's operational if needed. I kept visiting the camp and explaining to them who we were, what we were planning, and when, but I never got a firm commitment that they would join us. In the week before the strike, I began to bring workers from the other camps with me to meet the Jamaican workers, to demonstrate to them the support we had. I had invited the Jamaican workers to the rally the night before, but they didn't come. I was sure glad to see them supporting the strike that morning. They told me that they didn't want to be strikebreakers but that they had few resources and could not be unemployed for more than a few days. The next day, they simply left, with no farewells.

I told the cheering workers that Obreros Unidos had filed for an emergency Wisconsin Employment Relations Commission (WERC) hearing and was asking the commission to order an emergency certification election. We expected the commission to grant us the hearing and were confident that an election would be granted before the season ended. If not, we were prepared to go on strike and to stay out until our demands were met. This was not a plan that we favored. As I said, a strike lasting more than several days would imperil the summer crop, but we were ready to take that step if our demands for union recognition were not met.

That afternoon, I met David Loeffler, Wisconsin State AFL-CIO's attorney from Goldberg, Previant and Uleman, who had driven from Milwaukee at dawn to join us. Schmitt had allowed us to use the same law firm that the state organization retained. The previous year, we were already on strike when we obtained legal services. Schmitt ensured this would not happen again. We would have access to legal assistance from the inception of the labor action. This was crucial. We hoped the walkout would send an urgent message to Wisconsin's labor board that it should call an emergency meeting and hear our petition for a certification election. WERC knew from our previous unfair labor practice hearing that we continued to organize across the area. The committee agreed to hear our petition for a

Workers gather after the planned walkout at Libby's. PHOTO BY DAVID GIFFEY; WHI IMAGE ID 92960

WERC-mandated election to determine if, in fact, we were the bargaining agent for the five-hundred-plus workforce. Loeffler was an outstanding labor lawyer who would effectively argue our rights before WERC by first of all organizing the testimony for the emergency meeting and then laying the groundwork for and overseeing the election. He would advise Obreros Unidos in preparation for hearings and later negotiations.

At the WERC emergency meeting held in the Waushara County Courthouse, Obreros Unidos's petition for a certification election was granted. Under the terms of the proposed election, about 450 migrant workers would be allowed to vote out of a total estimated workforce of 700, counting the children. Although children under twelve years old were part of the harvest, the union supported the enforcement of child labor laws and did not argue that migrants under sixteen should be allowed to vote.

The other major issue was the location and staffing of the election. We argued and won the right to have a minimum of three polling stations, one for each of the counties' growing areas. Further, we won the right to have union members staff and observe at each of the voting sites. We made sure that the polling places reflected the Borderland communities that made up the workforce: in Bancroft, Texas Valley workers; in Hartford, Crystal City migrants and Laredo workers; and so on.

Once we had the idea of how the certification ballot would look, we had worker and voter education training sessions in the labor camps. Most of the union members had never exercised their right to vote. Those from Crystal City who had participated in the political revolt several years prior had voted then for the first time, but Texas Valley workers made up the majority of the workforce at Libby's. Unlike Crystal City, where they had fought for and won the right to the franchise, for most of the migrant workers, the union election was their first election. We won 405 to 8!

The workers had almost unanimously voted for Obreros Unidos. We were sure the eight votes against the union were worker errors. The victory spread like wildfire across the industry. The election result put to rest the arguments that the workers were happy and that the union didn't represent most workers. Most important was the feeling of pride, of being victorious in our attempt to collectively improve our working and living conditions by coming together and forming a union. The election had

Attorney David Loeffler speaks to the Wisconsin Employment Relations Commission on behalf of Obreros Unidos.

taken place in the next to last two weeks of the harvest and workers were leaving to the next crop, elated in their victory.

—ıı—

The organizing had begun five years earlier, when I returned to the labor camps in 1962 to ask families to remove their children from the harvest and send them to the emerging migrant schools. It had taken four more years, including organizing in the winter along the Texas Borderland, undertaking an eighty-mile march, and enacting the first labor strike the previous fall in the potato industry, to achieve recognition.

I gained important background on migrant issues while joining Professor Brandeis testifying before Wisconsin state agencies demanding the enforcement of Wisconsin's progressive legislation. In the last year and a half, we had found a more meaningful way to improve our working and living conditions. At that time the workers felt that they were marching to Madison to gain "respect," and their march became known as the March for Respectability. I didn't know how it would be received by the public. We wanted our work to be valued. That is why we wanted to call ourselves *Obreros* rather than *Campesinos*. We cultivated, hand-harvested, and processed the bounty of the fertile soil that the receding glacier had left us. We wanted an improvement of our living and working conditions. Important to us was that our contribution be recognized, as stated by the poster we devised calling for the workers to come together to:

Hablar para ser Reconocidos,
La Raza Tiene Causa.

Hablar means "to speak" in Spanish. We meant more! We meant to stand and speak. To stand and speak was to protest our miserable wages and working conditions. That's why we marched eighty miles to the State Capitol.

That's why we came together through Obreros Unidos: to be heard. But, to simply petition our patrons was insufficient. In spite of the fact that the majority of workers at the Burns potato-processing plant in Almond wanted to be recognized collectively, Burns would not recognize us. He disregarded the fact that we had the great majority of the seasonal labor force signed as members, or that we could demonstrate in a fair election that according to Wisconsin statutes, we enjoyed the support of his workforce. We needed him to bargain in good faith with us. We lost the strike because Burns broke the law. He later was found before the WERC board to have committed unfair labor practices, but it was not a timely decision. The commission did not hear our complaints until months after our labor action.

At Libby's, we organized a walkout instead of a strike and petitioned WERC for an emergency meeting calling for a certification election. This turned out to be a more effective use of Wisconsin's labor law.

Our strategy allowed us to avoid what had happened in the Burns strike the previous fall, when we had to call off the picket after three weeks. At that time, we enjoyed the support of the great majority of the Burns workers, and we had signed membership to prove it, but it had not led to union recognition. It was naïve of me to think that because I could prove that the majority of his workers wanted to bargain collectively Burns would respond affirmatively to our demands. I didn't want to make the same mistake with Libby's in the summer of 1967.

The most effective way we could prove that we represented Libby's workers was with a WERC certification election. This could only happen if WERC met in an emergency meeting and ordered one from the bench. This was not typically how WERC made decisions. We tailored the labor action to begin this process with a walkout and not a strike so that workers would not lose their income or housing. We succeeded! WERC responded to our demands for an emergency meeting and granted the workers the right to determine if they wanted a union through a certification election. We won the WERC certification election, 405–8!

Most of the workers would leave central Wisconsin for the next crop in the days that followed, believing that upon their return next year, they would have a union contract. The celebration was short lived. Libby's refused to negotiate in good faith that fall and then informed us at our first meeting that they were moving their multicounty cucumber operation, which employed more than five hundred workers, out of state. Libby's claimed it was not obligated to negotiate its business decision with the union.

I arranged meetings with Schmitt and Loeffler in Milwaukee to discuss suing Libby's for unfair labor practices. We all felt that Libby's was moving its operations out of state to avoid the union, but we had to prove it to the WERC board.

Even if Libby's decision was exclusively related to its bottom line—that is, that the company could produce cucumbers cheaper out of state—Loeffler felt that the company had to negotiate with us on the impact of its executive decision. Further, its claim that any cucumbers planted in Wisconsin could be harvested mechanically was not feasible. Based on evidence, the union did not believe that quality cucumbers could be developed, grown, and machine harvested. In fact, the market was moving the other way: continuing to cultivate and harvest select cucumbers, sell them in packaging other than jars, and more effectively marketing them.

Two decisions had to be made, one Schmitt's and one mine. Schmitt agreed to represent Obreros Unidos throughout the WERC legal process. Attorney Loeffler informed us that the WERC decision could be appealed by either party in Wisconsin courts beginning with the county courts, now the Wisconsin Circuit Court. The lower court decision could make its way to the Wisconsin Supreme Court. Schmitt committed the Wisconsin State AFL-CIO's legal firm to represent the union through the whole legal battle. This was an extraordinary decision. Obreros Unidos was an unaffiliated union. We were becoming self-sustaining only with the broad support of other Wisconsin unions and could not afford to pursue a lengthy legal case. Schmitt saw that decisions like Libby's, which chose to move its cucumber operation south to avoid unionization, were occurring throughout Wisconsin's industrial sector. Plants were moving to nonunion states in the South. Soon, whole manufacturing operations would move to Mexico and beyond. The Libby's case could have far-reaching implications for all Wisconsin union workers. Loeffler worked for the law firm that represented the state AFL-CIO. Previant and Uleman was one of the best labor firms in the state of Wisconsin. We were confident we were represented by the best lawyers in Wisconsin.

But Loeffler couldn't guarantee that the whole legal process would be exhausted by planting time the following year, in the spring of 1968. I had to inform the workers of the possibility of there being no cucumbers planted for them to harvest in the state of Wisconsin the following spring. If this happened, it would throw nearly seven hundred workers and their families out of the work cycle in the Great Lakes region. Many workers hoed and thinned sugar beets along the Red River Valley during the early spring and then moved to harvest cucumbers in central Wisconsin in early summer. Some would return to Texas after the cucumber harvest, but most would go on to harvest tomatoes in the lower Great Lakes region of northwestern Illinois along the Indiana border. Other migrants would move farther east to harvest tomatoes in Michigan and Ohio.

Libby's not planting cucumbers in Wisconsin would severely disrupt the migrant cycle with a gap of six to eight weeks of downtime, with no viable alternative for such a large number of workers. We had to alert workers as soon as possible so they could make plans. Union workers were no longer in Wisconsin during the break in negotiations, so I traveled to Texas to inform them. Still, the union had other options that I wanted to discuss with the members in Texas, to force Libby's back to the negotiating table by organizing workers at the Libby's food-processing and canning operations in Hartford, Darien, Jackson, and Janesville.

We also approached Teamsters Local 695, which represented the organized truckers who hauled the processed goods from the field to the processing plant and retailers. We wanted their support for our planned walkouts at Libby's the following harvest in 1968. Schmitt insisted I also

meet with the meat cutters union, which represented those workers at
Libby's Hartford plant. This could restrict local support. Further, I could
not ask the meat cutters to walk out of their jobs in violation of their
contract.

The Libby's plant at Hartford was the key to getting Libby's back to the
negotiating table. It had the most extensive canning and processing operations in central Wisconsin, and it had the potential to be the most effective, as it included migrant seasonal workers from the Winter Garden
region and my old hometown of Crystal City. I spent the winter organizing
the Libby walkouts, planned for the summer of 1968, beginning with my
first visit to spend the holidays with family and fellow union members in
Crystal City.

Before leaving for Texas in the winter of 1967, I met with Fred Kessler,
a lawyer from Milwaukee, for an update on legal cases that had emerged
from the volunteer lawyer's weekend visits to hear worker complaints.
Although we were planning for our winter fundraiser and pursuing a
worker's compensation case that had arisen the previous summer, the
most important legal case was preparing for the forthcoming court hearing before Judge Norris Maloney in Madison to determine whether the
piece rate system in cucumbers met the Wisconsin minimum wage law.
A key aspect of the legal case was determining who was the employer,
the grower or the processor. Loeffler was busy with the Libby's case, so I
asked Kessler to approach Milwaukee County Assistant District Attorney
E. Michael McCann to help out with the case. McCann agreed to be a volunteer lawyer for Obreros Unidos as well. Further, we needed the testimony of Professor Brandeis and the rich data that she had uncovered
during the UW–Madison Institute for Poverty's wage study of 1965 to
demonstrate the fact that the multinational processors like Libby's, not
the growers, were the employers. Additionally, Mark Erenburg had done
further field studies on migrant wages that supported Professor Brandeis's
assertions and agreed to help as well.

The following spring, with the testimony of Brandeis and Erenburg,
McCann's skill in the courtroom, and Loeffler's reasoned arguments, we
won the day. Judge Maloney found that the piece rate system in the cucumber industry that employed nearly five thousand workers did not equal
Wisconsin's minimum wage. It did not provide a living wage for women,

failing to meet the intent of the protection of the law. Most important, it found that in the cucumber industry, the employer was the processor. It was the large processors that would be responsible for maintaining records to ensure that the piece rate system equaled the state's minimum wage rate. It was a tremendous victory! It would begin to enforce one of Wisconsin's most important pieces of progressive legislation. The beneficiaries were all Wisconsin workers who worked in field harvesting Wisconsin's fruits and vegetables. Besides cucumbers, cherries and other harvests were also based on a piece rate system. Further, Wisconsin minimum wage law would later be modified to provide protection to all workers, men included. Judge Maloney's decision began to clarify other migrant worker issues of Wisconsin administrative law as enforced by the Wisconsin Industrial Commission, later the Department of Industry and Human Relations.

—II—

Several issues arose after the 1966 march to Madison and the Burns potato strike that guided the strategies for future union organizing. One of the main reasons Wisconsin protective legislation was never enforced was the lack of clarity as to who was the employer of Wisconsin migrants. Because of this, there had never been a successful worker's compensation claim by a migrant until we came along. That's not to say no one had ever been injured during those years. Working with farm machines and implements that were being developed and utilized in the automation of the agricultural industry was perilous, especially if workers were not properly trained. Now those workers' right to compensation for injuries sustained on the job would be recognized.

Clearly, the migrant seasonal worker was not an independent contractor, as the multinational food processors had claimed. National companies like Libby's actively recruited workers all along the Texas Borderland, directly or through agents such as crew leaders. Others used radio ads and flyers. In some cases, companies provided advance funds to cover the expenses of these crews to travel to the Great Lakes region.

The question of who was the employer in labor relations was at the heart of all collective bargaining agreements. Employers make the decisions that matter. You have to demonstrate an employer-employee relationship to have a labor agreement and thus a union to bargain over wages and working conditions.

Although the California farmworkers were engaged in labor actions against grape growers and Obreros Unidos's first strike had been against a potato grower, we felt that future organizational activities should target the large processors that were expanding into food processing and canning. The selected target was to organize Libby's seven hundred workers for the 1967 Obreros Unidos organizing campaign. Yet our whole organizational effort was threatened by the dislocation of more than five hundred families. Obreros Unidos was the elected representative of Libby's statewide cucumber operations. We claimed they were moving their operations out of state to avoid the union and that workers enjoyed rights to employment wherever future operations were located. The threat of walkouts at multicity processing and canning operations, we hoped, would eventually lead us to the negotiating table.

12

BUILDING SUPPORT

Much of what I knew about labor rights I learned in Wisconsin from Professor Brandeis and the many others who helped our cause. But most of what I knew about organizing workers and running political campaigns I had learned in my hometown of Crystal City, where I had participated in organizing voter education and registration drives and promoting political rallies before I began to organize workers. I had learned that elections are won by voter turnout and that the location of polling places and the role of registrants and poll watchers were crucial.

A major concern of union organizing among these families was that most of the workers had never exercised their right to vote. The Voting Rights Act had been passed just two years earlier, in 1965, and only some of the workers, mostly those who had participated in the political revolt of 1963 in Crystal City, had ever voted.

After Libby's refused to meet and informed us they were moving all Wisconsin cucumber harvesting and processing south, we sued, charging them with unfair labor practices. But we would not wait for the WERC board and counterappeals in the courts to determine the outcome. We would take our fight to Libby's food-processing and canning companies spread throughout central Wisconsin.

Because of the short growing season in Wisconsin, we had continued organizing in Texas for the Libby strike during the previous winter. In the winter of 1967–68, Crystal City's Chicano population continued to challenge the minority Anglo colonists who ruled with support of some middle-class Mexicans. In the Texas Valley, the Texas Rangers were called in to deal with the La Casita striking farmworkers in Starr County. Arriving when I did, I did not bring good news, as there would be no planting, cultivating, or harvesting at Libby's in the summer of 1968, only plans for more labor action across Libby's remaining and still extensive Wisconsin food-processing industry.

Throughout the winter, the home base of Obreros Unidos was in Crystal City. Obreros Unidos offices were established in our former residence beside the restaurant that my father founded in the early 1940s. The café was now being rented by Los Veintecinco (The Twenty-five): twenty-five employees of Del Monte canning company, mostly men, who rented my father's bar and formed an association to pay the rent. The dining room area was not rented and was used as a small meeting hall. Adjoining the open meeting space were Obreros Unidos's offices in our former front living room, which had now been converted to office space for Uncle Julian's justice of the peace responsibilities.

Julian had struggled in his role as justice of the peace. Although as a World War II veteran he was not physically threatened by the Texas Rangers, Zavala County deputies and Crystal City police would not bring any cases for him to adjudicate. He was convinced that this was illegal. He felt that residents charged in his district had to be tried there by him, but there was nothing he could do at the time. Although he did perform some marriages, he could not keep his office open based on these fees alone. Like thousands of other loyalists, he joined the migrant stream in those years following the counterrevolt. In fact, Uncle Julian had been part of the organizing drive in the Libby's walkouts and the WERC emergency election in the summer of 1967.

The political revolt of 1963 had energized the youth of my generation, and we played a significant part early on. The insurgents who were leading the fight for the franchise had a very special role for us: the future. We were the first generation that had been schooled. We were the first to be shown how to come together as in the local mutual aid society, Sociedad Funeraria Miguel Hidalgo. They first showed us that organizations are for self-help. That is, the reason we form organizations is for the common good, which presently was access to the franchise. Young local activists supported our organizing of workers in their home base, especially in Crystal City where the political revolt was now five years old. In spite of the fact that they had just come of age, by 1968 the youth of Crystal City were veterans of three city council elections and a countywide election.

My 1967–68 winter recruiting included expanding the organizational capacity of Obreros Unidos. Three of the main field organizers of Libby's Wisconsin processing plants came from Crystal City and were veterans of the political revolts and counterrevolts. In addition to being migrant workers, they were personal friends and former classmates of my brothers and me from when we all attended school in the segregated Crystal City Independent District.

The 1968 summer organizing activities were focused on putting pressure on Libby's to abide by the WERC union certification election and to return to negotiate a contract with Obreros Unidos. We wanted to maintain a position of strength in case we met to negotiate at any point during the legal process. We organized their seasonal workforce throughout the processing and canning industries. They had extensive contracts with growers that provided them with vegetables at three food-processing plants at Hartford, Jackson, and Janesville. We wanted to appeal to the migrant and seasonal workers at those plants to support Obreros Unidos and to negotiate. This we would do by organizing walkouts at all three plants simultaneously. We wanted to undertake these operations against Libby's while continuing our organizing of cucumber harvesters in central Wisconsin. This meant we needed an expanded organizational staff.

The winter organizing in Texas and in Wisconsin appeared to give us the capabilities to undertake such an operation. David Giffey, a dear friend and wonderful companion who had set up the union newspaper *La Voz Mexicana*, had returned to the Texas Valley with my brother Manuel to organize farmworkers in the Borderland, but we had recruited Chuck Miller, a gifted photographer, to publish the newspaper for the summer in his place. He would continue to support Obreros Unidos's union and grape boycott activities beyond the summer. From UW–Madison's High School Equivalency Program, one of the students who had been most supportive with the California grape boycott was Ricardo Enriques, a former migrant. After graduating with his GED, Enriques committed to volunteer in Wautoma for the 1968 summer. He was followed by Maria "Cookie"

Torres, who became one of the most effective union organizers. They both joined the statewide grape boycott later that fall. UW-Madison student Joan Porter coordinated the boycotts.

The largest and the oldest of the three targeted processing plants that we were organizing was at Hartford, where migrant workers from Crystal City dominated the workforce. Three of the key organizers for the 1968 Obreros Unidos campaigns were Francisco "Panchillo" Rodriguez, Rodolfo Palomo, and Ezequiel Guzman, all experienced political activists from Crystal City. They were migrant workers with extended families in the labor camps. Panchillo was the most well known of all of us. Named after his father, he was the son of the neighborhood barber, one of the most respected people in the *rinon*, the segregated Mexican commercial district. He lived with his wife, Anita, and their daughter two blocks from our home on Crockett Street. The barbershop was behind my father's café.

Panchillo and Anita were my family's most constant companions and friends over the years we migrated. As migrants, we had lived together in a number of labor camps. Panchillo's father now worked in a canning plant north of our union operations.

Rodolfo and his family migrated to central Wisconsin that summer and were living in a nearby labor camp. For personal reasons, his father, Don Adrian, had left for our hometown, Crystal City. Don Adrian left Rodolfo in charge of the Palomo extended family. Once Rodolfo found us, he spent more time organizing on behalf of Obreros Unidos than picking pickles.

Because Libby's Hartford plant was an hour away, Rodolfo frequently traveled with Panchillo and did not return until late. He was married with children. Concerned about them, I invited them to join us in the Wautoma "solidarity house." The house the union had rented had two bedrooms upstairs and a small one in the basement. I offered Rodolfo's family the basement bedroom, and Rodolfo happily moved in and spent the rest of the summer with the other union organizers and volunteers who came from Milwaukee and Madison and crashed on the living room floor. The organizing of Libby's could not have taken place without the full-time organizing of Panchillo and Rodolfo, and later of Ezequiel Guzman. While the walkout was best represented in Hartford, Ezequiel effectively got the Teamsters to honor the walkout and shut the plant down in Janesville, Wisconsin.

Ezequiel, who was the son of my uncle Teofilo's boyhood friend, inherited his father's nickname, Chumina. The Mexican families called a bloodhound dog, one with a keen sense of smell, a *chumina*. It was alleged that during Prohibition Ezequiel's dad could sniff out from across the border any bootlegged tequila that was hidden in the brush. My uncle Teofilo, the elder Chumina, and their cohorts would find it and raid it.

Chumina was active on the picket line after harvesting cucumbers with his family and on weekends. He joined Obreros Unidos and was crucial in the organizing of the walkout at the Libby's plant in Janesville in support of Obreros Unidos negotiations. Chumina persuaded the Teamsters truckers to temporarily halt the hauling of Libby's products in support of our union during the walkout. This relationship with the Teamsters was crucial in further organizing the canning companies. Chumina would later join the Milwaukee grape boycott and help organize the first political campaign by a Latino in the barrio in 1970.

Wherever we established solidarity homes, families and couples anchored the living quarters. As former migrants, the majority of us were used to living with our extended families in cramped quarters. Everywhere we organized labor actions, whether organizing migrants or supporting the California grape boycott, we established residences where we all huddled together. Manuel, with his keen eye on labor history and the local support of the International Office of the United Auto Workers in Milwaukee, had named these residences solidarity houses after UAW President Walter Reuther's union offices. When whole families joined the movement, everything was done to accommodate them and give them some privacy and time for each other. Children were the most welcomed and enlivened the busy households. My brother Manuel, after returning from the US Army in Panama and moving to Madison and organizing the grape boycott, would leave his young son Benjamin with Lloyd Guzior and others in a Mifflin Street solidarity house while he was on the picket line.

Rodolfo Palomo's wife took over the kitchen duties from Panchillo so he could travel more often with Rodolfo to Hartford an hour away. Panchillo was a great cook and he ensured that we were always stocked with enough staples for everyone: tortillas, rice, beans, and so on. He was a smart and considerate cook, and all the volunteers appreciated him.

There were always leftovers for the organizers who came in late from the field. But Rodolfo's wife's tortillas were better, everyone said. And over the course of many shared meals, as well as chores and tasks taken on by so many, it was clear that a strong community of people dedicated to our cause was forming.

13

ORGANIZING FROM THE PICKET LINE

Two incidents, both completely unanticipated, made us change our strategy for organizing the Green Bay Foods workers and Libby's canning company worker walkouts. By June 1968, when the cucumber harvest had started and the pea harvest was at its peak, the organizing at Hartford's canning company had already begun as migrant seasonal workers, many from Crystal City, were arriving.

First, the Valenzuela family was fired for wearing a union button while picking cucumbers on the farm of Jon Wilcox. As was the practice, they were not only fired, but also thrown out of their living quarters in the labor camp. Wilcox's father was the principal owner of the Green Bay Foods Company, which was being sold to Dean's Food. Although we had not planned any labor actions in 1968 against Green Bay Foods until the Libby's case was settled, we were actively organizing their workers, many from the Winter Garden region. The Valenzuela couple were both Obreros Unidos members who defended their right to wear our union button.

The union offered the Valenzuela family legal aid. We immediately contacted the Wisconsin State AFL-CIO's labor firm and got the assistance of attorney David Loeffler, who was also handling the Libby's case. Loeffler thought we should file a complaint of unfair labor practice with WERC and sue Wilcox in the local county court system.

In the meantime, the most immediate problem was where to house the Valenzuela family. We assured them that we could locate a unit at a labor camp that supported the union. But they were upset and wanted to protest the firings. They had been fired at the workplace, in the fields, in front of

Eva Valenzuela, who had been fired for wearing her union button, speaks to supporters at the downtown Wautoma tent city.

other workers. They felt that Wilcox had openly attempted to intimidate and humiliate them in front of their coworkers. Eva Valenzuela was particularly offended and wanted to challenge Wilcox's arbitrary and unlawful violation of her rights. The word would soon spread that workers were being thrown out of their camps for supporting the union. Something needed to be done! The Valenzuelas thought we should do something to stop the firings in Wilcox's and other Green Bay Foods labor camps where we enjoyed support. Eva insisted that workers should not have to face such humiliations.

The Valenzuela family decided to set up a tent city at the Wautoma Mill Pond Park in downtown Wautoma, next to the newly opened union gas cooperative. The tent city could be set up away from the parking area and deep into the park. The family could enter and exit the gas co-op through the back, out of view. They could get water from the gas station and use its toilet. The less we impinged on city property, the longer, I thought, we could stay in Mill Pond Park. We had no permit or authorization to camp, nor did we feel that we had to ask anyone whether we could set up camp there. It was public property, and we felt we had access to it. Migrant workers almost exclusively used the ample parking lot where they could park their tandem trucks when they came to shop in the two-block Wautoma downtown. If Wilcox fired other workers, we could expand the tent city throughout the rest of the park. In addition to providing a place for displaced workers to stay, the tent city in a public location would draw attention to our cause.

To stay ahead of the spreading of fear about the union, we agreed there should be a public demonstration against Wilcox. We had to spread the word that what Wilcox was signaling to other growers, to fire workers arbitrarily and without cause for wearing a union button, was illegal. Obreros Unidos would fight that to the end. A rapid legal response was necessary, but we felt it would be insufficient on its own. We all agreed that we should hold a rally and inform the workers how we were going to fight this infringement of our rights.

The sacrifice that the Valenzuela family undertook moved all of us who gathered. The organizational meeting that began in the union office on top of the shoe store would go late into the night. We began the discussion anew when the field organizers came back from the labor camps, which were spread over a multicounty area, and the Libby's Hartford plant an

Migrant families applaud in support of Obreros Unidos at the downtown Wautoma tent city in the summer of 1968.

hour away. Once we and the family decided to set up the tent city, our thoughts turned to security. We agreed that at least two staff had to be at the gas co-op so that one could service the station and the other could communicate with the camp, the union office, and the Wautoma solidarity house. Maintaining and securing the grounds for the Valenzuela family's stay would take our organizers' and volunteer staff's time that could have been spent organizing and servicing union members. But the organizers and volunteers had voted to defend the family; it was the right decision. We gave the Valenzuelas a key to the gas station so they could use the toilets any time of day or night. Most important, we agreed that we should call for a Sunday afternoon rally at the park in front of the tent city to make our case against the unfair, illegal act of Wilcox.

We had not had a demonstration in downtown Wautoma since the rally that announced the march to Madison two years earlier. The 1967 Libby's organizational efforts, the labor camp meetings, and the rally on the day of the strike were all held in Portage County in Almond and Bancroft Villages. The public building housing the sheriff's department and the city police was next door to the courtyard. We had informed them of our peaceful, nonviolent protest, and there had been no incidents. The following year, when more than five hundred workers walked out en masse at a predetermined time and drove to Bancroft to meet in the open air at Libby's cucumber grading and processing plant, there had been no police presence. Over the intervening two years, there had never been any confrontations with the local police. Area law enforcement authorities had no reason to doubt that our presence and planned demonstration at Mill Pond Park would be anything other than lawful and peaceful.

The Valenzuela firings and their subsequent public protest of their homelessness drew widespread interest. Obreros Unidos supporters extended an invitation to Wisconsin Attorney General Bronson La Follette to speak at the rally along with Obreros Unidos organizers, and La Follette accepted. The press followed the attorney general's tour of the migrant labor camps before the rally. At the rally, La Follette sided with migrant families who were inviting Obreros Unidos organizers to visit their individual homes at grower-owned labor camps. Processors and growers argued that the labor camps were private property and that they had the right to dictate to the families who they could have as visitors and guests. La Follette's remarks were warmly received and appreciated by Obreros Unidos members, their families, and our supporters.

But the most significant moments of the rally were the presence and remarks of Eva Valenzuela and Cookie Torres. Women and children, who made up a majority of the migrant workforce, had been well represented at the 1966 rally and other organizing activities, but it wasn't until 1968 that women's role in union activities became more prominent. At the rally, Eva and Cookie spoke to the crowd as migrant workers, as members of Obreros Unidos, and most important, as women. For the rest of the summer, the major organizational effort, the grape boycott, and the downtown picketing would include as many women as men.

—‖—

The second incident that changed our course that summer was a conflict with a local grocer. In addition to organizing the walkouts, Obreros Unidos had also taken on the labor-intensive task of promoting the grape boycott to support California farmworkers. It began when I took it upon myself to visit Wautoma-area food stores to inform them of California workers' issues and to explain why we were asking them to stop selling grapes. The grocers all knew who I was. Our family had been living in the town for the past nine years, and the Salas family restaurant bought groceries from these businesses. Further, this was the third year of Obreros Unidos's presence, and by this point we were highly visible in Wautoma. In addition to the café, we had the office space above the shoe store, where we had painted the windows with thunderbird signs, the solidarity house, and the gasoline co-op in downtown Wautoma, with a three-foot-high thunderbird and the name of the union painted on top of the front wall of the building. All of the local residents were aware of our activities, so no one was surprised by our issues or tactics. They had been negatively covered by the local newspaper throughout this time, but we and the workers had ignored the coverage. As long as we remained peaceful and nonviolent, our determination to have a presence in downtown Wautoma, where thousands of migrant workers' families came to buy their weekly groceries and shop, was not deterred. We would begin to have rallies in support of the Valenzuela family and set up a seven-day-a-week picket line in downtown Wautoma in support of the grape boycott.

No grocer was happy to see me or hear of my request to remove the boycotted grapes, but none was so bold to react as did one downtown grocery store. Wryzinski, the smallest of the local grocers but the most visible because of its downtown location, not only refused to remove the grapes from the store, but the owner also became offended that I had asked him to remove them. He informed me that I had no right to dictate to him how to run his business. He would not stop selling grapes and in fact would promote their sale. He was not only against what we were doing but also wholeheartedly supported the California grape growers' right to refuse to meet with their workers. The local newspaper featured his anti-union views throughout the summer and beyond.

Our major concern was committing organizers' and volunteers' time to setting up a picket line to keep the primarily migrant families from shopping at the store. Initially, it hardly seemed like it was worth the effort. In terms of the volume of grape sales, Wryzinski's was very small. Normally, when we set up a consumer boycott of a particular store, we went after grocery chains that handled large volumes of grapes. We chose the store's location of the chain where we would have the most impact. For instance, when we began to boycott the Kroger Food Stores in Madison,

Wisconsin attorney general Bronson LaFollette and state assemblyman Lloyd Barbee join me as we demonstrated at Kroger Food Store in Madison.

we chose the location on University Avenue where mostly university students, state office workers, and young couples lived. We then demanded that all Kroger's stores cease to purchase grapes, not only at the store we were picketing but at all outlets. If they didn't agree to remove the grapes, we would then set up pickets and proceed with a consumer boycott of the product. While the informational picket line was going on, we organized labor, religious, and student groups to write letters and make phone calls to the store's headquarters on behalf of the California farmworkers. While in Madison we proceeded to get school, city, and university institutions to stop buying grapes and inform California grape growers to negotiate with their employees. By comparison, the small food store in Wautoma would take almost the same effort but with smaller results. Further, we could not mount the external pressure from local institutions and supportive organizations that we did in urban areas such as Madison or Milwaukee, where local and non-Latino organizations might support us. We had to depend entirely on the migrant population for an effective grape boycott.

From the initial communications with Wryzinski, we were left with the impression that he would not relent and remove the grapes. Further, he would be a thorn in our side, as we were sure he would continue their sale with in-your-face promotions and support for the California's grape growers. We had no alternative but to challenge him. This would not be our typical picket. It was not going to center on consumer information on the issues facing the California farmworkers. This was about Obreros Unidos and our right to organize and support farmworkers, and in this case, to organize in support of our brothers and sisters who were demanding their rights on the West Coast as we were here in Wisconsin. The picket line would not be just about the boycott of grapes, but about farmworker rights, of exhorting workers and the broader community to join Obreros Unidos.

After the organizers' and volunteers' meeting at the solidarity house, we decided that the picket would be an all-week affair. We would picket seven days a week, from late afternoon until the store closed at nine in the evenings on weekdays, and all day, beginning after lunch until night, on weekends. Our goals included demonstrating to local businesses that farmworkers would not shop at designated stores that challenged our fundamental right to organize. Most important, local businesses in downtown Wautoma depended on tourists and migrant worker families. When migrant families came into town to shop and thousands filled the streets, the tourists stayed away on weekends and shopped at the small general stores on the outskirts of town. We focused on migrant families that came to church, attended the local theater, and did their weekly shopping.

An unanticipated consequence of the picket line was the support for Wryzinski's business. Supporters came in droves and walked out eating grapes and taunting us. Led by the local police and Jon Wilcox, the grower who had fired the Valenzuela family for wearing a union button, they included former classmates and teammates of mine. Mary Hotvedt's father, who owned a cottage across Silver Lake where we had designed the masthead for *La Voz Mexicana* before it became a union newspaper, would drive by, yell, and call us "pinkos" and "communist sympathizers" as he circled the pickets in his car.

We never allowed these taunts to develop into confrontations with the locals. First of all, we were too disciplined. Before we set up the picket line each and every one of the union organizers and volunteers who participated was trained to not be provoked. We knew that the police would be of no help. In fact, when the locals appeared to support the store owners, the police officer in charge threw neutrality aside and joined the grape buyers, eating grapes as he oversaw us being taunted.

Since I had begun organizing farmworkers into a union and made public our demands for an improvement of working and living conditions, my relationship with the townsfolk that had developed over the years had begun to deteriorate. Worst of all, I lost some of my friendships with former classmates and teammates. Among our taunters was someone with whom I ran track and played football in high school. Back then, he knew that I had earned my place on the line through tenacity, going against players who were much bigger and heavier than I was. At my father's restaurant, with few customers after the migrant and tourist season ended and with little to do, I used to box with fellow athletes. We used the sixteen-ounce gloves my father had brought from Texas, meeting in the alley between the café and the shoe store on the corner. I used to take on all comers, notwithstanding their size or weight, sometimes three or four of them in the same afternoon. As we faced each other across the picket line, he knew I never backed away from a challenge. He knew better than to get physical. There would have been consequences! Happily, the counter-protest never went beyond taunts, and Milwaukee volunteer lawyer Fred Kessler was always present when needed.

Although we were initially concerned with the inordinate time commitment of a seven-day-a-week picket line, it was the best organizational effort of the summer. Yes, it did consume a lot of our staff effort, and no, the amount of grapes that we stopped consumers from purchasing was not large. But the picket line became an organizational moment. We spoke to the workers who came into town to purchase their groceries with a picket sign in our hands. We asked them not to cross the picket line. We asked them to support the California farmworkers who were on strike against the grape growers. We asked them to stand in solidarity with their brothers and sisters in California who were on strike to improve their working and living conditions. This they understood as farmworkers living in deplorable conditions and earning lousy wages.

The summer-long grape boycott of Wryzinski was unlike any other Wisconsin picket line. Generally, the pickets that we established against grocery chains throughout the state were intended to inform the public about our cause. At the time, most of the customers were women, homemakers who were responsible for maintaining and feeding the household. They did most of the shopping. At night and on weekends, we would see more couples and families. The attempt was to inform the consumer why we were there, but if the women stopped to talk, we would converse about the conditions of the farmworkers who harvested grapes and other fruits and vegetables. The most compelling part of our message was the use of herbicides and insecticides in the cultivation of grapes. At the time, we didn't have much information on the long-term effects of these toxic chemicals in the food chain or the impact of the lack of sanitary facilities in the fields during harvest time. Women, and especially mothers, were very much concerned about what products they fed to their children. Chávez and Huerta realized this and began to publicize the unfettered use of herbicides and insecticides in the food chain.

The picket line in support of the California grape farmworkers in Wautoma in the summer of 1968 was different. Since many of the consumers were fellow farmworkers, we asked them not to shop at Wryzinski in solidarity with their fellow farmworkers in California. They could identify with this message. At the picket line, we not only passed out bilingual leaflets explaining the reason for the protest, but we also made available our union newspaper, *La Voz Mexicana*. To those who were most interested in our cause, we passed out union buttons and asked them to join the union. This type of organizing from a picket line was very different from talking to workers about the benefits of the union down the street in the park, or while we visited them in the labor camps. But we found that it worked! Very few if any of the thousands of seasonal workers who came into town to shop for their groceries crossed the picket line.

The success of our picket was largely due to the role of our women organizers and volunteers led by Eva Valenzuela, who became known throughout the summer as the symbol of the protest. It went beyond the industry's attempt to keep the workers from expressing their support for

Obreros Unidos. It denied the right of the workers to welcome friends and guests to their homes, and importantly, it blocked their access to the migrant educational, health, and social service programs that we had organized over the past five years. Eva and Cookie spoke to the primarily female shoppers as fellow workers, as young women, and as mothers. Cookie would wear her colorful Mexican embroidered blouses at the rally and in the picket line, showing pride in her Mexican heritage and art. The farmworkers' families responded. They stood in solidarity with Obreros Unidos's support for the striking California farmworkers. In the end, Wryzinski couldn't survive without the migrant workers' business. They closed their doors for good later that fall.

—⊩—

While the grape boycott was ongoing, Panchillo, Chumina, and Rodolfo had been successful organizing in the three Libby's processing plants, especially at the Hartford plant, which included many Crystal City neighbors and friends. We had to be extremely careful with the Hartford plant, as it had already been organized by the meat cutters' union. John Schmitt, the president of the Wisconsin State AFL-CIO, had suggested that we meet with the meat cutters union head, Matt Pinter, to avoid any problems. The meat cutter's union contract at the Hartford plant favored full-time non-seasonal workers at the expense of seasonal and especially migrant workers, but we hoped they would support our efforts.

I met with Pinter and the local head of the union in Hartford to explain what Obreros Unidos planned to carry out. I told them we had won a union election against Libby's and the company had refused to honor the results of the election, instead moving its operations out of state. Obreros Unidos sought to compel Libby's back to the negotiating table. We wanted Hartford's union of full-time nonseasonal workers to honor a multiplant walkout that included Hartford's. In order not to impact their contract, we were organizing a walkout among migrant seasonal workers during their lunch hour. As I organized the Hartford plant, I found major complaints with the union contract. I related this to Pinter, but I did not make it a major issue when I met with the meat cutters' local leaders. I wanted their support, but it was obvious that the plant's seasonal workforce supported Obreros Unidos and were going to walk out.

In the early part of the summer, we also met with the head of Teamsters Local 695, who was interested in having Obreros Unidos join the Teamsters' efforts to organize Wisconsin's processing plants. It was an interesting proposal, as the Teamsters would assume Obreros Unidos's attempt to establish social unionism with a full range of services for seasonal workers. This was unlike the meat cutters' type of contract that favored primarily full-time nonmigrant workers. Furthermore, the Teamsters controlled aspects of the transportation of processed food products from the three Libby's plants that were essential in impacting Libby's statewide operations. Obreros Unidos had maintained its unaffiliated status even after the California National Farm Workers Association (NFWA), César Chávez's original union, had merged with the Filipino-led Agricultural Workers and formed the United Farm Workers Organizing Committee (UFWOC) AFL-CIO. Besides, Frank Lyons from the University of Wisconsin Extension's School for Workers, who had been instrumental in providing access to summer workers' training sessions and pass-the-hat activities to raise funds for our efforts, cautioned me not to rush into a decision to collaborate with Teamsters Local 695. He laid out the pros and cons, and it appeared that we would sacrifice our ability to engage in the political revolt in Crystal City, as we presently did, as well as continue to oppose the war and involve ourselves in Wisconsin progressive politics, if we went forward with the collaboration. I respected Frank's experience and knowledge of the labor movement and had developed a close working and personal relationship with him. Further, he warned me that if I linked up with the Teamsters, I would eventually end up opposing the California farmworkers' union efforts on the Teamsters' behalf in California, as they were now raiding previously organized UFWOC's plants and signing "sweetheart" contracts.

In addition, if I opposed the meat cutters and joined the Teamsters, it would mean an end to the multiyear relationship with John Schmitt. No one had been more helpful in Obreros Unidos's efforts to organize farmworkers, and I couldn't do anything that would risk rupturing our relationship. Chávez had begun to pressure Schmitt to end his assistance to Obreros Unidos by having the national AFL-CIO lean on him. The national office was prioritizing the organizing of California farmworkers. Chávez assured me that once they won in California, he would help us organize in Wisconsin. I don't know why I believed him, but I did. I decided to stay the course instead of joining with the Teamsters.

I suggested we split Obreros Unidos's activities into two. Manuel, who had just returned from military service and was in Madison helping out with the grape boycott, and Bill Smith, who was now helping us full time, would continue to head the Waushara County field operations and keep the union office open, including the gas co-op and the union newsletter. George Vasquez, recently returned from Vietnam, would join Obreros Unidos's organizational team in the canning companies. I would move to Milwaukee to direct the grape boycott office out of the state's largest metropolitan area. Later, Panchillo, my brother Frank, and Chuck Miller would follow.

The city of Milwaukee was at the moment sizzling with political organizing. When I moved there at the end of the field operation at the end of summer of 1968, the city had just concluded two hundred consecutive days of protest for an open housing ordinance by the Black community. Riots had ensued, and the Wisconsin National Guard had been called. Lives had been lost and there were nightly images of police attacking and arresting peaceful protesters. It was a difficult time, but one full of potential for change.

14

Intersecting Movements

Obreros Unidos greatly expanded its organizing operations as more former migrant workers joined as organizers and support staff. This had allowed me to spend more time outside the main offices in Wautoma seeking support and raising funds. Beyond reaching out to Wisconsin's other labor unions, I was now being invited by churches, universities, and other progressive groups to speak. Milwaukee was the home base for more than a dozen attorneys who were part of the free migrant legal services, which were entirely paid for by union fundraising. David Loeffler was one.

When I first moved to Milwaukee, the Loefflers allowed me to stay at their place until I secured a multibedroom flat nearby. Although I needed only a small space for myself, when additional organizers moved in to assist in carrying out the boycott operations, we would need a home with several bedrooms to establish another solidarity house. Rent was cheaper on the near south side, where the Milwaukee Archdiocese's Centro Hispano had allowed us to use a backroom for the grape boycott effort at 524 West National, only several blocks from where my brother Carlos and Salvador Sanchez worked. We would also be closer to the targeted area of picketing on the near east side by UW–Milwaukee, where the United Auto Workers International Union offices were located and where I was warmly welcomed by its leaders, Harvey Kitzman and Charles Heymans.

The Milwaukee grape boycott had gotten off the ground out of Milwaukee's Archdiocese-funded Centro Hispano. Chicano activist Avelardo "Lalo" Valdez, along with Hollis Stewart, had initiated boycott activities. Centro Hispano director Father John Maurice had invited me the previous year to address Centro staff on Obreros Unidos issues and later helped in hosting Chávez's first visit to Milwaukee. He allowed us a small space in the back of the Archdiocese-funded program with phone access to expand the boycott.

After conferring with Wisconsin State AFL-CIO President Schmitt, we made arrangements to bring a boycott support resolution to the Milwaukee County Labor Council. Schmitt's former union, Brewer's Local #9, had over the years supported Obreros Unidos activities. I had met Angelo Verdeen, who was most helpful in introducing me to affiliated unions in the area labor council.

At the time, we were assessing moving the planned informational pickets in the near east side from Downer Street near UW–Milwaukee toward the recently unionized Black community that was patronizing the newly constructed Kohl's Food Store at Capitol Court, the multistore shopping mall along Capitol Drive. Kohl's was not responsive to removing grapes and was an early target in addition to the Kroger boycott that had begun in 1967 in Madison and would soon spread to Milwaukee.

The landscape had changed on Capitol Drive west of Oakland by the bustling Tower Automotive plant and across the viaduct that brought

An officer escorts me and other demonstrators out of Kohl's Food Store during a direct action.

thousands of employees, many of them Black, to its cavernous factories and warehouses. The finished products were railed to the automotive industry in Kenosha and Janesville, as well as east to Michigan's auto assembly centers. A growing number of Black families who were employed in this industrial sector were buying homes and shopping in the newly constructed Capital Court at Kohl's Food Stores. Initially we thought they would remove their grapes, but we were unable to reach an agreement on their removal, and we targeted them in this area after approaching consumers in the near east side's smaller stores.

—||—

Besides working with area unions, I reached out to Assemblyman Lloyd Barbee for help in getting Milwaukee's Black leaders, including elected officials, to support the grape boycott. I dearly wanted to meet renowned activist Father James Groppi and Vel Phillips, the first Black alderwoman elected to the city council, and ask them for their support. They were leaders of the recently concluded Freedom Marches, two hundred consecutive days of demonstrations for a City of Milwaukee open housing ordinance. Barbee had earlier supported the grape boycott activities in Madison and had joined the picket line to publicize his support. He was able to connect me to Groppi and Phillips.

After our meeting, Alderwoman Phillips agreed to organize support for a press conference urging the Black community to support the California grape boycott. But it was Father Groppi and the NAACP Youth Council leaders who most dramatically changed how we organized the grape boycott and later the Spanish Speaking Outreach Institute (SSOI) at UW–Milwaukee, by adopting the direct action tactics that followed the Freedom Marches in the fall of 1968.

As we were in the process of moving Obreros Unidos operations to Milwaukee's Walker Point neighborhood, the NAACP Youth Council initiated a demonstration, supported by Centro Hispano staff and volunteers, against Allen Bradley's discriminatory employment practices. I joined the multimonth Allen Bradley protests and met Father Groppi there. When Barbee organized a protest for mistreatment and discrimination against Marc's Big Boy, the restaurant at the recently built Juneau Village, I again joined NAACP Youth Council members at the picket line.

Father Groppi joins grape boycott organizers who were camping and fasting at Kohl's Food Store in Milwaukee in the fall of 1968.

In addition to the activities that the grape boycott generated, personal and Obreros Unidos issues drew me several blocks down the street to Eighth and Greenfield, at the multistory former orphanage that housed both United Migrant Opportunity Services (UMOS) and Social Development Commission's (SDC's) Concentrated Employment Program. My older brother Carlos now worked for the Concentrated Employment Program, the employment and outreach office of the SDC, a federally funded antipoverty program. Salvador Sanchez, a former union organizer, and Ernesto Chacon, who had joined the grape boycott picket line, were now working for UMOS, which had recently moved its operations from Waukesha. I frequently met Carlos, Salvador, Chacon, and Dante Navarro at nearby Mexican cafés and bars for dining during the day and socializing at night. My visits to the UMOS building also had to do with policy issues.

Although we had informed Obreros Unidos members during our winter organizing visits to the Texas Borderland to avoid coming to Wisconsin for the cucumber harvest in the summer of 1968, as Libby's was not planting cucumbers, migrant families still came to Wisconsin looking to fill the gap in the midwestern migrant cycle with any type of work before the tomato harvest in early fall. Many workers had no choice, whether due to economic necessity or the simple fact that the seasonal migrant stream depended on their being employed six weeks in central Wisconsin. Thousands traveled to the area with no guarantee of work or housing. They were subsequently displaced, with weeks of unemployment on the horizon, as other crops, principally tomatoes, would not be ready for harvest until later in the season, usually after August. These workers needed UMOS services and support. This brought us in conflict with UMOS administrators who had sworn not to involve themselves in our challenges to the processors and growers to improve migrant families' working and living conditions. They were afraid that providing services to dislocated migrants who had supported Obreros Unidos would imperil their grant, they informed us.

UMOS had other obvious administrative and operational issues. First, none of UMOS's administrative leaders were Latino. Most of the Latinos, primarily Mexican American former migrant workers, were employed only as outreach workers. But more important, UMOS was in violation of Office of Economic Opportunity's (OEO) Migrant Division mandates for maximum feasibility of participation. UMOS was obligated to include migrants and former migrants on the board. The Migrant Division had previously cited UMOS administration for this deficiency. It would take a lot of effort and internal change for UMOS to be an effective supplier of assistance to migrant workers.

15

CHICANO AND LATINO
SELF-DETERMINATION

We were not asking UMOS to support labor union activities. But during the winter months of 1968 we testified and lobbied for enhancement of the migrant housing code with a certification process based on more timely inspection. We sought to establish an out-of-state labor recruitment process based on formal work orders that reflected the acreage they were planting, the specific need for workers based on that acreage, and the certified housing available. Professor Brandeis and other civic leaders had founded the Governor's Committee on Migratory Labor exactly for this purpose: to deliberate, debate, and recommend to Wisconsin state agencies as well as to the Wisconsin legislature the implementation of policies that would improve migrant working and living conditions.

Religious leaders from southeastern Wisconsin had founded UMOS in 1965 to provide services for migrant children. The 1966 grant was an expansion of a child care program that had been funded by the State of Wisconsin Division of Children and Youth since 1962, the same program that funded the day care program that saw my entry into migrant workers' issues after college. The program had expanded to more than half a dozen sites over the next three years. Although wonderful and very needed, these services were insufficient. They did not address the overcrowded, unsanitary housing conditions or the violations of Wisconsin's social and progressive legislation, or, especially, its minimum wage law.

We demanded that UMOS address the working and living conditions of Wisconsin seasonal farmworkers. We supported a broader mission for UMOS besides providing child care. We supported the recently added initiative to assist in the resettlement of migrant families, but we wanted to incorporate adult basic education as well as job training programs for both men and women. We challenged the UMOS board to end its discriminatory policies of not including qualified migrants or former migrants in its administration.

Most egregious was UMOS's complete disregard of their mandate as an OEO-funded program to incorporate migrants and former migrants in all aspects of the program's delivery system, including in the board of directors that set and oversaw the carrying out of UMOS policies. The incorporation document created a nine-member board of directors made up of three representatives of the three religious orders that had founded it in 1965.

After being informed by UMOS administration that they would not assist displaced Libby's migrant workers, we enacted a plan to openly demand changes to the administration, staff, board structure, and policies. The UMOS demands were developed at a community meeting of migrants, former migrants, and Milwaukee community activists. Most of the Obreros Unidos Chicano organizers who were in the process of moving to Milwaukee in support of the grape boycott were former migrants with longtime ties and familial relationships with UMOS participants and staff. We began to reach out to certain UMOS board members for support.

On the UMOS board was Gladys Zophy, an original UMOS incorporator from southeast Wisconsin and dear friend of Genevieve "Beba" Medina. Both had been on the inaugural UMOS board, and Ms. Medina, as we called her, had known me all my life. Our fathers were friends and her family had lived only one block away from us at our homestead. Additionally, on the UMOS board was Father Maurice, who also was one of the original board members and had worked for years organizing support for migrants and immigrants and providing office space for the grape boycott. He was responsive to our demands. Further, we received early support on the board from Bill Koch, whom I knew from my work with UW–Madison Extension's migrant outreach programs.

As well organized as the former migrants and their community supporters were, the nonmigrant, non-Latino UMOS administrators underestimated us. In spite of the fact that the OEO had warned the administration in 1967 to enhance migrants' and former migrants' representation in both planning and operations, UMOS administrators were taken aback by our broad-based challenge.

A group including Navarro, Sanchez, Ernesto Chacon (founder of the Latin American Union for Civil Rights), Dolores Aguirre (a former UMOS student), present UMOS staff, and myself began to meet in the fall of 1968 to plan to apply pressure to UMOS. On November 25, 1968, a large number of Latino community members met at UMOS's offices to protest UMOS mismanagement and to present a list of twelve points, including the demand for hiring former migrants and advancement of those presently employed. Not only was the lack of migrant participation on the UMOS board negligent, we argued, but all five of the top administrative positions were also held by non-Latinos.

UMOS administrators responded that Latinos were being "phased in" and that dramatic changes in administration would imperil the OEO grant. The administrators went to the press to publicly demand contracts for the five top administrators, a guarantee from the UMOS board that their jobs would be secure against a "Brown Power" attempt to unseat them. (The UMOS educational coordinator offensively referred to our efforts as "chili power.") When we presented our demands, Auxiliary Catholic Bishop Jerome Hastrich stated that former migrants presently employed or community leaders recommending changes were not ready to assume leadership of UMOS. That is, we were not capable. If we tried to take over the program tomorrow, it would fail and be the end of the program, he stated.

Navarro effectively argued against the Catholic bishop, stating that it was the UMOS administration that was failing to provide adequate housing and jobs for former migrants. Sanchez and I, who were given permission to address the board, argued that the present program's core staff, with board and community support, could effectively improve the program. In the early hours of the morning, the board agreed with us and refused to grant the five administrators their contracts. The administrators resigned en masse, and UMOS was left leaderless and in jeopardy of losing its grant. I felt responsible for this, but I thought that I could assist in the reorganization, get funding reinstated, and set the organization on course as not exclusively a service provider, but as an advocate for migrant issues. I applied for the director's position.

16

UMOS, MIGRANT ADVOCATE

Obreros Unidos had committed to support the California grape boycott by moving its operations and coordinating the effort in the labor-rich Milwaukee area, but Chávez wanted us to focus completely on supporting the California grape boycott. He had qualms about our engaging in ongoing Milwaukee issues such as open housing, employment discrimination, and school desegregation. He assumed that upon my moving to Milwaukee, we would cease to organize in the field. But Manuel and Bill Smith were planning to follow up on our 1968 success of organizing walkouts in three Libby's processing plants in support of negotiations with Obreros Unidos. George Vasquez, like Manuel a Vietnam-era veteran, left the migrant stream and joined Manuel and Bill in organizing the Wisconsin processing plants in 1969.

Another issue that created tension between Chávez and myself was our continued winter organizing efforts along the Texas Borderland. Manuel and David Giffey spent part of the 1967–68 winter helping NFWA Vice President Antonio Orendain in the Texas Valley, while I committed to visiting Crystal City's Obreros Unidos members and bringing them up to date on the lawsuit against Libby's. At that time Chávez's disagreements with Orendain and the Texas farmworkers broke out into the open.

Crystal City's political revolt had continued and expanded into the Texas Valley after the organizing of Obreros Unidos in 1966. That year, the melon workers in Rio Grande City, Texas, went on strike and marched to the state capital, Austin. Farmworkers were still on strike and picketing when I visited Wisconsin migrant families in the Texas Valley in the winter of 1968–69.

Chávez and I disagreed about the amount of time I was spending in Texas and away from the grape boycott, but the disagreement went further. I thought he should have been more supportive of the Texas farmworkers.

After returning to Wisconsin, I wrote to Chávez disassociating myself from his Texas strategy and telling him I would cease to coordinate the grape boycott full time. Few knew that I had severed my relationship with Chávez, and I continued supporting the boycott as a volunteer among my other activities. When the first contract was signed between a grape grower and the union, Schmitt brought several cases of beer to our near south side backyard, and we celebrated the five-year-long struggle. I decided to focus on the reorganization of UMOS the following month, and I was hired to lead UMOS in March 1969.

During the summer of 1968, while frequently traveling to Madison, I had met and dated Glorie, then a senior at UW–Madison, who I would later marry. In the spring of 1969, Glorie moved to San Francisco, pregnant with our first child. While busy with my work for UMOS, I was overcome with happiness over the birth of our son Miguel Emiliano in the first week of March in San Francisco. I had thought he would be born several weeks before, so with a loan from John McAlpin, one of my few remaining friends from Wautoma, I flew to greet my son's arrival. My wife, Glorie, did not give birth on that trip, so I flew again to see him hours after he was born. We were indigent at the time, and I thank San Franciscans, especially the neighbors of the old Mission Street neighborhood where he first resided, for their generosity. Emiliano's first crib was a cardboard box. I brought both Miguel and Glorie home to Milwaukee's Riverwest area east of Meinecke Street and began the process of transferring all union responsibility to my brother Manuel, George Vasquez, and Bill Smith. Busy with my new family and UMOS, I informed attorney David Loeffler that all pending Wisconsin Supreme Court decisions on Obreros Unidos should be addressed to them.

George Vasquez and Manuel had targeted several canning companies for the summer 1969–70 union activities. But after our falling out, Chávez began to pressure Wisconsin state-affiliated unions not to support Obreros Unidos. Schmitt and Manuel were on opposing sides in the organizing of migrant food-processing workers in the fall of 1969. Schmitt had to support the meat cutters against Teamsters Local 695, which was on the

César Chávez (middle) and my brother Manuel Salas (left) address reporters at a press conference in Milwaukee prior to the grape boycott rally at Steelworkers Hall in 1969.

ballot for union recognition of the Fall River Canning Company workers. Obreros Unidos remained an independent, unaffiliated farmworkers union. It had not joined the Teamsters, who continued to reach out to seasonal workers in processing plants where they provided trucking services.

The Milwaukee boycott activity was at its zenith in the fall and winter of 1969. We enjoyed strong labor support and had the most successful grape boycott rally in November 1969 with more than five hundred community and union supporters welcoming Chávez to Steelworkers Hall. Manuel and Chávez carried out the press conference in support of the grape boycott. I, meanwhile, had my hands full with getting my nomination as UMOS's director confirmed by OEO and getting funding for the reorganized program renewed in less than 120 days.

OEO's Migrant Division staff supported the changes of migrant and former migrant worker participation on the UMOS board, but it would be a challenge to get them to approve my appointment in April 1969. Waushara County processors and large growers, led by Jon Wilcox, who was now a Wisconsin assemblyman, continued to organize against Obreros Unidos. Now he opposed not only my appointment as UMOS director but

State assemblyman Lloyd Barbee, pictured with me, helped to organize labor and community leaders in support of the California grape boycott at Steelworkers Hall.

also UMOS's ability to receive funding later that spring. He wrongly claimed that I was going to use UMOS to continue organizing in central Wisconsin. He now proposed legislation that would go beyond barring migrant families from inviting union organizers into their homes in labor camps owned by processors and growers. Wilcox sought legislation that would disallow social service agencies such as UMOS to enter Wisconsin's labor camps without the owner's authorization as well. We began to organize with the help of labor, religious, and civic groups to lobby against Wilcox's proposed legislation.

In Milwaukee, my application for UMOS leadership had been entirely vetted by Obreros Unidos organizers and volunteers. At the end of the Obreros Unidos 1968 summer organizing campaign, the union had split its focus. Manuel and Bill Smith, and later George Vasquez, were put in charge of field operations as I moved to Milwaukee to head the grape boycott. Chuck Miller also moved to Milwaukee after publishing the last summer issue of the union newspaper along with boyhood friend and union organizer Panchillo Rodriguez. Miller and Rodriguez—along with my youngest brothers, who had dropped out of high school to support our union efforts—joined me in the recently established solidarity house. Ezequiel "Chumina" Guzman followed and headed our first voter education and voter registration effort.

But other Chicano activists and local community leaders whom I had recently begun to work with had concerns about my leadership of UMOS. In late October 1968, as we were organizing and developing the demands to present to UMOS administrators, the question of personal interest arose. Would we use the reorganization of UMOS for personal gain? All present disavowed it. I publicly stated that I had no personal interest in UMOS. For this reason, in response, I felt that I had to publicly announce when I declared for the directorship that my tenure at UMOS would be temporary. I would stay at UMOS for only two consecutive funding cycles. That is, I would stay only long enough to stabilize the transition that UMOS was going through.

The hiring of an UMOS director was a two-step process. After a candidate was selected by the statewide UMOS board, the OEO's Office of Migrant Affairs would review the selection. I made a visit to Washington

DC where I met Migrant Affairs staff, and I made sure that I stopped at the office of Senator Gaylord Nelson to seek his support in the ongoing challenge from central Wisconsin growers led by Assemblyman Wilcox.

After my return to Milwaukee, a letter of appointment to the board followed. This did not guarantee funding for the program, however. To receive funding, we had to develop the grant proposal for program year July 1, 1969, to June 30, 1970. The grant had to be effectuated by early June, the end of the previous program year, for their consideration. I was confident that the UMOS board decision not to offer contracts to the five non-Latino administrators was because they felt confident that the migrant, former migrant, and community leaders had made an effective case for reorganizing and directing UMOS. The UMOS board supported us because it saw a reinvigorated staff with a committed core of former migrant workers with a plan that enjoyed strong community support. My aim was to get a reorganized board, a redirected UMOS program, all moving in the same direction. This could not be mandated. We all had to come together to accomplish the reorganization plan for UMOS as a migrant advocate. UMOS had been created by three major religious groups primarily to provide migrant child care programs. The present program was expanded to include a migrant resettlement program with a nascent adult basic education program.

At the time, the conditions for the grant funding included designating Peat Marwick & Mitchell (PM&M) to oversee and coordinate the training for UMOS board members and proposed reorganized administrative staff. I agreed to have PM&M consultants assists us in the reorganization by designing and redrafting our organizational chart, writing new job descriptions that spelled out UMOS's mission and emphasizing that administrators and staff would advocate, not simply be of service, on behalf of migrants; that we would address migrant issues beyond providing day care services; and that UMOS would address overcrowded, unhealthy migrant housing conditions, violations of minimum wage laws and unsafe working conditions.

UMOS redirection would only work if we came together to plan, design, and establish new guidelines that would reorganize the program to be an advocate for the implementation of the Wisconsin statues and administrative law that Obreros Unidos had been demanding. Most importantly was the focus on community development. The training for UMOS's reorganization was to be broad-based and continuous. Training was a process. It had to be ongoing. UMOS's board of directors as well as all staff members were to be included in the training sessions. Every monthly board meeting was an opportunity to enhance the knowledge of board members regarding ongoing programmatic and staff changes. Annual meetings were planned, not only to report and inform, but also to be advised.

Changing UMOS's basic mission was in line with the core principle of the agencies and organizations fighting poverty, which reflected community needs and incorporated input of those most affected. The community-based organization was to assist low-income community members to help themselves. We challenged UMOS to live up to those values beginning with its governing board. We had demanded that migrants and former migrants be elected to the board to determine its new future. The national office agreed. It was the UMOS board, now in collaboration with a Chicano-led administration, that guided the development of the new job descriptions and training for all present and future employees.

We foresaw not a top-down organizational structure, in which the direction and all decisions come from administrators on top, but one that was sustained and directed locally. The nearly ten years I had spent working with migrant programs and issues, including the last four in building a union, had taught me to trust the old mutualista model of encouraging individuals to help themselves and their communities. UMOS had to alter the program-client relationship promoted by ongoing service organizations to reflect this principle, as Obreros Unidos had done. To this end, UMOS organized advisory-area councils of migrants and former migrants to direct UMOS activities in the Racine-Kenosha, Madison, and Sheboygan areas, as well as seasonally when the highest number of seasonal migrants were concentrated in Wautoma, the home of Obreros Unidos.

Although we felt the consulting firm was there to keep an eye on us, I sensed that there was real support at the OEO Migrant Divison for UMOS as an advocate agency on behalf of migrants. The OEO Migrant Division funded statewide programs throughout the Great Lakes region, where more than one hundred thousand seasonal migrants turned the household industry into a national provider of processed fruit and vegetables. We deeply desired that the consultants, led by Jack Charles, incorporate our experience and our ideas to expand geographical services to central Wisconsin, including programmatic changes that focused on family resettlement with a more extensive adult education program.

Father Maurice, with his dual roles at Centro Hispano and UMOS, was most helpful in establishing a firm relationship between Milwaukee Area Technical College (MATC) and the two Latino community-based organizations in our education and employment and training programs. We both became delegate agencies of MATC. Certified teachers were to be stationed in our classrooms, and MATC would engage our participants on-site. Former migrants could take advantage of the varied job training programs, guaranteeing a smooth transition to MATC's vocational and certificate programs. Child care programs that had dominated the previous funding were to be used to provide family support so men and women could attend educational and training classes.

Following our years of organizing Obreros Unidos, we had a very concrete idea about the role of a community-based organization to build a sustainable community. Obreros Unidos was a membership organization that provided needed services: legal services, a gasoline co-op, a newspaper, recreational activities including softball games and dances, and more. This has been called social unionism. At the time, I had never heard the term or known that it was a model of organization. In fact, my sense of community organization was rooted in mutualistas. However, we continued to acknowledge Chávez and Huerta's foundation of farmworkers organization: that if workers want a union, they have to pay for it, and if they can't afford it, they have to work for it.

The PM&M on-site consultant, Jack Charles, was a talented and easygoing trainer. Charles was most helpful in rewriting the job descriptions for the restructured organization that would now be led by a program coordinator rather than an executive director. I would coordinate rather than direct area advisory boards, which would be empowered in guiding the new area centers, including hiring area coordinators. I reduced the level of pay for the whole administrative staff, including mine. These savings would be redirected to the newly designed area coordinators whom we now saw as being recommended for hiring by the area advisory board. Giving the area council the right to select its own coordinator was a plan to give them ownership of the emerging local, community-based organizations in Racine/Kenosha, Madison, and later Sheboygan, and to have them forge their own path. Further, in addition to asking OEO for authorization to expand services to central Wisconsin to have outreach service in the area with the greatest number of migrants, I structured monthly meetings with the new coordinators.

The new structure was most evident in the Racine/Kenosha area rather than the newly designated Madison region. The Racine/Kenosha area included the original incorporation by the local church groups and now operated day care centers. I wanted a link to the Racine Hispanic center to collaborate on expanding educational and vocational training programs. I reached out to the Chicano UAW members for support in the hiring of UMOS applicants to the area auto industry. The Malacara brothers, who both worked in the auto industry, introduced me to Jaime Castaneda, to be hired by El Centro to teach UMOS former migrant job applicants blueprint reading as part of the adult education effort. Castaneda was a Korean War veteran, and his wife, Helen, was hired as the first bilingual teacher by the Kenosha School District.

UMOS hired Irene Santos, widely supported by area volunteers, as the Kenosha area coordinator. Genevieve "Beba" Medina, also widely supported by the local community, was hired for the Milwaukee region. Here we broke with the Texas Borderland mutual aid societies, in which leadership roles were mostly filled by men, a practice that started to be challenged following the political revolt. By contrast, UMOS's area coordinators were dominated by women. Irene Santos had organized early voter registration and get-out-the-vote efforts during the political revolt before joining the seasonal migrant cycle and resettling in Wisconsin.

By default, we assumed ownership of UMOS corporate offices at the former four-story orphanage on Eighth Street and Greenfield Avenue in Milwaukee's near south side. The old building presented several hardships but ultimately allowed us to fulfill our mission. At one point the coal-fired boiler failed, and installing a new one with corresponding ductwork cost almost as much as the building's assessed value. OEO, although not on record as allowing its funding agencies to acquire and purchase property, acceded to us purchasing the building based on cost and expenses of the new heating system. The purchase of the building allowed us to make major renovations to expand educational services, including developing a certified child care program. This meant establishing a kitchen with a menu developed by a nutritionist, adequate space for child care activities to support families in educational and training programs, and a recreational area with a fenced playground. We recruited from Madison a most talented director, Patricia Probe, to provide the leadership that led to our certification.

One of UMOS's most innovative initiatives was carried out in the area of housing. While we vigorously demanded the enforcement of Wisconsin's migrant housing code in the labor camps and now as part of the resettlement of displaced seasonal workers, we undertook the challenging task of finding large households with low incomes adequate housing in Wisconsin's urban neighborhoods. We further took steps to assist former migrants who were gainfully employed to find housing in the outskirts of the Racine/Kenosha/Janesville industrial complex that included a mix of automotive and farm implement industries that employed tens of thousands of workers. All along this area was some of the finest soil blessed with abundant water that made it ideal for a variety of crops that were processed and canned. Wisconsin was a national leader in the canning of these products, which included corn, peas, and cabbage (for the making of sauerkraut). This area was ideal for a self-help housing program. Migrant extended families could continue to enjoy this rural link and have the potential to be employed by companies paying some of the highest industrial union wages in the state.

Following the decentralization plan of the top-down organization to one that was locally directed, we applied for and received a grant to initiate the Southeastern Wisconsin Housing Corporation. With the grant secured, we spun off the housing corporation and engaged the local community in selecting its director, Arturo Gonzales. Gonzales and his team organized small groups of former migrants to help each other build their individual homes. Their dedicated work was part of a sweat equity, a down payment on their new home. Key to this program was the training of selected families in working as a group through a process of multiple construction phases. Over the next couple of years, they built scores of homes.

—⊢⊢—

Chávez had been adamant in the need for organizers to be trained before directing informational grape boycott picket lines. Organizing the 1967 walkout of more than five hundred workers in three counties of central Wisconsin required that all the organizers and family heads be in tune with one another. The 1968 Libby's walkouts included a larger area led by a larger group of volunteers, including three additional full-time principal organizers, Palomo, Rodriguez, and Guzman, along with myself, organizing a labor action in three food-processing plants in three different cities. As part of UMOS, I oversaw not only the rewriting of the job descriptions, but also the organizing and training of area boards and staff. I didn't have to start anew. We had spent nearly a decade organizing area support for the early migrant education programs in the early 1960s and at the close of the decade organizing Obreros Unidos and our support for the California grape boycott. Organizers began to meet statewide for all-day training sessions in collaboration with our new network of community-based organizations. We finally collaborated with SDC's Concentrated Employment Program to establish a semiautonomous Latino-focused employment and training office at Fifth Street and National Avenue. Down the street, Father Maurice's voluntary resignation from Centro Hispano had resulted in all three community-based organizations coming under Latino direction. Most exciting was the emergence of the Latin American Union for Civil Rights (LAUCR), which incorporated a youth recreational component as well as the emergence of the Brown Berets, a local chapter of a national movement of activists.

The UMOS initiative became part of a larger Chicano/Latino movement for self-determination on Milwaukee's near south side. There was broad-based support for the old Walker's Point community to receive an equitable distribution of the citywide antipoverty programs administered by the SDC. We demanded the SDC's support for neighborhood initiatives and more effective delivery of services in the area. This became a major issue. We advocated for a separate board for the employment and training arm, the Concentrated Employment Program, and more autonomy for the Inner City Development Program (ICDP) neighborhood initiatives. The ICDP's near south side office was more culturally diverse than other programs, and they supported our efforts for Latino self-determination. We collaborated on a number of community development issues. This coalition made efforts to address the dangerous working conditions of the entry-level jobs that resettled migrants held in tanneries, foundries, and machine shops, which resulted in large numbers of unattended worker injuries. Ted Uribe's organizing of worker support networks, along with Ted Seaver's broad-based view of building sustainable communities, began to take hold.

Our attempts to reorganize the UMOS board went to the core of the issues: the participation of migrants and former migrants in the administration. When we demanded parity of services from the SDC Concentrated Employment Program funds for the poor on Milwaukee's south side, we insisted on independent south side advisory boards to direct those funds. We wanted to ensure that the low-income, ethnically diverse residents participated in the direction of the employment and training programs to go along with UMOS's and El Centro's model adult education and child care programs, such as Head Start. UMOS's board composition was key to the successful expansion of educational services beyond child care to include services for children and youth, employment, training and job development, assistance for seniors, and health and dental services. Whereas some developing community-based organizations began to include civic and philanthropic leaders from the community at large, UMOS maintained a board primarily made up of migrant, former migrant, and Latino public servants.

At UMOS, we foresaw providing employment development linked to local Wisconsin state employment services from our offices. We petitioned them to station their services and Wisconsin's employment services personnel in our community-based organizations so they would be more accessible to UMOS's and Centro Hispano's program students. After Father Maurice resigned from the Archdiocese-funded program and called for a Latino to follow him, Carlos Sevilla was hired as director of Centro Hispano, and former Obreros Unidos organizer Ezequiel "Chumina" Guzman was later chosen to fill the recently created credit union directorship. Further, Delfina Guzman (no relation to Chumina) was chosen to direct the education and citizenship classes at El Centro. My brother Carlos was selected as director for the near south side office of the Concentrated Employment Program. Also important was the founding of LAUCR by Ernesto Chacon. The year before, Chacon had joined the grape boycott and had

Ernesto Chacon addresses young people at a police brutality protest as Luis "Tony" Baez awaits the bullhorn.

encouraged and supported, along with Roberto Hernandez, the publishing of Milwaukee's alternative, bilingual newspaper *La Guardia* by Avelardo "Lalo" Valdez.

Chacon's founding of LAUCR was a key moment in the early days of the Chicano/Latino civil rights movement. He was a key player in reshaping the UMOS board by supporting the addition of migrant and former migrant representatives. He would later become chair, following Luis Trevino, who had overseen the transition of my being hired and restructuring of the UMOS board. Chacon amplified the self-determination movement from a Chicano-based migrant farmworkers movement made up primarily of Texas Borderland activists to an urban barrio focus. It was a unity of all Latino youths in the near south side community, especially Mexicans and Puerto Ricans. Chacon and Hernandez also later supported Armando Orellana's struggle to create access for Latinos at UW–Milwaukee.

In addition to the strategies developed for what would later be called the "takeover" or "Latinization" and expansion of social service agencies, we used tactics that were adapted from Chávez's nonviolent, peaceful picket lines and marches. When we arrived in Milwaukee to organize the grape boycott, more than two hundred days of open housing marches had ended inconclusively. The marches continued, but the City of Milwaukee still refused to accede to Black Americans' demands for an open housing ordinance to desegregate its neighborhoods. Tensions continued between City Hall and the Black community. It wasn't until Dr. Martin Luther King Jr. was assassinated in April of 1968 that Milwaukee began to move to incorporate national fair housing guidelines.

Black and Latino residents joined efforts to continue dismantling segregation policies and employment discrimination in public and private sectors. The grape boycott pickets, access to UW–Milwaukee, and the welfare marches, as well as other Latino community initiatives adopted direct action tactics that were developed by Father James Groppi and the NAACP Youth Council's Freedom Marches.

17

DIRECT ACTION AND SELF-DETERMINATION

My collaborating with Wisconsin's Black leaders had begun before I moved to Milwaukee. I had stayed in Madison to conclude Professor Brandeis's Migrant Study supported by the recently funded Office of Economic Opportunity (OEO) grant to UW's Institute for Poverty in the fall of 1965. As a means of sustaining myself, I joined the Laborer's Union and was hired to work on the construction of Sherman Plaza in Madison. There I worked alongside Bill Smith, who was doing graduate work at UW–Madison. Bill lived near my Mifflin Street one-bedroom efficiency on Bassett, one block across West Washington Avenue. Bill introduced me to a vibrant UW–Madison campus engaged in support of the civil rights movement, ongoing in the Deep South, as well as protests against the Vietnam War. He was the one to introduce me to attorney Lloyd Barbee, who was elected to the Wisconsin State Assembly in 1965. Although elected to the assembly from Milwaukee's segregated north side, Barbee had roots in Madison and was helpful in getting support from Madison's Black community for Obreros Unidos and later for the grape boycott. He joined Obreros Unidos's publicized picket of Kroger Foods in Madison in 1967.

During the Milwaukee Public School System's desegregation lawsuit, Bill Smith and I were invited to the Barbees' Milwaukee residence, where nearly a dozen parents were organizing and providing testimony for the desegregation lawsuit against Milwaukee Public Schools. I had contacted Milwaukee Alderwoman Vel Phillips to obtain support for grape boycott

activities in Milwaukee. Phillips would help get other Black elected officials and community leaders to hold a press conference with Ernesto
Chacon supporting the grape boycott.

I had moved to Milwaukee after the two hundred consecutive days of
protest for an open housing ordinance. The Freedom Marches, as they
became known, began when the NAACP Youth Council marched across
Milwaukee's Sixteenth Street viaduct en route to Kosciuszko Park for a
rally and were met by thousands of white counterprotesters on August 28,
1967. On the second night of the protest more than ten thousand hostile
white counterprotesters shouted racial epithets and threw bottles, bricks,
and other objects at the protesters. In the midst of so much turmoil, we
were grateful for the support of Black leaders and learned from their
strategies.

Earlier in the year, on March 24, 1967, Father Maurice had agreed to
host a reception for César Chávez. After the 1967 summer field organizing,
we focused on organizing pickets in Madison as well as in cities in the Fox
River Valley. I would move to Centro Hispano's back room, where Obreros
Unidos had been granted offices to expand the grape boycott in early fall.
Several blocks down from El Centro's office on National Avenue was the
most imposing building in the old Walker Point neighborhood, the Allen
Bradley Company's five-story building that employed thousands of workers from the surrounding area. The NAACP Youth Council targeted the
company's discriminatory employment practices against Black workers. I
joined the Allen Bradley protests and later marched with the Youth Council
in support of Barbee's protest against discrimination by Marc's Big Boy
restaurant on Juneau Street. Although we had been marching, striking,
and setting up pickets throughout the state, I had never seen anything like
those political manifestations: young Black protesters, veterans of scores
of marches on behalf of open housing and other civil rights issues, marching proudly, loudly, unafraid of the menacing, heavily armed guards who
were there to keep them in their place.

As it is known, we had marched to Madison in the summer of 1966,
organized a strike at James Burns Farms that fall, and walked out of Libby's
the following summer. Later in 1968, we would set up an all-summer
picket in downtown Wautoma against a local grocer who had refused to
remove the grapes. In Madison, we began a sustained attempt to remove

grapes from state and local institutions and a long fight against Kroger. Throughout those years, following Chávez's nonviolent tenets, none of us had ever been arrested. In Milwaukee, we couldn't stay out of jail! Milwaukee expanded disorderly conduct statutes and implemented further restrictions of our First Amendment rights with the passage of a misconduct on public grounds statute. We could be arrested for simply exercising our rights before public officials in public buildings.

I had faced going to jail during my antiwar protest in 1964 and my resistance to being drafted in 1965. Because I thought that the Vietnam War was illegal and largely being fought by unfairly drafting nondeferred minority youth, I had considered going to jail as an option as I mulled how to oppose the draft and the war in Vietnam most effectively. On the picket line, alongside Groppi's Youth Council members, protesters went to jail in a flash.

Every time we assembled, Milwaukee's finest were out in full force. As we would find out many years later through freedom of information requests, Father Groppi was being monitored by the FBI and this information was being shared with the local police force. They knew his whereabouts and his activities at every moment. All serious agitators for justice knew that we were being monitored and followed. Our private conversations were heard and, worst of all, used to manipulate and alter our course of action through agent provocateurs.

This frequently led to a paranoia that not only altered the way we interacted with each other, but also tended to confine strategy sessions among a few. Some thought that direct action could be planned by a small group and that the masses would support the initiative in solidarity. My experience made me skeptical of this strategy. I could not forget the first strike at Almond in the fall of 1966 that led to more than two dozen workers not only losing their jobs but also being thrown out of company-owned housing. Workers wearing union buttons were fired. Others were forced to sign affidavits that they were not a member of Obreros Unidos. Being openly for the union was perilous. Participating in a labor action involved putting the whole family in harm's way. But all these actions were predicated on workers and their families being aware of the bosses' likely reaction to their standing up for their rights. Although some things were unanticipated, most of the migrant families who joined us in these actions knew the consequences of their actions. Planning actions in a way that did not allow participants to know all the consequences of adopting those actions was something I did not support.

Organizations that survived this period of turmoil did so primarily due to the support of those who were engaged openly in support of a stated cause. Very early on the farmworkers movement stayed away from support groups that advocated such strategies where only a few knew and planned the initiatives. We thought everything had to be done in the open. At the very first rally to protest migrant wages and working conditions, I publicly asked for volunteers to march the eighty miles from Wautoma to the state capital. Later on, when Obreros Unidos planned sit-ins at UW–Madison's Chancellor's Office, these actions were openly discussed and voted on, and individuals freely volunteered to commit civil disobedience and be arrested. This is the way we had always organized farmworkers in the field and how we would organize in the barrio and later on the university campus.

Now in Milwaukee, we ensured that individuals who decided to commit civil disobedience met with experienced organizers and were instructed on how to carry it out peacefully. Most important was not to provoke aggressive reactions from the riot police. We made sure that the press was on-site to record the arrests and that lawyers were available to seek the setting of bonds and release of the arrested. We also reviewed how to respond to police questioning during the arrest and booking process. Most of the time these events were witnessed by movement photographers, David Giffey in the early years of farmworker organizing, and later Chuck Miller, who photographed the events in 1968 when we split field operations and I moved to Milwaukee to coordinate the statewide grape boycott. Chuck moved to the solidarity house on Frederick Avenue in 1969 and recorded our political manifestation for the next three years.

One of the ways I avoided any potential snooping, whether by the FBI or anyone else, was not to have a personal phone. Long after the government had any reason to be concerned about our activities, I continued to avoid personal phones. We used office phones while at work and public phones for personal calls. This lasted for more than twenty years. I used a public phone in Salas Café during the organizing days, and I had no home phone during my activism in Milwaukee in the late 1960s and early 1970s.

While in graduate school in Madison in the seventies, I couldn't afford a phone, so I used the University of Wisconsin's Latino student organization phone. I did not have a home phone until the 1980s, when family life necessitated one. During this whole time, I never spoke on the phone about anything that might land me in jail.

At the time, in the Black/Chicano coalitions, I never got the sense that being subjected to arrests on whims of timid public officials in public buildings mattered much to Father Groppi. He didn't exhibit any concern. Over the years, we never planned subversive activities, by phone or in person, so there was never anything to hide. Father Groppi had joined the picket line at Kohl's Food Store on Capitol Drive in the fall of 1968, marched against Allen Bradley protesting their minority hiring practices in Milwaukee's near south side, and later held mass during Latino protests. Although Father Groppi and I were arrested at one point for the "takeover" of the Wisconsin State Capitol, we never planned to overthrow the government, damage public property, or hurt anyone during the sit-in at Wisconsin Assembly Room during the welfare protest. We were simply trying to exercise our rights.

No one in my circle ever spoke about the surveillance. We spoke with our lawyers about our arrests and charges resulting from revised state statutes designed to quell our expression. Eventually, our attorneys warned us that we might not be allowed to post bail in future arrests. In the early 1970s, federal judge James Doyle issued two important rulings on the rights of protesters. One, he disallowed the Wisconsin Legislature's arrest of Father Groppi, and two, he ruled that the expanded statutes of disorderly conduct and misconduct on public grounds were unconstitutional. These decisions would come too late for us. At the time, the picket line was a source of conflict and inevitable arrest.

One of Father Groppi's greatest contributions to the civil rights movement was his organizational ability. He executed the notion of direct action most effectively. In fact, he openly spoke about it, and he alerted irresponsive public institutions and public officials to its use. Those who participated in direct action knew that tensions would increase the longer demands were disregarded or not acted upon. Direct action also exposed the recalcitrant public institutions to our demands for equity. It was a question of power. They didn't want us to share in their decision-making: to hire minorities, to provide housing, to provide for a meaningful education, to enjoy the franchise.

When I arrived in Milwaukee in late summer of 1968, whole blocks of white-owned retail and commercial businesses were becoming vacant on the city's near south side. Open housing and a desegregated public school system were unbearable to the nonminority Walker Point residents, and they were leaving in droves, leaving block after empty block of retail space on Mitchell and Lincoln Avenues in the business area. Latino community development organizations and commercial and retail businesses later filled these empty storefronts.

Fear and violence had not deterred the primarily Black youth from dreams of inclusion in American political society. Most impressive was how fearlessly Milwaukee's inner-city youth advocated for their long-denied rights. Two hundred days of marching had changed almost nothing. Petty apartheid continued, and there was little evidence that Milwaukee was moving to comply with recently enacted civil rights laws.

While businesses in the downtown area were forced to serve us, they expected nonwhite customers to know their place and "behave." At Marc's Big Boy on Juneau Street, protesting the restaurant's mistreatment of Wisconsin state assemblyman Barbee, we formed a picket informing potential customers not to eat there as they discriminated against us. Later, I joined the NAACP Youth Council protesting job discrimination at the Allen Bradley plant in the near south side. The Youth Council's picket lines were the most well organized and lively I had ever participated in.

Without anyone giving orders, the marchers would assume particular responsibilities: establishing the perimeters of the march, designating who would carry the picket signs, deciding who would represent the group with the police or the press, what slogans to utter, and which songs would be sung and when. Wherever Father Groppi went, without an order being issued, a circle of Youth Council commandos would follow him. Most importantly were our public manifestations, which were also ringed by extensive security detail.

They marched against apartheid and petty discrimination with non-service at public places, such as restaurants and downtown businesses, tired of being shut out from public institutions, postsecondary schools, and vocational institutions. Police protection was for the citizenry who wanted to maintain Milwaukee as the most segregated community in the nation. When Father Groppi and advocates for open housing marched onto the south side from downtown Milwaukee crossing the Sixteenth Street viaduct, they were met by flying bottles, rocks, and a menacing, angry crowd of thousands of whites yelling racial epithets. But the protesters were not intimidated by the mobs or by the police. They were resolute in their mission to exercise their right, to join protest marches and challenge authorities that sustained apartheid and denied equal treatment under the law. The marches continued as lively and animated as ever. At the Marc's Big Boy, youngsters taunted the police by changing the lyrics of the then popular song "Whose Making Love" but maintaining the rhythm: "Whose making love to your old lady/While you're out taking care of me?" The songs were directed not in general but to specific police officers whom I suspected they knew from previous protests. Every time we circled in front of the restaurant, the singers would raise their voices as we approached a particular riot-equipped officer. These pickets, I found, were much different from the ones I had been carrying out.

The farmworkers' picket lines in front of grocery stores had been informational. We wanted to stop grocery stores from selling grapes but also to inform and appeal to consumers, mostly homemakers, as they approached the doors. We wanted them not only to stop buying grapes but to demand that the grocers stop handling them, to stop shopping there altogether if the store continued to carry the grapes. Following Father Groppi's direct action strategy, we began to escalate our demands, adjusting our protests to be more aggressive in our dealing with the entering and exiting customers. If the grocer still would not respond to our demands, we would enter the store with our picket signs and stand between the customer and the grapes. This was clearly problematic and perhaps illegal; we did it symbolically, as we would, after a moment, exit the store, before the police arrived. Thereafter, there would be a police presence at that store and customers would shy away from such a confrontational scene. On several occasions, after weeks on the picket line, we committed civil disobedience, creating a blockade inside the store in the produce section in front of the grapes. Here we would stay inside the store with picket signs between the customers and the grape displays. The protesters who volunteered to enter the store were trained before they went in. We went over all contingencies, even role-playing angry customers who wanted to buy grapes and who were intent on provoking a fight. Only those who were committed to nonviolence were selected.

The resulting pressing matter was dealing with arrests, bookings, and jail. We had to have legal services and cash for bail available. The best protection against Milwaukee's finest was the press. We wanted to document that our efforts were peaceful and nonviolent and that if there were arrests, that the detained be treated fairly. Reporters were there to document any infractions. If members of the press were absent, we had a photographer to document the peaceful manifestation. Further, our aim was informational and the more times that the issue of the grape boycott was reported, the better. Our reason for employing direct action strategies was the increased attention and pressure that came with it. Again, these scenes would scare off all but the most committed customers.

Not only did Father Groppi and these youngsters embolden me to continue our cause for the farmworkers, but they also led me to adopt their strategies of direct action. In other words, the grocer would face consequences for refusing to respond to our demands. We did not simply ask the recalcitrant store owners to remove their grapes, we threatened them with direct action for failure to act. We began by escalating our actions from an informational picket on the grape boycott to boycotting the business itself. We began to be more aggressive with our pickets, actually interfering with the coming and going of the customers. We would no longer wait for the customers to walk to the store. We would walk over to the parking lot to discourage them from coming in. Soon thereafter, security details would appear, to no avail. Finally, local police would be called. Confrontation and arrests would follow. Most shoppers had no taste for shopping in locations where these conflicts were being played out.

Direct action allowed us to be proactive, to be in control of the tempo of the negotiations rather than simply waiting for the grocer to respond in support of the California farmworkers grape boycott. Arrest was a last resort. Initially, most of us had never been arrested. Again, we did not want the arrest to be handled haphazardly. We chose the day and the time. We found that getting arrested on Fridays or at the end of the week was a bad idea. There are no judges around on weekends, which meant that rather than an overnight stay, one would be looking at a weekend stay in jail. We never went to jail without having an attorney and bail money available either. Unplanned mass arrests were most unpredictable as some of those detained might have had run-ins with the law or had outstanding warrants. This would complicate matters and delay protesters being released. We needed to review the backgrounds of the individuals facing arrest to avoid lengthy incarcerations. Mass arrests also meant raising large amounts of cash for bail money in a short period of time.

—ıı—

For the great majority of us, even those of us who had been involved in labor actions where picketing was common, committing civil disobedience was not a spur-of-the-moment decision. Father Groppi had been involved in the early civil rights protests having joined other priests and religious leaders in support of the Deep South's protest against apartheid before Milwaukee's 1967–68 Two Hundred Days of Freedom. Father Groppi had been arrested a number of times, but in spite of his reputation as an agitator, he always avoided conflict. In fact, direct action did not mean a promotion of violence. He was foremost a priest, a man who preached love, peace, and justice. Both of us were most intent on preventing violence.

If someone didn't know a thing about Father Groppi's political activities, they might be hard pressed to ascribe to him the firebrand status for which he would later be known. I recall his support for the grape boycott and his stopping by one afternoon in the parking lot at Kohl's Food Store on Capitol Drive in the fall of 1968. He approached the picket line with his customary huge smile. It was an infectious smile that compelled people of goodwill to respond in kind. I walked toward him, we embraced, and he began to joyfully greet the other protesters before settling in to talk. I sat by the fender of a car, covered by a blanket, as we had slept there overnight, and the vehicle's fender was cold and damp. He stood by talking, gesturing, laughing, and lifting all our spirits.

In happier times, he and Father John Maurice officiated the wedding of my younger brother Francisco to Barbara David. Barbara had been an early participant in the open housing marches the year before with the NAACP Youth Council. It was a wonderful evening, joining Obreros Unidos organizers with Groppi's Youth Council commandos, all enjoying ourselves instead of facing menacing riot police. Since the wedding was in Milwaukee, our father and mother drove from Wautoma and spent a most enjoyable evening with the two priests and the young activists. Father Groppi had a great sense of humor and easily expressed his joy with a huge smile and laugh. It was not a "drop your jaw, throw your head back" kind of laugh. It wasn't loud; it was visceral. He expressed himself wholly. This, combined with the spiritual sense of his priesthood, made him one of the most extraordinary individuals I have ever met. Besides Chávez, he certainly was the one who influenced me the most in terms of organizational strategy and tactics.

18

ACCESS TO HIGHER EDUCATION

I enrolled at UW–Milwaukee in the fall of 1968. The main reason the Salas family had relocated to Wisconsin a decade earlier was for educational opportunities. Our parents thought that if we had access to an education, we could do something other than migrant seasonal farmwork. My focus on organizing farmworkers had interrupted my postsecondary studies that began in 1961 when I graduated from high school, not ended them as my parents feared. I enrolled at UW–Stevens Point during the organizing of the potato strike in the fall of 1966, and I took a UW–Extension correspondence course before my enrollment at UW–Milwaukee.

Although I had performed adequately my first two semesters at Oshkosh State, my poor academic training during the ten years of migrating had taken its toll. My dedication to the migrant cause and later my opposition to the draft and the Vietnam War seemed at the time more important than attending college. My last semester at Oshkosh State University, while in Texas during the political revolt, I did not officially drop out of college and earned failing grades in all my courses. Thereafter, because of my poor academic record, my application to Stevens Point and later to UW–Milwaukee was resolved in appeals to the respective chancellors' offices. At Stevens Point, Chancellor Lee Dreyfus recommended I be admitted, and at UW–Milwaukee, Assistant Chancellor Ernest Spaights advanced my application to the School of Education. I received my bachelor's degree from UW–Milwaukee's School of Education in 1971.

Throughout this decade my brother Manuel and I had been the only Chicanos at Oshkosh State and at UW–Stevens Point; I don't recall another

Latino enrolled. At UW–Milwaukee in the 1968–69 school year, out of a
student population of more than twenty-five thousand students, all the
Latinos could sit around one table at the recently built Memorial Union. At
the time, among the few of us who were enrolled, all had links to emerging
Latino educational and training programs. Several barriers stood in the way
of increasing Latino enrollment: the lack of Spanish-speaking instructors,
limited support for or outreach to Latino students, and unreliable transportation from the neighborhoods where these potential students lived.

The UMOS reorganization in the spring of 1969 and our collaboration
with El Centro Hispano's Adult Basic Education/English as a Second Language (ABE/ESL) programs allowed us to provide migrant participants
with seamless transition to Milwaukee Area Technical College's vocational
and technical programs. As MATC's delegate agencies, we expanded our
sole funding base. UMOS collaborated with El Centro's survival ESL curriculum and adopted it to serve relocated Mexican American migrants
through bilingual, Spanish-language instruction. MATC administration,
encouraged by our collaboration, designated us as delegate agencies. This
outreach effort included on-site MATC faculty assisting us in developing
curriculum and instruction plans to meet the needs of our participants.
Further, Latino community efforts were successful in persuading the Social
Development Commission (SDC) to establish a Concentrated Employment
Program office with a corresponding advisory committee and an employment and training office on the near south side, giving south side residents
access to the State of Wisconsin's Employment Services job openings.

The primary focus was to make these services available to barrio residents, complementing UMOS's and El Centro's MATC vocational training
and job development initiatives. This was especially important in hyper-
segregated Milwaukee, where minorities were kept in their respective
ghettos and barrios, thus denying and limiting social and employment
services by zip code. This was also the reasoning behind the growing Latino
demand for improved access to education at UW–Milwaukee. It had to be
an outreach model with services and classes in the neighborhood.

Among the Latino students enrolled at UW–Milwaukee were Lorenzo
Tovar and Graciela de la Cruz, both involved in community agencies.
Graciela was teaching part-time at El Centro's ABE program and was
intimately aware of adult learners' educational needs. Additionally,

Rosé Guajardo, a bilingual teacher, like Graciela, was enrolled in UW–Milwaukee's Master of Education program. Her sister had been hired to teach at UMOS. Alejandro Nieri had been selected to direct UMOS's Educational Department and was urging the whole instructional staff to enroll for postsecondary educational training at UW–Milwaukee.

From this group of students with connections to community-based education programs emerged the need for an organization that was broader than those of the three main organizations, El Centro Hispano, the Concentrated Employment Program, and UMOS. They felt that an "organization of organizations" vehicle was needed and identified themselves as the Council for the Education of Latin Americans (CELA), a name that speaks volumes. This was important since the Obreros Unidos former organizers were all Chicano as were most of the migrant seasonal workforce. The UMOS takeover had been undertaken by Chicanos. Just as in the founding of the Latin American Union for Civil Rights by Ernesto Chacon, the founding of CELA attempted to overcome the Latino movement's tendency to be exclusively Chicano.

CELA selected Armando Orellana as its chair. Armando had earlier worked for Wisconsin's Migrant Ministry, and his wife, Patricia, was an executive secretary at UMOS. Both were migrant advocates in support of CELA. CELA representatives included Reverend Jaime Davila, pastor of the Evangelical Baptist Church. CELA was unique in that it brought together the Milwaukee Archdiocese-funded El Centro Hispano with the outreach activities of the Christian Center, which supported youth programs and the need for recreational programs and activities at the newly created community center The Spot. Roberto Hernandez was selected to the CELA board, and Marquette University professor Ricardo Fernandez was also present at one of the most crucial meetings. Ramon Caban, director of the newly created Spanish Center Credit Union, and Wilda Rosario, a bilingual teacher, joined them. None of the heads of the three main Latino organizations or LAUCR sought a leadership role in CELA. Chacon's and my contribution would emerge at mass community meetings where CELA representatives updated us on our demands and we directed the picket line in front of UW–Milwaukee's Chancellor's Office at Chapman Hall.

Beginning in 1969, CELA began pushing for university administrators to create a Spanish Speaking Outreach Institute (SSOI) to provide services

A candlelight vigil in support of fasting protesters at Chapman Hall in the fall of 1969 was attended by myself, Roberto Hernandez, Ernesto Chacon, Maria Ortega, Josefina Castro, Reverend Jaime Davila and his parishioners, Raul Flores, and others.

to Latino students, making a college education more accessible to them. CELA further demanded involvement in directing the proposed SSOI, insisting on an advisory board comprising Latino community members. This kind of self-determination was embedded in Obreros Unidos's mutualista model of organizing communities and had been effective in the reorganization of UMOS. What's more, we demanded a say in the selection of the director of the SSOI. This demand was rejected outright and delayed the establishment of the program. Part of the issue was the process of how faculty were selected and given administrative responsibilities in the respective university colleges and departments.

After presenting our demands to the Chancellor's Office and being utterly disregarded, tensions escalated. Each attempt to meet with the chancellor, J. Martin Klotsche, and his further nonresponse was followed by a more intense response on our part.

Community participation had been at the fore of the Latino drive for self-determination with the UMOS takeover, in which community participation was encouraged. We had effectively used this concept in redirecting the educational and service agencies under Latino leadership, and we would settle for no less at UW–Milwaukee. Most important was the need for enhancing the educational aspirations of the recently hired young Latinos in the emerging community-based organizations. The combined staff of the three agencies now numbered more than 150. We saw an immediate need for postsecondary training of the emerging Latino community activists who were now responsible for administering these community-based organizations. Many of the administrative jobs required postsecondary training, and many top jobs required a bachelor's degree. Moreover, the drive to Latino self-determination could not succeed without university training and its academic degrees. We encouraged Latinos to enroll at UW–Milwaukee and continued pressuring the university to try to serve their needs better through protests. Father Maurice and Father Groppi came together to conduct an evening mass during the UW–Milwaukee protests.

The efforts of CELA and others proved successful with the establishment of the SSOI, now the Roberto Hernandez Center, the following year. The multisemester campaign was an example of using direct action to achieve our aims. The establishment of the SSOI was not a direct route, from meetings, to protest, to sit-ins, and finally to the realization of the SSOI/RHC.

On the way to the establishment of the SSOI, CELA organized two major protests. The first one, in the spring of 1970, was called off when we found ourselves in over our heads. Although LAUCR and Obreros Unidos organizers and supporters were committed to a protracted struggle with the university, we had little experience in dealing with the complex hierarchy of a large university. I was aware of the distinction of the authority within the colleges and divisions by then, as I had attended both Oshkosh State and Stevens Point College, but I didn't know how they effectively interacted with each other, especially in relation to the Chancellor's Office at UW–Milwaukee.

Further, we miscalculated the initial response from the students. We were uninformed about the lack of an organized UW–Milwaukee student body. My first experience in the antiwar movement of the mid-1960s in Madison emerged from an engaged student body supported by a most progressive and active Madison community involved in the major issues of the day: the civil rights movement in the South and the Vietnam War.

The draft resistance and the civil rights movement had been brought to our attention through television images of savage responses to Black citizens demanding the franchise. The UW–Madison campus was abuzz with activity. There were faculty-led, campus-wide symposia and "teach-ins." Organizers who had participated in the dismantling of apartheid in the Deep South would return and make presentations. We would have follow-up meetings, make reports, and issue press releases after these symposia. Even during UW–Madison's recess and summer vacation, the campus and its surrounding bars and cafés became our daily destination. By contrast, the UW–Milwaukee campus became deserted by late afternoon, and there was a virtual lack of students between the end of the spring semester and the start of the summer semester. We had made some efforts to contact some of the student leaders of an antiwar protest earlier in the spring, but summer came and we temporarily lost track of them.

UW–Milwaukee at the time had not built the extensive residential halls that it has today. It was principally a "suitcase college," with students who commuted. There was very little happening on campus in the late afternoon and evenings, unlike at UW–Madison. UW–Milwaukee students had few expectations of a campus life other than attending daytime classes. This meant that the Latino protests on the UW–Milwaukee grounds in the late afternoon or evening were uniquely our own. We designed our efforts to not simply create a protest on the east side of town where UW–Milwaukee was located; our attempt was to create our own *ambiente*.

We not only picketed Chapman Hall, where UW–Milwaukee's Chancellor's Office was located, but also spread out to faculty and staff offices and classrooms to organize support. We organized Latino community activities and events on campus as well. These events were intended to establish our community's presence on campus; they were for us. We wanted to engage our community on the role of education on UW–Milwaukee grounds. We carried our outreach efforts to the faculty and staff; we reminded them of their mission, the Wisconsin Idea. This idea was set in stone on the UW–Madison campus, but the university's boundary was the whole state. We wanted to remind the UW system that its mission included outreach efforts to our segregated community across town. This was especially true in Milwaukee. For Latinos, the near east side of Milwaukee where UW–Milwaukee was located might as well have been on another planet. Most

Latinos on the near south side had no interaction with that part of the city, let alone the UW–Milwaukee campus. Earlier one of the challenges El Centro and UMOS faced in engaging Latinos with MATC was leaving their enclave to cross the Sixth Street Viaduct west of Milwaukee's downtown area where MATC was located. We had demanded expanded activity by MATC in our barrio because Latinos on the south side did not generally cross the Sixth Street Viaduct to take advantage of the educational and vocational programs or shop downtown, only several blocks down the street.

We were keenly aware of our friend attorney Lloyd Barbee's desegregation lawsuit, and we were also demanding not only the bilingual (Spanish/English) language education that we had developed and were using in our neighborhood community-based organization, but also a curriculum and instruction that reflected our lived reality. This included principally Mexican/Chicano and Puerto Rican history, in particular those events that were significant for us. There were walkouts in local schools when school administrators refused to respond to our demands, including those that required little resources, such as the recognition of el Cinco de Mayo and el 16 de Septiembre. Here, LAUCR, with the support of religious and lay groups, was most important in developing youth after-school activities, which we wanted Milwaukee Public Schools to support and expand.

Public protests need an audience, but there was no engaged UW–Milwaukee student body to appeal to. Most students weren't on campus for anything other than their classes. We had engaged a number of progressive faculty members and enjoyed the support of the education dean, but members of the so-called liberal community that lived in Milwaukee's near east side was preoccupied with their own issues and did not initially join us, so we had to organize their support. Eventually they responded most effectively.

—⊣⊢—

MATC was several blocks from downtown Milwaukee, where we along with the Black community were not welcome; UW–Milwaukee was even farther away on the northeast side of town, north of the downtown area. It was lily white. The university campus was in a neighborhood that was unknown to the Latino community. Outreach academic programs and support services located in the barrio were at the core of how we dealt with this issue. This is also why we wanted to be part of an advisory committee to collaborate with the newly selected director of the proposed SSOI. The UW–Milwaukee chancellor did not see a university role in the segregated neighborhoods and was not receptive to the idea of having a structured relationship with the Latino community such as a standing advisory committee.

The negotiations reached an impasse not only regarding our participation in the selection of the director of the SSOI, but also in regard to our disagreement over setting up an advisory council of Latino community leaders and campus faculty and staff to guide the establishment and direction of the program. Additionally, although UW–Milwaukee administrators generally supported the need to recruit more Latinos, they were not supportive of the proposed outreach activities that included staff presence and academic classes offered in the barrio. A number of community-based organizations, principally UMOS and El Centro Hispano, had pledged to provide classrooms and offices for UW–Milwaukee personnel to meet and enroll students to minimize costs. Nevertheless, the administration remained opposed to CELA having a say in the selection of the SSOI director and to the proposed advisory committee.

Key to sustaining the UW–Milwaukee protests was the agreement among the Latino community-based organizations to come together in an umbrella organization dedicated specifically to higher education advocacy. The emergence of CELA would eventually go beyond UW–Milwaukee access and involve Milwaukee Public School System desegregation efforts with the Milwaukee United School Integration Committee (MUSIC) and the establishment of a bilingual program as well as the Bilingual Education Act of 1968. The community meetings that had begun to come together during the reorganization of the UMOS board had expanded a south side Latino employment and training office, which now offered services at Fifth Street and National Avenue. The orderly resignation of Father Maurice at El Centro and the selection of Carlos Sevilla provided additional Latino support for the UW–Milwaukee access efforts.

Chacon's efforts in organizing LAUCR, which had launched youth walkouts at Milwaukee Public Schools on Mexican fiesta patria days, now collaborated in support of CELA. Chacon encouraged the Brown Berets to provide security, initially on the picket line, later at late-night vigils, and most important, while camping out in the open during the later stages of the protest. In the Latino community, CELA's large meetings now alternated between the UMOS and Concentrated Employment Program offices; both had large halls for the mass community meetings. Additionally, Chacon had established an office across the street from the Concentrated Employment Program at the Bernie Building (formerly Schlitz's Beer Tavern & Hall) and El Centro, which was only one block west on National Avenue.

There was unanimous support for the continued protest in front of the Chancellor's Office. People were furious that the chancellor continued to ignore our demands. CELA meeting reports on our written correspondence to the chancellor about our demands grew, with scores of families attending. The largest crowd attended when we began to discuss and plan for civil disobedience, a sit-in that might lead to arrest and jail.

During the day, when the campus was operational, we continued the picket in front of the Chancellor's Office, but we also marched and protested at academic support and administrative offices, speaking only in Spanish to demonstrate that they had no Latino or bilingual personnel to deal with our community needs. The protest of UW–Milwaukee was against the university as an institution, not against the employees, not the staff in registration, financial aid, or academic support services. In fact, we outwardly wanted to gain their support. Our goal was for a mass protest that would shut down the system, that would overwhelm and interfere with their services, but we would do so in an orderly, respectful manner. It worked!

On August 28, 1970, the Chancellor's Office received a letter of support for CELA's demands signed by two dozen of UW–Milwaukee's staff in registration, financial aid, and academic support services. Several days later a number of these individual walked off the job and joined the CELA protest. Unfortunately, two of the student workers were fired for their action. They protested their firings, and evidence was brought forth that these two students had also been involved in the spring antiwar demonstrations.

The daytime protests were led by volunteers, many of whom were staff, participants, and supporters of the three agencies that we had taken over and which now had Latino directors and advisory boards: UMOS, El Centro Hispano, and the Concentrated Employment Program. All three agencies bused participants and agency supporters to university grounds for the protests. In late afternoon and early evening, when people got out of work, our participation would grow, and we would hold events such as a mass just for the participants. We received support from the Catholic priests noted, in addition to Reverend Davila and lay members of the Christian Center. We also reached out to Latinos from the near south side and those who lived closer, in Riverwest. Non-Latino students seldom joined us. Most non-Latino supporters were activists whom we had collaborated with before, such as open housing veterans, antiwar movement activists, and grape boycott supporters.

We conducted large community meetings on the near south side to plan a strategy of direct action to be carried out in front of the Chancellor's Office. The events held at UW–Milwaukee brought hundreds to the site of the protests. Each of the actions taken in front of Chapman Hall represented what we stood for. During the UMOS board of directors migrant worker takeover, Father John Maurice openly supported migrant and former migrant participation and later my becoming its head. During the multiyear UW–Milwaukee protest, Reverend Davila and fellow parishioners Manuel Martinez and his wife were ever present. The denial of access of Latinos to the University of Wisconsin–Milwaukee was a moral issue. We asked both Fathers Maurice and Groppi to hold mass in front of Chapman Hall. In addition, we held a rally in front of the Chancellor's Office and then carried out a peaceful, candlelit march to the chancellor's residence on North Lake Drive. During the fair housing marches several years earlier, protest in the form of pickets of private residences of public officials had provoked lawsuits and restraining orders, but the chancellor's residence was not a private residence. The property belonged to the university. There was a question as to whether we would be permitted to march as we did north of the city of Milwaukee, toward the suburb of Shorewood, to get to his residence. Milwaukee's Lake Drive, where the chancellor's residence was located, was the "gold coast," lined by imposing mansions. We got away with it that night without being arrested, but we didn't try it again.

One of the main challenges we faced was the complexity of a research university with its administration, colleges, divisions, departments, and corresponding projects and programs; not to mention its academic and student services, which included registration, financial aid, food services, and more. Initially, we didn't understand the day-to-day operation of the colleges and departments, which were almost autonomous from the central administration that we had found in the private sector. Thus, CELA moved to contact and negotiate with these other spokes of the wheel. We did not want to depend on the Chancellor's Office to represent us with the School of Education. We went directly to the dean and faculty members for their support and to begin to discuss links with Latino community-based organizations.

The personnel at the School of Education weren't as helpful as we first thought they would be, but they were eager to learn. UW instructors, at the time, had little experience in offering adult basic education programs. University instructors knew less about how to teach adults whose dominant language was not English but Spanish. El Centro Hispano and UMOS had been challenged with these profound issues and, with few resources, had developed concrete ideas about how we could access UW–Milwaukee and the type of programs that were necessary for our community. UW–Milwaukee Department of Education Dean Richard Davis was extremely interested in the bilingual adult literacy and job development programs from El Centro, the Concentrated Employment Program, and UMOS. Davis and key staff members were excited about what was going on in the classroom at El Centro Hispano and at UMOS with a curriculum that was based on survival skills such as learning how to catch a bus, fill out an application, interview for a job, or enroll children at local schools. Helene Aqua, director of adult education, had successfully implemented this curriculum and instruction model in ESL classes at El Centro. El Centro also had a part-time instructor in Graciela de la Cruz, who was an ardent supporter of the SSOI and one of the few Latina women then enrolled at UW–Milwaukee. What the UW–Milwaukee complex had was a small number of outstanding faculty members who were committed to supporting Latino programs. El Centro Hispano and UMOS staff made presentations in School of Education courses. Sociology professor G. Kostas wrote on our community needs and aspirations, and some of us took courses from James Cockcroft, a Latin American Studies professor whose appointment would not be renewed, some of us thought because of his political views.

Throughout this process, CELA had the responsibility to present our demands to the university and negotiate on behalf of the Latino community. This was meant to diminish the influence of the leaders of the three main organizations, including myself, and to recognize other emerging groups such as LAUCR and others that advocated initiatives that were not being addressed by the three main Latino agencies. It included personnel from other neighborhood organizations, such as the SDC-funded Inner City Development Program's south side office staff, including Margie Meyer, Mary Ann McNulty, and the emerging workers' injury program led by Ted Uribe. Most important was the support of Latino businesses on the near south side that Dante Navarro was most helpful in organizing. This wide net of support proved crucial as we worked toward an agreement on the SSOI.

19

POLITICS AND PROTEST

Dante Navarro was a foundry worker who was known throughout the Latino community for having a Saturday morning radio program that played primarily Mexican music. Dante would buy the hour-long radio slot and sell advertisement spots to Mexican restaurants, bars, and storefronts on the near south side. He was one of the most extraordinary characters in our community, a joy to be with and great company. He was a foundry worker, but I doubt if any but his coworkers ever saw him in work clothes. He would shower after work and most of the time he would don a suit or sports coat and a tie. Convincing local businesses that "advertising pays," he promoted them on his Saturday morning radio show. He also urged all of us to shop at these Mexican establishments. Because he charged them a nominal fee to pay for the airtime, he was constantly visiting these businesses to discuss the latest promotions and collect the fees. To join Dante making stops at local Latino small businesses was to get a tour of Mexican retail, eating, and drinking establishments at every stop. With his connections, Dante was key in getting Latino businesses to support and join in community political manifestations and protests. He became the first Latino to run for Wisconsin State Assembly with broad support from this sector of the community.

There were two major criticisms of Dante's candidacy. One was his background. He lacked a formal US education. He had started his schooling in Mexico and had a wonderful command of the Spanish language. As a disc jockey, his narrative was well informed and enjoyably delivered, but he did not have a US high school diploma. He valued the need for education and training, and in fact, his later work included job development and related training as an UMOS employee. In spite of his lack of formal education, he had been quite successful and was one of the most ardent supporters of a broad community coalition that included the business community, comprising community leaders from his generation, in the formation of the Council for the Education of Latin Americans (CELA) to negotiate the establishment of the Spanish Speaking Outreach Institute (SSOI) at UW–Milwaukee. Later Dante joined the demand for equal employment opportunities by Milwaukee industry that the NAACP Youth Council had initiated against Allen Bradley in August 1968 and now was focusing on local breweries to hire Latinos. When the Congress of Racial Equality (CORE) began challenging Budweiser, local chapters stopped drinking Milwaukee beers until the brewing industry began hiring minorities. Dante organized a political action group that was supported by chapters of the emerging League of United Latin American Citizens (LULAC) to initiate a national campaign to pressure the breweries to hire Latinos.

The other criticism of Dante was directed at us, the core Obreros Unidos organizers and volunteers who were moving to Milwaukee following my

Dante Navarro, the first Latino candidate for the Wisconsin State Assembly, attends a campaign fundraiser in 1970. Seated at the head table are (from left) myself, Navarro's campaign manager Ezequiel Guzman, Navarro, and Salvador Sanchez of UMOS.

being assigned to coordinate the Wisconsin grape boycott in the fall of 1968. Many of the farmworkers were from our hometown of Crystal City and the four Texas counties known as the Winter Garden region. Local Latino activists reacted to the Crystal City "clique" in leadership positions in the south side community-based organizations. But the reality was that the surge in former migrant families relocating to Wisconsin included a large number of former Crystal City residents and many Texas Borderland former migrant seasonal workers. Most were Chicano and Norteños (Northerners) from Mexico Borderland states.

For our generation, which followed our parents' incitement of the political revolt in our hometown, to be active politically—that is, to participate effectively in the political process—was at the core of our being.

We encouraged Dante to run for office, and he filed for the State Assembly. Some thought he was "too Mexican." He was actively involved in Mexican fiesta patria celebrations and resisted efforts to call these "Hispanic" or "Latino" celebrations, which were the names being applied to us. We were criticized for not broadening his appeal beyond the Mexican community.

The Navarro campaign established an office in the middle of the barrio, down the street from the CEP and LAUCR offices and across the street from El Centro, off Sixth Street and National Avenue. Chumina Guzman was selected as campaign manager. Chumina had earlier been a member of Obreros Unidos during the 1968 organizing campaign and along with other organizers from Crystal City was an experienced political operative. We sought out Lupe Ledesma, a World War II veteran, also from Crystal City, who had exposed how the Texas veterans land assistance program was a sham and was defrauding Crystal City's Mexican American veterans. We asked Lupe if he would allow his daughters, Leticia and Maria, to volunteer to staff Dante's campaign office. Ledesma was one of our early heroes. He was a combat veteran who challenged the local political operators who were defrauding veterans from the land allotments they had been issued by the Texas legislature for serving honorably during World War II. As a result, he was deprived of his livelihood and forced to join the migrant stream and was now a relocated migrant in Milwaukee like the rest of us. Not only did Leticia and Maria volunteer, but they also got their cousins and neighbors, Barbara Medina, Irasema

Flores, and Sandra Rodriguez, to help. Barbara was the daughter of Genevieve Medina, tireless director of Milwaukee's UMOS local resettlement
and retraining center. Irasema was her niece. Mrs. Medina from the Crystal City Flores family had lived one block from my father's café. Sandra's
father and uncle had worked with my father in opening a gas and service
station in the late 1940s before joining the migrant stream and relocating
to the south side of Milwaukee. My youngest brother, Luis, had recently
moved into town, and he and Lois Alpert initiated outreach efforts to the
district's majority non-Latino voters.

Dante's run for the assembly seat was in the Democratic primary held
late in the summer of 1970. It coincided with our renewed efforts against
UW–Milwaukee. We had suspended our picketing early in the summer
when spring semester ended and only a few summer classes and programs
were operating. The university had no campus life between semesters,
so we held community meetings during the summer, but only to plan
for the fall events. Guided by our commitment to direct action, sit-ins, civil
disobedience, and jail were the discussion of the day.

—II—

One thing we had learned from Chávez and Huerta was that building a
sustainable community meant making a commitment for the duration.
It was open-ended. The first California farmworker's union contract took
five years of boycotting with almost continuous picketing. I recall meeting
with Chávez after the third year of the boycott, in 1968, when he informed
me that "we have some difficult days ahead." I was aghast! I didn't see how
it could get any tougher.

Although we found support for the California grape boycott on the
heels of Obreros Unidos organizing activities, the march to Madison in the
summer of 1966, the potato-processing strike that fall, and the successful
organizing of the Libby's strike and certification election that we won in
the summer of 1967, organizing the grape boycott was a bigger process.
First of all, it was greatly helped by the extensive union support that we
had earlier organized. Second, campuses were key to providing us with
support in the picket lines, especially at UW–Madison. But it was the information about the farmworkers' conditions and the issues we elaborated
that appealed to consumers at the picket line, mostly homemakers, and

their buying decisions changed the retailer's mind about carrying grapes or not. The same would hold true in challenging UW–Milwaukee to open its doors to the Latino community. Direct action would expose the closed postsecondary system. We needed to get the word out to the Latino community that CELA had a plan to address this void.

—ıı—

Adopting direct action tactics in the protests that led to the establishment of the SSOI at UW–Milwaukee meant that we would not simply be picketing in front of the Chancellor's Office. The longer he ignored us, the more militant our actions would become. His lack of response led us to burn him in effigy in front of his office and later to take over his offices, to conduct a sit-in, and commit civil disobedience. But agreeing to establish the SSOI came about after two actions, both of them sit-ins, unlawful occupation of Chapman Hall, the location of UW–Milwaukee's Chancellor's Office.

Those who volunteered to be arrested at the community meeting beforehand initially did not include Dante Navarro. A number of us who planned the civil disobedience spoke against Dante volunteering to be arrested. We all felt that it would imperil his chances of winning the assembly primary later that summer. As the first Latino to run for local office, Dante's candidacy was the first chance the Latino community had to exercise our right to vote to select our own local representatives. We knew we did not have the votes to challenge for a seat in the Milwaukee County supervisor election the way the map was drawn, and that the high voter turnout in the Milwaukee alderman election held in the spring made winning prohibitive. But the Democratic assembly primary election had the lowest voter turnout of all. It gave us the best chance to win. We didn't have anything to lose. We wanted to begin the process of voter education, registration, and voting among the Latino community, and it all began by participating.

It didn't appear that we could win without some non-Latino votes, but Dante Navarro was a unique Latino assembly candidate. He was Mexican and had originally arrived undocumented. Although he had stable employment, he was known mostly as a radio personality. He organized and provided the first and for some time the only hour-long Spanish music show on Saturday mornings. He knew all of the Mexican small businesses, as he promoted them and they paid for time on his radio show. We didn't want him arrested. His volunteering to commit civil disobedience would be seen as courageous in the Latino community, but it would cost us votes among the general voters. How many, we didn't know, but we were sure that we might not be able to put a positive spin on his arrest, that it would cost us votes, perhaps the election.

—⊩—

At the community meeting to discuss the sit-in at the Chancellor's Office, two major issues were contentious: one, who would be arrested (not Dante), and two, whether women would be "allowed" to be arrested. Neither discussion should have taken place. Dante should have never have considered being arrested, and women should not have been excluded from being arrested. The latter idea was quite ridiculous. The role of women in the movement was an issue at many of our community meetings because women were also challenging their role not only in general society, but also in our community, our families, and in the movement's leadership. Some of them saw us as chauvinist "machos," as perpetuating their mistreatment and inequality. For example, because it was not customary for women to drink at bars and we daily frequented certain watering holes after work or political demonstration, they felt left out. They knew that political issues and strategies would be discussed at these all-male social events, and they were not part of it. Consequently, they challenged the decisions that came out of these settings.

Their frustration culminated in their disruption at a community organizing and strategy meeting held in a UW–Milwaukee meeting room to discuss the future of the SSOI and other burning Latino community issues in January 1971. Women, without the majority of the male Latino/Chicano leaders suspecting, took over the stage and read a statement publicly challenging their status in the movement. Marla Anderson was later arrested at the Chancellor's Office, and her arrest needs to be seen within this context. Her arrest at the Chancellor's Office was not planned. Although Marla had argued at the pre–civil disobedience strategy meeting that women be included in the group to commit civil disobedience and be arrested, she was not among the group that had been selected for the occupation of the Chancellor's Office and risk being arrested, nor was any other woman.

The day of the sit-in arrived, and when the police entered the Chancellor's Office to remove the Latino community members who were waiting to meet the chancellor, all the community members except those who had pledged to be arrested left the room. As the arrest process began, officers dutifully informed us that we would be arrested unless we exited the premises, as the offices were closing. At that point, one of the protesters jumped out the first-floor window and another rushed out the door. Dante and Marla stayed in the room, contrary to the plan, and proceeded to get arrested. I was really concerned about Marla. She was the only woman arrested. If we had moved to include women being arrested at the sit-in, we would have selected a pair so they could go through the booking process and be jailed together. I felt that I should have spoken more forcefully on their behalf at the previous meeting. In the fields where we were organizing, women and children made up the majority of the workforce. Obreros Unidos was not solely about farmworkers' wages and working conditions; it was the emergence of a women and youth movement. Seeing Marla arrested, I felt bad that I had no notion where women were detained after arrests. I knew that juveniles were not housed with adults and could not be released to anyone but a parent, another reason why we didn't want underage youth to be arrested. Now Marla, alone, the only Latina woman of the five of us who were arrested, was taken downtown, and we didn't know where.

I made sure that Dante and I were placed in the same paddy wagon. I had hoped the two other men arrested would also stay together, but we lost track of each other when we arrived at the police station. I told the officers, untruthfully, that Dante did not understand English and that I could serve as an interpreter. It worked! Dante and I were booked jointly and ended up in the same cell. Once we got to our cell, I knew that it would take several more hours before the lawyers could find us and bail us out. I wanted to relax and hopefully get some sleep. Dante was anxious throughout and would not let me rest.

After making bail, we wondered what we should do next. My instincts were to return to the Chancellor's Office, as that was what we had agreed to. It was late in the evening, and we didn't know the whereabouts of the other three arrestees, Marla, Goyo Rivera, and Guerra. Moreover, we didn't know if the community protest was still going on or if anyone had

stayed at the Chancellor's Office after our arrests. We made the right
decision. We took a taxi back to campus and found a large group of community members waiting to hear from us. They cheered long and loud as
we got out of the taxi.

At the following meeting after the arrests, all the arrestees were
cheered, Dante and Marla most of all. Marla took the floor and began
excoriating the men who had spoken about excluding women at the previous meeting. "It was the men who jumped out the window, not the
women," she shouted. She went on to call them *sin huevos* (without testi-
cles). Then she corrected herself and said, *"No, les cuelgan pa' riba, como a
las viejas"* (No, they hang upward like a broad's ovaries).

Initially, everyone was stunned by her choice of words. Then, after a
moment, we all laughed at their colorful arrangement. The lesson was not
lost on this manifestation. In fact, in earlier protests, women had clearly
demanded a place at the leadership table. During the Welfare March from
Milwaukee to Madison, Marla and other welfare rights mothers, many
single moms, publicly declared that the march would be led by them. Father Groppi, Chacon, and I escorted them to the city limits at their request.
The welfare rights mothers would lead the march from there to Madison.
We were asked to meet them on the outskirts of the city four days later.

The fact that a woman had committed civil disobedience had a large
impact on the role of women in subsequent community meetings and in
later political manifestations of the Latino/Chicano civil rights movement,
including reinforcing their hiring and leadership roles in social service
agencies serving Latinas and Latinos. In the moment, it energized and
broadened the campaign against UW–Milwaukee for the SSOI.

The sit-in and arrest at the Chancellor's Office did not resolve the impasse between the parties. At the following CELA meeting it was decided
that we would undertake a fast on UW–Milwaukee Chancellor's Office
grounds. In implementing direct action, we had escalated our activities
from picketing, to conducting a mass, to marching to the chancellor's
residence, and finally to civil disobedience, a sit-in that led to our arrest.
This had not brought the chancellor to agree to meet and discuss our demands. This infuriated the community.

In selecting the next tactic, we were faced with further escalation,
more sit-ins and additional massive arrests. Once at this stage of the

Wisconsin National Guard members with fixed bayonets remove welfare rights protesters from the State Capitol in 1969.

protest, we had few alternatives but to escalate tension. This would be an organizational challenge to undertake and sustain, and worse, fraught with consequences, especially concern over bodily harm to the protesters undertaking these actions. So far, the arrests had been peaceful, but they hadn't gone as planned with protesters jumping out of windows and people getting carried away and joining in the fray, and I was worried about further conflicts.

We broadened our attempt to pressure the chancellor and alert the entire UW system about our demand for access for Chicano, Chicana, Latino, and Latina students by crashing the next UW Board of Regents meeting in Madison. The reorganization of the UW system had not been fully implemented, but we wanted to publicize the UW–Milwaukee chancellor's recalcitrance and nonresponse to the lack of access and programs for Spanish-speaking students. We also wanted to send a message to the rest of the UW system that they also had to act. We weren't on the agenda, and we had no guarantee that the regents would allow us to speak; nevertheless, we ventured to attend the next regularly scheduled monthly meeting and plead our case. We took a busload of protesters, so we were able to quickly fill the boardroom with community members and Madison supporters. After a tense moment, the regents president allowed us to make a statement, after which we left peacefully. It was a joyful ride back to Milwaukee.

We returned to the picket line with nearly a dozen protesters who had volunteered to undergo the next direct action, a fast. We wanted to defuse tensions, not increase them. We wanted to continue affirming that the protest would be peaceful and nonviolent. This was a message we wanted to communicate to the public at large, especially after our arrest. Chávez had used fasting as a strategy to publicly maintain peaceful, nonviolent protest and picketing in Delano, so the tactic was not original, but it had not been undertaken during the five years I had been organizing farmworkers in Wisconsin. It would be a public fasting; we would also camp out, sleeping outside Chapman Hall at the end of a day of picketing. We encouraged the community to join us. They came and stayed until dark and beyond while we lay on the ground on sleeping bags hungry and exhausted.

I announce to protesters at the chancellor's office that the vice chancellor has agreed to meet and has agreed to CELA demands to establish the Spanish Speaking Outreach Institute.

I think the people fasting could have continued longer, but those of us who were fasting were also picketing, and after several days the effort was quite debilitating. After nearly a week, with no response from the chancellor regarding our latest effort and I being the only one remaining who had not eaten, we undertook an outrageous ploy.

While we were fasting, we had negotiated with UW–Milwaukee's campus police to use the bathrooms, which were at the entrance to the Chancellor's Office at Chapman Hall. In other words, we did not have to enter the office area, as the bathrooms were on the hallway leading up to the administration's individual offices; the Chancellor's Office was on the second floor. At the end of the hallway was an open area with posters and campus literature for visitors. Adjacent to this were the offices of one of the assistant chancellors. During the fast, the front door was left open for us to use the bathroom, but campus security was present to ensure that in using the bathroom we would not go beyond this area into the offices.

That October morning when I got up to relieve myself at daybreak, I noticed that the night security had left and the daytime security guard had not arrived. In the meantime, one of the assistant chancellors walked in, left the door open, and stopped at the bathroom before going to his office. I called out to Panchillo Rodriguez and my brother Luis, who had been sleeping beside me, to help me lock the assistant chancellor in the bathroom by placing a desk and a sofa in front of the door and to secure the main entrance. Then, we let the other community members who had been sleeping on the grounds into the building and locked the office building behind us. We proceeded to call friends from the office phones, first those who lived closer, on the near east side, and later those on the south side, to join us as we were occupying the Chancellor's Office.

Before the guard appeared and informed the chancellor's staff what we had undertaken, we had an opportunity to organize buses and cars full of community members to join us. This time we weren't leaving the premises. We allowed the assistant chancellor to leave the building as we began the process of blocking entrances. The takeover of the Chancellor's Office changed the tempo of our negotiations with the university administration. By the time they realized what had happened, we had filled Chapman Hall with scores of supporters. Further, we had a bilingual leaflet printed that called for a late-afternoon rally with buses available to bring hundreds of supporters to ring Chapman Hall. The administration realized we were not going to leave the premises peacefully. There would be a confrontation. The only way we could guarantee our safety was to surround the Chancellor's Office with community members.

Later in the morning we received a phone call telling us Assistant Chancellor Ernest Spaights wanted to be let in to negotiate the final steps of establishing the SSOI. We made one more demand that wasn't on the original CELA list: we wanted to announce the proposed establishment of the SSOI ourselves. We reserved the right to call a press conference at LAUCR's south side office and to designate a spokesperson to make the announcement. We had the upper hand. They agreed, and both Roberto Hernandez and I appeared before the press the following day. Roberto read the official statement regarding the SSOI, and we both answered questions.

Several days after the Chapman Hall takeover and the announcement that the Chancellor's Office had agreed to the establishment of the SSOI, a School of Education professor released a letter signed by seventy-eight faculty, staff, and students in support of the SSOI with commitments to its implementation. Nearly two months earlier, on August 27, School of Education Dean Davis had issued a letter after meeting with CELA representatives that supported the concept of the outreach institute and agreed to hire a full-time staff member recommended by CELA who would "become familiar with the programs in the School, in order that the University can involve more members in the Spanish Community in its educational programs."

UW–Milwaukee's School of Education support for CELA was crucial during the protracted protests. No other UW–Milwaukee college or department was as important! In the demands, CELA saw a structural relationship with the proposed director of the SSOI and the UW–Milwaukee School of Education. We had approached Dean Davis during the protest, and he had agreed in principle to the idea. His August 27 letter and the October 21 petition pledged full departmental support for its success.

The following month, on November 20, the University of Wisconsin Board of Regents authorized the establishment of the SSOI and the hiring of CELA's recommended candidate, Marquette professor Ricardo Fernandez, as its first director. Thereafter, we began to recommend a site for the outreach office activities, including the offering of UW–Milwaukee classes in the barrio and a space that Latino students could use as a library to study. We saw the SSOI outreach activities as the heart of the Latinos' drive for self-determination, surrounded by El Centro Hispano, UMOS, CEP, and The Spot (precursor to the United Community Center). El Centro offered space for UW–Milwaukee outreach classes, and space for a library and study center was made available at 805 South Fifth Street. An early January community-wide meeting was planned, but first we would welcome the New Year with a celebration of our achievement. We wanted the New Year's Eve celebration of the Latino community gaining the SSOI to be held at UW–Milwaukee, where we would gather the community to plan for its future. We wanted to continue the Latino presence on campus. We weren't able to accommodate the New Year's Eve celebration on campus, but we did make arrangements for a community-wide discussion on the future of the SSOI with reservations for a large hall for a mass meeting, several smaller ones, and cafeteria services for more than two hundred participants.

20

LAS ADELITAS

The Latino effort to establish University of Wisconsin–Milwaukee's Spanish Speaking Outreach Institute shifted from exclusively using CELA board meetings with the Chancellor's Office and the exchange of correspondence about demands to an approach that included direct action led by the picket line leaders. Beginning with the August 1970 community meeting, we decided to undertake civil disobedience. Individuals publicly vowed to carry out peaceful actions at UW–Milwaukee's Chapman Hall that could lead to their arrests. Thereafter, we did not exchange written demands. Negotiations moved to the picket line where the Latin American Union for Civil Rights, the Brown Berets, and the United Migrant Opportunity Services, including many former Obreros Unidos organizers, conducted the final strategy for the SSOI from the occupied Chancellor's Office.

Dante Navarro's and Marla Anderson's involvement, and most importantly their arrests in UW–Milwaukee's Chapman Hall during the August sit-in, kept this phenomenon from being exclusively a youth movement. Marla had been active in UMOS's reorganization in 1969 as well as a supporter of LAUCR initiatives, including actively participating in the welfare reform demonstrations later in the year. We referred to Marla as one of the "Adelitas." The Adelitas were an iconic image preserved in the poems and *corridos* (ballads) of the *soldaderas* (women soldiers) of the Mexican Revolution. Anderson was joined by Josefina Castro and Maria Ortega, two other Adelitas in the Milwaukee movement.

Josefina was ever present in the welfare reform movement both in the protest and demonstration at the Wisconsin State Capitol and before the

Milwaukee County Board of Supervisors. Long after the demonstration subsided, she continued to advocate for child care services. UMOS would establish one of the first Latino child care services to allow former migrant women to enroll in basic skills and employment training programs. Lupe Aguirre, the first UMOS student representative on the board, had been a strong advocate for the program. Josefina thought similar child care programs should be available in all community-based programs to allow women to enhance their skills and thus be able to compete for jobs with fair wages. She called it *La Causa* (the Cause), the adopted name of the organization that would advocate for a comprehensive child care program for infants to preschoolers.

The last of the three Adelitas was Maria Ortega. She was the oldest of the three, the most reserved, and a very astute middle-aged woman who would go on to serve on the early LAUCR boards that mentored the young members of the Brown Berets and advocated for Chacon to pursue after-school youth academic support programs.

Las Adelitas represented the emerging role of women in Latino leadership building a sustainable community with effective community-based organizations that focused on bilingual adult basic education, employment training, health, and child care as a family matter: one that concerns every single community member.

Obreros Unidos, unlike the traditional labor movements, which organized mostly male heads of household, organized families and was predicated on the family-based workforce of the cucumber harvesters. In complete disregard for Wisconsin state child labor laws, every member of the family besides infants and the elderly were in the field. Later in organizing for the inclusion of migrants and former migrants on the UMOS board, the community meetings that came together in the late fall of 1968 in Milwaukee were filled with family units. The Republican Party–led Wisconsin Legislature's welfare reform platform, which aimed to end the safety net of social services, threatened the whole family of resettled migrant families, especially vulnerable families led by single parents, mostly women.

That is why when we came together late in 1969 and began to organize for the establishment of the SSOI, a campaign that would use direct action as a strategy, we organized families. The Latino movement was organized as a community effort that was family based and led by young male and female members, already multiyear veterans of the movement. It was primarily a youth movement, but it was also a women's movement. Las Adelitas were the face of the Latina women's movement. Although they may have been at the front of all of our past political manifestations, what was not at the forefront of the movement were their demands for equity for young Latina women in the workplace as the Latinization of the organizations continued, first at UMOS and El Centro Hispano and later in the SDC-funded barrio initiatives that were more diverse and included non-Latino community organizers who were collaborating with us. When we organized the first SSOI community-wide meeting at UW–Milwaukee in January 1971, Latina and non-Latina women community organizers and leaders staged a demonstration demanding equity, which included equal say in setting the agenda and priorities for the SSOI and other community issues. I was at the podium at the lower end of the hall when more than half a dozen women dressed in Mexican regional dresses, rebozos and serapes, took the microphone and proceeded to take the stage and state their case. Taking us completely by surprise, the women who read written statements included my then-wife, Glorie Salas, and Irasema Flores, niece of UMOS's area coordinator Genevieve "Beba" Medina. Leticia Ledesma, an UMOS employee and, along with Irasema, former volunteer for Dante's campaign for the Wisconsin Assembly, was also dressed in a Mexican blouse in support of the women's demonstration.

At the women's meeting, two non-Latinas who took a leadership role were Mary Ann McNulty and Mary Lou Massigianni. No one viewed Mary Lou as a non-Latina. She was Italian born and spoke Spanish as well as her native tongue. She was a Marquette University mathematics teaching assistant who had joined fellow faculty and staff in their antiwar stance. For this, her visa status had been challenged, but with the support of both the Latino community and Marquette University, she was found not to be in violation. She was an anchor of support as a math and science teacher for the recently created Chicano/Boricua's GED program. Mary Ann McNulty, SDC's Inner City Development Program organizer and a supporter of the neighborhood and injured workers projects, was intensely interested in voter education and registration initiatives and was later elected as a City of Milwaukee alderwoman with the support of the Latino community.

One of the most extraordinary demands was for an all-women caucus to be part of the ongoing community meeting that would meet and make recommendations to the general assembly. The other face of the Latina protest that was not seen but was felt was the accusation of machismo. The Spanish colonial status of women as unequal and with few rights was challenged by Las Adelitas, who joined the armed revolt of the Mexican Revolution. Additional challenges to the Mexican male-dominated society arose through the mutualista movement of the Partido Liberal Mexicano and the women who all along the Texas Borderland had set up mutual aid neighborhood programs in the 1920s and 1930s. Still, in Milwaukee in the late 1960s, many Mexican bars did not welcome Latinas. Fellow Latina organizers and volunteers would chide us during sustained protests for patronizing bars, discussing the political manifestation of the day, and making decisions that they had not participated in or been part of. The disagreements could have divided our community of leaders and organizers, but they did not. We stayed united as women took on roles of more leadership in the movement.

The camaraderie we shared proved important as we faced bad news. Several days earlier, Dante had lost the election for the Democratic Party candidate for Milwaukee's near south side Wisconsin state assemblyman. However, his candidacy had promoted political involvement and voter registration, and his loss did not deter his participation for the establishment of the SSOI.

21

COMMUNITY ORGANIZING
AND LATINO POLITICS

Dante lost the election, but we won the support of Milwaukee's near south side Latino community. Many of the local businesses that supported Dante's radio program on weekends, which during the campaign included voter information and registration instructions, also supported his candidacy. Business support was crucial for other related community activities, youth programs, and especially support for our demands to celebrate fiesta patria activities, including later support for our demands to have Fiesta Mexicana's 16 de septiembre celebration at the Summerfest grounds on the lakefront. Dante's candidacy engaged the community in electoral politics. We conducted the first voter education and registration activities ever to be carried out in our community. Knocking on doors, we got a view of the community that one doesn't simply get by driving down the street. We began to create a database, our own census of our community.

The early 1970s political activity led us to carve out a sense of a political universe that would continue to be based on the south side of the Menominee Valley, in the old Walker's Point settlement, the oldest of the Milwaukee neighborhoods. The 1970 redistricting process, instigated by the County Board of Supervisors, included a plan to combine the downtown political district with the near south side. I called Fred Kessler, who not only had coordinated the Milwaukee-area lawyers to provide migrant families legal services for Obreros Unidos, but who also was extremely interested in the Wisconsin redistricting process. He informed me how to proceed to make a claim for a Latino south side district. Later, Chacon and I and others publicly opposed gerrymandering at public hearings. Nevertheless, the plan passed the first hurdle in the redistricting process and all the later ones. At the Milwaukee County Board redistricting hearing, our position against the downtown supervisor's district put us in conflict with the Black leaders who supported the plan. Later, our opposition against Milwaukee County Supervisor Harout Sanasarian's plan for his district to cross the Menominee Valley and represent the core of the Latino neighborhood had nothing to do with him personally. We supported Supervisor Sanasarian's tenure on the county board, but we wanted Latinos to have a voice in their choice of candidates in their barrio. Our only alternative was to sue, an effort that would be slow but would eventually provide the basis for a fairer 1980 redistricting process. Latinos would coalesce around Mary Ann McNulty for Milwaukee City Council following the redistricting, but a Latino would not be elected until the 1990s, more than twenty years after Dante's candidacy in 1970.

After losing the assembly race, Dante led the Latino effort of the Black/Brown coalition for increased minority hiring that had earlier targeted Allen Bradley and now was challenging Milwaukee brewers Miller, Schlitz, Blatz, and Pabst. Dante's effort was most effective in how he made the brewers' hiring of minorities into a Latino national campaign. He had been an ardent supporter of the League of United Latin American Citizens (LULAC). He had helped organize LULAC Council 302 in southeastern Wisconsin and later reorganized Council 380. In 1962, he was named the Wisconsin LULAC state organizer by LULAC's national office. Through this state and national network that he had developed in more than a decade of organizing local LULAC initiatives, he initiated a letter-writing campaign in support of Latino hiring by Milwaukee brewers. By late December 1970, we were already meeting with brewery representatives and had written responses for a scheduled meeting for January 1971 with all major breweries with the exception of Pabst.

Dante recommended the community deal with Pabst differently, for several reasons. First, Pabst was the most popular beer in local Latino bars and restaurants in Milwaukee's near south side, and Dante thought the brewery should lead in the effort to hire Latinos. Dante had found that out of 5,100 Pabst employees, only 54 had Spanish surnames. We demanded that Pabst immediately respond to a list of demands that included the hiring of 120 Latino employees or face a national boycott. We had long-time experience with consumer boycotts, as we were successfully carrying out a national boycott of grapes in support of California farmworkers. CORE was engaged in a boycott of Budweiser beer bottled in St. Louis. We thought we could undertake an effective campaign against a Milwaukee brewer, and we targeted Pabst at the direction of Dante and fellow national LULAC councils and local Latino businesses and community leaders. In the end, Miller Brewing would have the most impact on the hiring of Latinos. All of the brewers responded affirmatively and hiring began at all levels, including the delivery of the beer in the barrio. Most significantly, both Schlitz and Miller began to support local recreational programs as well as cultural events. Budweiser would hire Tony Torres for this purpose, and Miller would later hire Jose Ruano, who became an important source of support for local cultural and sporting events supported by Miller, including the celebration of Fiesta Mexicana.

But during the process of gaining support for Latino events, community leaders agreed to protest the alleged lack of support from Milwaukee brewery union leadership. Brewery Workers Local 9 had been for years one of the most ardent supporters of Obreros Unidos. John Schmitt had emerged from the breweries to lead the Wisconsin State AFL-CIO as president in the fall of 1966, during our potato strike. He had invited me to address the state labor leaders at the convention and passed the hat to secure drastically needed cash to support the union. Later, he provided extensive legal assistance in our efforts to petition the Wisconsin labor board for recognition and helped our multiyear legal fight against Libby's when the company refused to negotiate after we had won the WERC certification election.

The support of local brewers for minority hiring could be won, I thought, and I decided to go along with the pickets before the brewers union meeting in order to talk to Schmitt and union leadership. It was a poor decision. The fact that a picket line had appeared greatly offended the brewers, and when I walked inside the union meeting with other Latino leaders to meet with the brewers, a scuffle broke out. I was charged with being an "ingrate." I should have found another means of meeting with

Schmitt and local brewers union leaders. Later, the issue would be cleared up. The brewers union would not oppose an affirmative action campaign and Black and Latino workers were hired and became active union members. But at the time, I felt that I had failed. First, I was unable to dissuade Dante and fellow Latino community leaders from picketing the brewers union meeting. I was voted down. And second, I had not devised a means to clear up the issue, personally, through the long-term relationship that I enjoyed with Schmitt, rather than from a picket line.

I found that there were no personal decisions in community organizing in the barrio. In labor unions as well as in community-wide initiatives, what one of the leaders of the coalition decides affects the whole organization and, for us at the time, the Latino community as a whole. But labor unions differed from community organizations. We reached decisions differently. We, most of all, attempted to speak as one. The most effective decisions occur when labor unions are active membership organizations that deliberate openly and, with personal interests to the side, act as a unit. The only way that community organizations bond as labor unions is through sustained effort.

22

UMOS and Welfare Rights Manifestations

The reorganization of UMOS as a community-based organization that not only provided needed services but also openly advocated on behalf of migrant issues took years to put in course and sustain. The essence of organizing is not only its design but also its effective application. On migrant labor issues, this meant a long battle to support and sustain these community issues. When Obreros Unidos split its field operation and committed to intensifying grape boycott activity, it moved union organizers to Milwaukee to coordinate the statewide effort. Our task was primarily to engage our counterparts, the Milwaukee area's unionized community of workers. But we had had several years of organizing among Wisconsin university campuses, especially at UW–Madison, and we wanted to continue organizing. The focus on UW–Milwaukee went beyond obtaining student support for the grape boycott to Latino access to the university system. The attempt to establish the SSOI also was a multiyear attempt, and the Latino community's continued involvement shaped its future for the long term. Lastly, the Welfare Mothers' March on Madison sought to maintain Wisconsin's safety net of social services for impoverished families, many headed by single mothers, and to oppose the Wisconsin Legislature's welfare reform proposals. With not a single Latino representative and only one Black representative in the Wisconsin Assembly, the issue was resolved, not in legislative chambers, but in the streets. The welfare rights protest would lead to the takeover of the State Capitol, and the Milwaukee protest correspondingly grew more militant. The farmworkers movement intersected with the Freedom Marches, demands for equal employment, and maintaining a safety net for the impoverished.

Before the protest that led to the takeover of the capitol building and the calling of the Wisconsin National Guard for our removal, we had traveled to Madison to testify at a hearing, advocating on behalf of migrants and informing the legislators on the negative consequences of the legislative changes. Although we opposed other aspects of the proposed reforms, we were most concerned that the establishment of a longer waiting period, exceeding a month before any benefits would be available, would disrupt the migrant resettlement program and deny thousands of migrants needed emergency aid. With a waiting period longer than a month, none of the fifteen thousand workers who came to Wisconsin would qualify for services, including food and shelter assistance, if they suffered an emergency. The harvesting period for the variety of Wisconsin fruits and vegetables was less than the thirty to sixty days that were being proposed. It threatened UMOS's resettlement of migrants who were losing their jobs primarily to automation, as well as the thousands of Black residents who had fled Southern apartheid and were finding work in Milwaukee's bustling industrial sector, foundries, and tanneries. In fact, the new residency requirement was meant to deter Black families from moving to Wisconsin; politicians argued Black families were moving here to enjoy what were seen as more generous welfare benefits than those found in neighboring and Southern states.

Republican legislators listened, but they had already made up their minds regarding the cutbacks. Their view was that minorities moved to Wisconsin not to work, but to depend on welfare to sustain their idleness. This was wrong, and it was racist. Both Black and Mexican Americans and Mexican migrants had been migrating to the Midwest and Wisconsin for decades to work. Since there were no social services in the late 1950s and early 1960s in Waushara County, migrant families who suffered emergencies were mostly in need of food for their children. If they couldn't find a grower that had housing or needed workers, the family had to move on without resources to look for fieldwork outside the area. They would come to my father's restaurant to inquire about aid, and we would feed them, and I would take them down to the Waushara County administrator and request assistance by translating their needs into English. At the time, before food stamps, basic assistance was commodities. The county administrator would take us to a small warehouse that held canned and dry goods and make them available to Waushara County's indigent and in some cases migrant workers.

The proposed welfare reforms would disrupt UMOS's relocation and training programs for former migrant workers who were resettling. UMOS matched Milwaukee County's first month of rental assistance with a stipend for multilevel educational programs that might include UMOS English classes, referrals to the Concentrated Employment Program (CEP) for job assessment and development, and referrals either to MATC vocational programs or to in-house employment services or job openings. Some UMOS participants also attended evening and weekend ESL and citizenship classes at El Centro Hispano one block west of the Concentrated Employment Program office. The same core of Latino community-based organizations that had carried out the effort on behalf of the establishment of UW–Milwaukee's SSOI also collaborated in the protest of welfare reform. Across the street from CEP were the offices of the newly established Latin American Union for Civil Rights (LAUCR), headed by Ernesto Chacon. For the Latino community, local welfare reform community hearings and meetings took place before the Milwaukee County Board of Supervisors, who directed and administered the federal and state social services for which changes were being proposed. UMOS, CEP, El Centro, and LAUCR staff, participants, and supporters all coalesced with the north side Black organizations in protest of welfare reform. The proposed changes would affect us all directly.

For the Latino community, there were two major focuses of protests. One was the Welfare Mothers' March on Madison that led to a direct confrontation with the Wisconsin State Assembly and the sit-in at the Wisconsin State Capitol that has been extensively written about. Less well known are the local protests, principally at the Milwaukee County Building but also carried out in Milwaukee's downtown. The most massive of the Black marches to downtown Milwaukee was, in fact, after the Freedom Marches. It was a day of mourning following the assassination of Dr. Martin Luther King Jr. in April 1968. Only then did the nation slightly relent, beginning to dismantle the cornerstone of racial segregation, open housing laws and real estate covenants that prohibited the interaction of races and ethnic groups.

South side welfare rights mothers, including many Latinas led by Las Adelitas, coalesced in their support for the march to Madison and gathered in front of the UMOS building on the near south side. Father Groppi, Chacon, and I, as well as other male members of the Youth Council, were asked to escort the women out of the City of Milwaukee. Thereafter, the women could handle the march on their own. The leadership of these women is a little noted part of the history of the welfare marches. They argued that whenever Father Groppi appeared in support of welfare and women's rights issues, the press inevitably were drawn to him. The evening news featured Father Groppi's statements rather than women issuing their own. The leaders of the welfare rights mothers rightfully wanted the focus to be on themselves and their issues, so they led the march.

Father Groppi and I did not join them again until they were at Columbus, just outside of Madison. When we met up with them, the women were deliberating on their plan to walk into Madison over the weekend and hold a rally at the steps of the State Capitol upon their arrival. I argued that they would be walking into a deserted town over the weekend, as all the state employees would be off for the weekend and state offices would be closed. I proposed they stay outside Madison until Monday and then march into the capital. I further suggested to march to campus first, plan a rally at UW–Madison's Library Mall to gain student support, and then together march down State Street to the Wisconsin capitol building. All liked the idea and after the meeting I began contacting former Obreros Unidos supporters and UW–Madison student groups to sponsor and organize the rally for the Welfare March. No one in a leadership position ever proposed the takeover of the State Capitol that ended up happening.

The morning sun greeted the rallygoers at the foot of the University of Wisconsin Memorial Library steps. Students continued to join us as the rally and march progressed up State Street. The march grew to thousands as we entered the Wisconsin State Capitol. The Wisconsin Assembly was in session.

Milwaukee minority community leaders had earlier appeared before legislative hearings opposing the elimination of the family safety net of social services, known as the Republican Party leaders' welfare reform package. On this day, the legislative chamber's door had been locked, but with more than a dozen of us pushing, we forced the door open as the surprised assembly members scurried from their desks and began running the opposite way. Protesters poured into the chambers and filled it to the brim with all corridors and walkways packed. Welfare rights leaders and the NAACP Youth Council spread throughout the chambers, insisting that care be taken of the desks of the representatives who had fled as soon as we entered the chambers. Many had left personal items on their desks, but protesters insisted on maintaining order and respect of public property. This was essential as speakers wishing to be heard stood on top of individual desks.

As the afternoon wore on, there appeared to be no positive response to our presence. Although the assembly leaders had retreated to their offices that ring the capitol, they refused to meet or respond to our demands. There arose a sense that we would not leave the chambers until the Wisconsin legislators met with us. We refused to vacate the premises, but by early evening no order to remove had been issued. As time passed, we suspected that they would not force us out of the building until late at night when there would be no witnesses. We sent word outside for the protesters to stay around the capitol and await our removal. We later heard that the Wisconsin National Guard had been called to remove us by force. We let the capitol police know that we would leave peacefully, but as the mass of people inside the chambers moved outside, we heard cries as members of the National Guard used their rifle butts to push the peaceful demonstrators out. Many of us felt real concern for our physical well-being. When riot police had been called during the Freedom Marches, officers attacked peaceful demonstrators, including with deadly force. Three people had died from gunshot wounds, including a Black college student who was shot by police. In Madison that day, the NAACP Youth Council and Latino youths linked arms in front of and behind Father Groppi and me to keep the National Guard, with their bayonets drawn, away from us as we peacefully left the capitol.

Except for those in the rear who were pushed out, we were simply walked out by the National Guard. There were no arrests of anyone. As soon as we realized this, we wanted to prevent any further confrontation. At this time, there were many more students than welfare rights mothers among the protesters, and the students didn't want to go home. They wanted to continue the protest by camping overnight. I was employed by UMOS and was expected to be in the office the following day. I had not taken the day off, so I called to inform them of my plan to miss work. I had to officially take the following day off so that I wouldn't be acting on UMOS's behalf at the capitol.

Among the Latina welfare rights leaders and welfare rights mothers were supporters from the community-based organizations that had formed the core of the group for Latina/Chicano self-determination. They included staff, board members, and volunteers for UMOS, El Centro, CEP, and the ever-growing number of youths who joined different aspects of LAUCR initiatives. But the struggle had brought other allies: other neighborhood organizations, including welfare rights and worker's rights groups.

Initially, the Wisconsin legislature ordered Father Groppi to be arrested for the takeover. Federal judge James Doyle threw out their case as the legislature had no authority to call for his arrest, Judge Doyle claimed. Subsequently the Wisconsin Assembly charged Father Groppi and me and several of the Welfare March leaders with a civil suit for the damages caused to the State Capitol during the takeover. We were also charged with "misconduct on public grounds."

I was not worried about the charges. In fact, the disorderly conduct law had been expanded, and the misconduct on public grounds charges were so broad that they were also thrown out in court. My main concern was OEO reaction to my arrest. I had told the staff that I was taking the day off. I called the OEO offices in Washington to make sure they knew my arrest had not come while working at UMOS. They supported me when the calls for my firing and the defunding of the program came. We never stopped marching. In August 1971, UMOS would again lead a march from Milwaukee to Madison, this time protesting the Wisconsin state agencies' lack of enforcement of Wisconsin social and progressive legislation and administrative law.

23

FREE CHACON AND PUENTE PROTESTS

At one of the downtown Milwaukee welfare demonstrations, LAUCR director Ernesto Chacon and member Jose Puente had been arrested and very quickly sentenced to six months in jail. After lengthy community meetings, we decided to alter our focus of the welfare protests and attempt to get recently elected Democratic Governor Patrick Lucey to grant Puente and Chacon pardons. The issue was clouded in that the downtown marches had resulted in scuffles with the police, resulting in arrests. At the time, Milwaukee police would treat any type of peaceful demonstration, large or small, as a riot, especially those that were undertaken in downtown Milwaukee. City of Milwaukee leaders, since the Freedom Marches of 1968–69, were aggressive in maintaining their segregated turf, especially its downtown commercial retail and corporate space, as well as Milwaukee County and City municipal offices.

Milwaukee County administered the state's welfare programs that included corresponding budgeted social services for its residents. Milwaukee County welfare policy and budgets were deliberated at the Milwaukee County Courthouse. Black protesters marched from their north side segregated neighborhood, and Latino protesters would arrive from their enclaves on the south side through the same Sixth Street to get to the courthouse several blocks west of downtown Milwaukee. Neither minority community was welcome in downtown Milwaukee. Welfare rights demonstrators were approached by riot-equipped police officers with helmets, masks, and batons as soon as we appeared.

Paddy wagons were always nearby to remove the "disorderly." Those arrested were subjected to expanded state statutes relating to protests, including the "misconduct on public grounds" statute the legislature had established to apply to protesters at public buildings. Local judges were notorious in their unfairness, particularly Judge Christ Seraphim, who would personally insult and berate minority protesters who came before him. He gleefully handed down maximum sentences.

The times I was scheduled to appear before Judge Seraphim, my attorneys requested a change of venue. We anticipated that any conviction would be appealed, as our protests were always peaceful and nonviolent and we could easily prove protesters had broken no laws. The authorities, whether UW–Milwaukee's chancellor or the Wisconsin legislature, simply wanted us off their premises, thus the limitations of protesting in public buildings. Father Groppi and I had appealed our earlier charges to federal courts, but the case had not been heard as we were being arrested for the same charges in ongoing peaceful protests. Attorneys were concerned that the ongoing appeals process could compel authorities to issue further charges and may lead to the refusal of or higher bail. Father Groppi and I were forewarned.

At the protest sites, it didn't matter what the charges were. Riot police and/or the Wisconsin National Guard were called to intimidate us to deter us from exercising our rights with their military-like presence. Their orders were to remove us by armed force, beaten and bound. We would be charged with the latest statute or ordinance and be jailed and booked. First, we attempted to keep the case from going to court by getting the felony charges reduced to misdemeanor status. Those cases that were brought before local magistrates, if found guilty, we would appeal. The whole process—from the response to our political demonstrations and protests, to our contact with the police, to the role of the district attorney's office and the judicial system—was geared to convict us. But the purpose went beyond punishment. The system seemed designed to quell the protests. It was meant to be so outrageously unfair that we would fear being caught up in its web of injustice. They hoped we would be so fearful of the consequences that we would stop demanding the franchise, equal opportunity, and access to the state's segregated educational systems. They were wrong.

The sentencing of Chacon and Puente had not been based on fair legal grounds. They had been criminally charged and were found guilty and sentenced to prison unjustly. The Latino community felt that it was not a crime to support welfare rights mothers seeking to keep food and maintain shelter for their families. In fact, it was the moral thing to do. Large numbers of families attended meetings and marches to free them.

—◁||▷—

Many already knew Chacon, as he had been instrumental in early activities of the Latino/Chicano civil rights movement, including the UMOS takeover, establishing SSOI, the school walkouts, and very early on, welfare and women's rights. We as a community could not allow Chacon to be unjustly incarcerated, removed from our community, of which he had become such an integral part. Several years before, in the summer of 1968 while we were picketing in front of Wryzinski Food Store in support of the California grape boycott, he had shown up at the picket line. When I asked who of the Obreros Unidos organizers had recruited him, the response was "*Solo vino*"—he came on his own. *Solo vino* in Spanish has several other meanings also, principally of personal independence in decision-making and daring.

Chacon's genius was in establishing LAUCR with private and foundation funds so that it was not beholden to federal and state laws that limited political activity by employees. Because UMOS and CEP received their funds from federal sources, staff were restricted in some of their political activities. Chacon, along with Roberto Hernandez and other LAUCR leaders, had no such restrictions and were at the forefront of many political manifestations from which some of us who were employees of federal- or state-funded programs were restrained. Chacon was an excellent organizer and unselfishly supported the creation of ad hoc groups to direct activities that demanded particular focus, such as education, social services, and especially youth programs that required extensive community support, such as CELA. In the intensive negotiations with the UW–Milwaukee Chancellor's Office, Chacon and Hernandez had demonstrated their leadership qualities. At UMOS, Chacon had supported the decentralization of administrative power and the creation of area boards in Racine, Madison, and other outreach offices.

I made sure I was not officially working for UMOS while I demonstrated and faced arrest. Nevertheless, it was very obvious that my tenure
at UMOS would adhere to my promise to serve for only two funding periods. My participation in ongoing civil rights activities that were resulting
in my being arrested and charged threatened UMOS's funding. I couldn't
let that happen.

Chacon faced no such restrictions, and those of us working for federal-
and state-funded community-based organizations depended on his office
to be the vanguard of the movement. Although it is well known how
LAUCR organized Milwaukee's Brown Berets and undertook solidarity
visits to Corky Gonzalez and his Chicano Youth Liberation meetings,
Chacon also organized a core of young leaders to attend Sal Alinsky's community organizer training sessions in Chicago. Chacon's focus on training
went beyond organizers, to Latino emerging community-based boards in
Milwaukee and surrounding communities. He not only supported UMOS
staff and board training, but he also called for all Latino organizations
to review their missions after their Latinization and make sure that their
job descriptions included advocacy of community issues. They also had to
be diverse and inclusive, representative of the whole Latino community,
the majority of whom were Chicano, Mexican, and Puerto Rican.

The fact that Chacon called for a Latin American union in the middle
of a Chicano movement speaks to his view that the core principle of all
civil rights issues would be broad based, diverse, and elaborate. It would
be led by Puerto Ricans, Chicanos, and other Latinos who were arriving
daily. It would reflect our own uniqueness as La Raza, a people, those of
us who identified with *Chicanismo*, who reached out to the general Mexican American and Mexican immigrant members of the community for a
self-identity.

We had addressed this issue at the inception of the Wisconsin farmworkers movement five years earlier when we began to organize the migrant workers from along the Tejano Borderland. Five thousand of the
fifteen thousand migrant workers who came to fertile fields west of the
Wisconsin Kettle Moraine area and north to the Central Sands came from
both sides of the Rio Bravo. In Texas, the workers came primarily from the
four-county Winter Garden region, the twin cities of Laredo and Nuevo
Laredo on both sides of the border, and the Texas Valley south of San

Antonio. As workers, it was essential that we consider ourselves as
obreros, workers united to improve our working and living conditions,
rather than being from Crystal City or Laredo, from this side or the other
side of the border. I addressed this issue at the labor camps and in my first
public interview, in which I identified our union as being made up of workers from both sides of the border. This would later distinguish us from
Chávez's campaigns, which dealt with unauthorized Mexican immigrants being used by growers to break strikes. It drew us closer to Antonio
Orendain, vice president of the National Farm Workers Association, who
was sent to organize farmworkers in the Texas Valley and who felt that
farmworkers from both sides of the border needed to be organized into
one union.

Chacon's legacy also endures because of his contribution to the orga-
nizing of Fiesta Mexicana, now celebrated on Summerfest grounds by
Lake Michigan. These celebrations had been going on since the arrival of
Los Primeros, the early Mexican settlers who came to Milwaukee's Walker
Point neighborhood at the turn of the twentieth century. Chacon tied the
fiesta patria celebration to the Latino demand for a culturally relevant,
bilingual education that reflected our reality in the desegregation of the
Milwaukee Public School System, then being led by our friend, attorney
Lloyd Barbee. Chacon organized barrio public school walkouts when local
principals refused to recognize and celebrate fiesta patria holidays.

The students who walked out met in front of their respective schools
on el Cinco de Mayo (marking the Battle of Puebla when the Mexican army
held off the invading French troops at Puebla, Mexico, in 1863). Later these
walkouts became celebrations at block parties with political speeches,
music, and Mexican food. This was not uncommon in Milwaukee, where
ethnic and even religious festivals were celebrated by the closing off of
streets.

What LAUCR and the emerging Latino community-based organizations did was to politicize the fiestas patrias, first to focus on the desegregation of the schools, but most importantly for Latinos to demand relevant
bilingual curriculum. The school walkouts would be not only a protest,
but an event that included political speeches, music, and daylong celebrations at a block party to follow El Centro's sponsored parade. Later it
evolved into an entire weekend celebration of Fiesta Mexicana on

Latino students celebrate el Cinco de Mayo with a school walkout and march on May 5, 1971.

Summerfest grounds on the lakefront with a variety of Mexican businesses promoting their specialties. We all felt that public institutions should honor our heroes and recognize our fiestas. LAUCR was one of the first to demand bilingual public education and to confront neighborhood schools to teach Chicano/Latino history and celebrate our fiestas patrias.

Centro Hispano's staff, in collaboration with the Christian Center offices and with strong support from the religious community and other Latino community-based organizations, gave rise to The Spot, a youth center that would later become one of the most effective educational and recreational programs for young people. Assisted by Jose Ruano and Oscar Cervera, Chacon also raised funds for particular youth activities, especially *futbol* (soccer). Roberto Hernandez was a most effective organizer for these activities. He was a role model for the youth, a Vietnam vet, foster parent, and courageous leader in the street demonstrations that were being carried out. Cervera and Ruano sold Christmas trees during the holidays to raise funds for uniforms for youth soccer teams. Chacon, Cervera, and Ruano later organized businesses led by Dante Navarro, "Tacho" Dorantes, Salvador Sanchez, and others to support the development of a whole league of multilevel, multi-age soccer teams for boys and girls.

—‖—

We were not going to allow Chacon's unjust jailing. At community meetings we decided that we would make known our efforts to "Free Chacon
and Puente" through public protest, individually focusing on the impact
of their jailing on our community and in collaboration with other welfare
rights organizations. We also developed a letter-writing campaign to demand a pardon from Governor Lucey. Besides organizing letters of support
from other welfare rights groups, Latino community-based organizations,
labor unions, and other community allies, we also sought out churches,
church groups, and human rights groups to write letters on their behalf.
Since Obreros Unidos, El Centro Hispano, UMOS, and the NAACP Youth
Council had long-standing support and relationships with religious leaders, we also reached out to them to write letters to Governor Lucey. None
was as effective as the union's petition to the Archdiocese for support.

—‖—

My relationship with the local unions that had supported Obreros Unidos
during the farmworker organizing of the mid-1960s continued after I
moved to Milwaukee to organize the grape boycott. Besides John Schmitt,
former Milwaukee brewer and then president of the state AFL-CIO, none
had been more helpful than United Auto Workers (UAW) leader Harvey
Kitzman, who had sent Charles Heymans to central Wisconsin to help us
organize in the summer of 1967. Raymond Majerus would follow Kitzman at the UAW's international offices, and he and I became acquainted.
Majerus, who would later become a national UAW leader, was also active
in the Milwaukee community and was a member of the Archdiocese's
human rights group. With his and Father John Maurice's help, I was also
appointed to the Archdiocese human rights board.

   We held a community meeting to select the group who would meet
with the Archdiocese. Attendees included several who were not active or
practicing Catholics, including myself and many young Latinos. The
group selected to meet with the archbishop was composed of active members in El Centro and the Bruce Guadalupe Church, not just community
activists. At the community meeting to select who would attend, we also

discussed the pardon. Some of the young members wanted to make sure that we weren't visiting the archbishop to ask for *perdon*, the Spanish word for "forgiveness." Some challenged the selected group not to kneel or kiss the archbishop's hand. On the other side of the discussion, the true believers insisted that the archbishop be addressed as His Excellency.

After the meeting with the archbishop, fellow activists poked fun at my hypocrisy. I had not been selected for my religious fervor, but I wanted the archbishop's continued support for El Centro's adult basic education program, in addition to his support of the pardons for Chacon and Puente. Fathers Becker and Maurice helped to arrange the meeting, which turned out to be successful. The archbishop would later send a letter to Governor Lucey in support of a pardon for Puente and Chacon.

—⊣⊢—

We were concerned about our ability to conduct future peaceful protests such as the Free Chacon and Puente marches downtown to the Milwaukee County Courthouse complex where we wanted to publicly present our case. I can't stress enough how the nature of the police response to our assembling in public buildings in Milwaukee's downtown area became more aggressive when we dared cross the Sixteenth Street bridge (now the James E. Groppi Unity Bridge) or the Sixth Street Viaduct that spanned Milwaukee's industrialized Menominee River, which separated us from the downtown area. It was a psychological barrier too. Families of color, in particular Black and young Latino males, were not welcome in downtown Milwaukee.

Similar barriers, some geographic and others psychological, had divided previous generations in Crystal City, where we were separated by railroad tracks, just as in Milwaukee, where a fortress of white privileged neighborhoods were sealed off from us. On Milwaukee's near east side, the bridge between the Riverwest area and the east side formed one of these boundaries. West of the river was the north side Black community. Even though the near east side ended next to a beautiful park and beach along Lake Michigan, seldom did Black families in the late 1960s cross the bridge to enjoy it. The retail area on North Street was sandwiched between Farwell and Prospect, and all around these businesses there were still moderate housing prices that attracted working-class families and students.

Some Black families, Latinos, and students lived in the "buffer zone," the Riverwest area, between the Black neighborhood west of Holton and the bridge to the near east side; but minority families did not cross the imaginary barriers: the viaduct on North Street or the parallel one on Locust Street. The several-block area east of these bridges included upper-income families, and on Lake Drive were impressive mansions with block-long front yards. Seldom was a face of color seen in this area.

Demonstrations in downtown were a challenge to organize, not only because we had to urge Latinos to penetrate the psychological barrier and walk en masse from the south side of the Sixth Street Viaduct and across the downtown to the Milwaukee County grounds where the Board of Supervisors met. We inevitably met the real menacing barrier made up of riot police, outfitted with sidearms and billy clubs, ready to pound us in place. Behind them paddy wagons waited to cart us off to the downtown jail across the street from MATC. Riding up and down noisily on Sixth Street were locally made Harley-Davidson motorcycles instead of horses to keep us in line. Marching without a permit meant that we had to stay on the sidewalk.

Leading the demonstration across the Sixth Street Viaduct in protest of Chacon and Puente's sentencing, I felt this was not going to turn out well in spite of our intention to keep it peaceful and to avoid confrontation with the police. The loud, sputtering Harley machines, more effective than any horse, were aggressively forcing us onto the sidewalk anytime we squeezed out, almost running us over. It didn't bode well for a peaceful, nonviolent march.

In fact, keeping us on the sidewalk extended the march. This actually was more dangerous. It took longer to get us downtown because we marched behind each other stretched out in a long line and interfering with traffic at the corners of the east–west lines. We marched the two blocks spilling onto Fifth Street, not concerned about using the sidewalk until we reached the Sixth Street Viaduct, with families joining us on the way. Raul Flores and I were marching at the top of the line, side by side. No sooner had we stepped onto the drawbridge than we were arrested.

Raul was accosted by a patrolman who saw him put his hand inside his jacket pocket as he marched. Alleging that Raul was going for a weapon, the riot-clad officer used his club to separate Raul from the crowd and

Hundreds of Latino protesters march across the Sixth Street viaduct from the Walker Point barrio to downtown Milwaukee while protesting the jailing of Chacon and Puente.

began to confront him. Raul was the nephew of UMOS's janitor who had recently arrived from Mexico. During the winter, he had slept in a bed in the corner of the basement, stoking and regulating the overburdened boiler, which needed almost twenty-four-hour oversight during extreme use in winter months.

I immediately attempted to keep the police officer from Raul, yelling that Raul did not speak or understand English and did not understand his commands. There was no other way to protect Raul other than grabbing the officer's club. I had to do it without causing the officer to fear that I wanted to disarm him or that I wanted to use the club as a weapon against him. As I moved between him and Raul, I grabbed the bottom end of the baton and placed all my weight behind my hands. I wanted to look him straight in the face so he would realize that I meant no harm to him. My act was not one of aggression.

My plan did not work. Soon a whole number of other police officers came to the aid of the now arresting officer. But it allowed for a split second in which Raul escaped the swing of the baton by the first officer. Raul did not get clubbed. The confrontation would lead to our arrest, but we were at the moment unharmed. The next task was to avoid being taken down. If we were to be arrested, we wanted to walk into the paddy wagon, not be thrown in headfirst and handcuffed.

Other police arrived, as well as fellow supporters, as Raul and I were both arrested, handcuffed, and detained. Out of the corner of my eye, I glimpsed a possible confrontation between a riot police officer and a man with a cowboy hat. The police officer went down, and all I could see was a cowboy hat bobbing back to the barrio. I hoped it wasn't my brother Frank, who was wearing a Stetson that night. I continued to repeat out loud to all involved that Raul did not speak or understand English. This was only partially true, as no one misunderstands the language of violence and threats and how our bodies react to such. Raul understood the predicament we were in and what had been averted, but neither of us knew what we further faced, both of us now handcuffed with our hands behind our backs.

Confrontations and the clash of bodies and billy clubs seemed to occur at the speed of light around us. In other moments, events seemed to happen in slow motion.

As the paddy wagon arrived to pick us up, I looked south and saw "El Vesugo" Mendoza and other Brown Berets move toward Raul and me and the surrounding officers. I didn't want to give any indication that we needed their intervention. In fact, I wanted my body language to convey that we were not hurt and did not feel threatened. We were escorted to the rear of the paddy wagon with a wall of police between us and the rest of the protesters. As the paddy wagon moved north on the steel bridge, toward downtown where the city jail was situated, Mendoza jumped on the back bumper and forced the back door open. He urged us to jump out and flee. Mendoza did not know that there was a police officer inside with a club on his lap beside us, making sure we did not make a move. Nearby police moved to close the door and prevent anyone else from interfering with their taking us downtown and booking us. We did not know until later that night that fights had broken out and over half a dozen more protesters were jailed. A number of police officers, it was reported, needed medical assistance. Because of my arrest early in the night, I had not been able to discourage the violence.

Our booking inside the downtown police station went well as I continued to insist that Raul could not speak or understand English. I hoped this would keep us together, as none of the officers spoke Spanish. It worked, and we were booked together and jailed in the same cell. Soon we could hear other Spanish-speaking detainees being booked and joining us. The news that came trickling in was not good. Some of the protesters jailed were being charged high bails, and some we couldn't get out. These included minors, whose parents had to be present for them to be released. Because we had planned for arrests, lawyers were available. As the first to be arrested, Raul and I had our bail set for us, and we were the first to be released. Soon thereafter, we met with supporters who were waiting for us outside the municipal building and drove us to the LAUCR office. We decided to break into groups to go into supportive businesses to raise funds to bail the large number of jailed protesters. Even though Topitzes' Groceries was closed, we thought the owner would be helpful. At nearly midnight, I knocked on the door of Argamenon "Memo" Topitzes, who was known to us in the neighborhood as the "Mayor of Walker Point." No one contributed more money than Memo. In small bills, he counted off all the money we asked for. It was to be a loan. I assured him that all the arrestees we released would show up to court and would return his savings. The most challenging, most painful part of the evening was yet to come.

We began to knock on doors of sleeping families to tell them that their underaged children had been arrested and jailed. We had the money to get them out, but they could not be released to us because we weren't their parents or guardians. They had to come downtown to see to their release. When we got to the police station with the family member, some of the children had already been sent to juvenile detention, and we had to wait for them to be brought back. Before that night, I had been unaware what happened with detained underage youth. Over half a decade of organizing, our efforts had always been to protect women and children in the picket line. I was terribly worried, as I hoped the youngsters remained unharmed as they were being moved between the municipal building and the juvenile detention center, which I had never visited. I did not get home until morning when all of the protesters had been released and the youth returned to their parents.

After the confrontation with the police, my brother Manuel had told Francisco, my brother with the Stetson hat, to go home and stay there. Manuel came back to the municipal building and waited with me until everyone arrested had been released. We stopped at a George Webb café that was open all night to have breakfast before going home, where we faced more bad news. The morning newspaper, the *Milwaukee Sentinel*, described the demonstration to free Chacon and Puente as Latinos attacking the police.

Later that day, we began to organize in response to the mischaracterization of the protest; it had been a peaceful protest until the police charged and attacked us. Most important, the call for a community meeting was to continue completing our task: marching downtown to present our case for Chacon and Puente to be pardoned before the county and the public. We met and in spite of the forecast of blustery cold, we planned to march to the Milwaukee County Courthouse as we had intended several nights earlier. The announcement drew the attention of Mayor Henry Maier's office, who became concerned about our proposed march across the same Sixth Street Viaduct where the "riot" and "attacks on policemen" had broken out days earlier. Woody Welch, Mayor Maier's assistant, responded to our calls proposing a meeting with the mayor and the Milwaukee chief of police. We wanted to affirm the fact that we would continue to seek pardons for Chacon and Puente and do so in public demonstrations, but that we would do so peacefully and nonviolently. I wanted to clear up any misunderstanding of the police confrontation with Latino youth.

Publicly, Harold Breier, chief of police, had gone on record that he would not meet with protesting groups, but the invitation had come not from us but from the mayor. The mayor's assistant asked us not to publicize the meeting arrangements. Nevertheless, word got out that a meeting had been proposed and agreed to, and the newspapers wanted to know who would attend and what would be discussed.

Chief Breier agreed to meet with us at Mayor Maier's office. Most of the narrative concerning Chief Breier during this period was negative. This was not one of those stories. In the barrio meeting beforehand, there were some disagreements on the number of people who would attend the meeting and who was going to speak on behalf of the community. There was a lot of interest from LAUCR, the Brown Berets, and other youth who were sore at the police for attacking the protesters at the Sixth Street Viaduct demonstration. I thought that we should stay focused on the intent of the march, seeking pardons for Chacon and Puente, and reaffirm our constitutional right to make our views heard in a peaceful, nonviolent manner. It was agreed that we would focus on the pardons and affirming our right to peaceful protest. A larger Latino group than agreed upon showed up at the mayor's meeting at the municipal building; this couldn't be helped, as there was tremendous interest among the Latino community. Several of us moved to sit around the mayor's desk, while the rest formed a ring around the outer walls of the mayor's office. The press was not allowed in and remained outside.

Chief Breier completely disarmed me early in the meeting. During our introduction, he interjected that his daughter had attended Oshkosh State and had known about my role in student government when I was enrolled in the early 1960s. Everyone was taken aback by our chatting about the connection. The congenial exchange was a great opening and reduced the tension, after which the rest of the discussion was constructive with little or no recriminations. Chief Breier made no public commitment other than that the police would continue to maintain safety and order in a fair manner, but his demeanor and his early comments about his daughter attending OSU spoke volumes about the success of the meeting. We got a glimpse of the chief that was counter to his image on the street. Mayor Maier surprised all of us by taking it upon himself to call Governor Lucey informing him of our meeting to discuss the pardons. The Milwaukee mayor asked the Wisconsin governor to look into it, and the governor, we understood, agreed to do so.

Before the meeting broke, Mayor Maier instructed Woody Welch to arrange for him and me to meet with the press outside his office. We were going to make a statement. On the way out the door, Woody told me that I should make the statement and answer any questions the reporters might have about the particulars. He would stand beside me and speak if needed. I took care to represent the meeting fairly, and there was never any need for Woody to speak other than to open and close the interview.

The following weekend, we finished the march that we had started several days before. At the community meeting ahead of the second march, we reported back on the meeting with Mayor Maier and Chief Breier. Everyone was elated, and we pledged to march peacefully and to fill the march with our families. Volunteers agreed to call the Racine/Kenosha

UMOS-supported center to participate. I brought my two-year-old son Miguel, and we marched to the Milwaukee County Courthouse grounds to plead our case for the pardons. At the county grounds, empty except for the several hundred Latino participants, the main speakers were Roberto Hernandez, Marla Anderson, Lalo Valdez, and me. It was a cold day, snowy and blustery. We walked back proud that we had been able to demonstrate peacefully our support for the pardons. On the way, Miguel became tired and I carried him almost all the way back across the Sixth Street Viaduct, where I had earlier been arrested and where Latino youth had confronted attacking police officers.

The process to gain the pardons for Chacon and Puente accelerated after the meeting with Mayor Maier and Chief Breier and came on the heels of the archbishop's letter, among other advancements. We continued to push the letter-writing campaign, sending letters to the Governor's Office in support of pardons. At the time, Governor Lucey's legal counsel was Sandy Williams, a competent and extremely thoughtful attorney. We urged him to review the charges, which we thought were unfair, and the conviction and sentencing, which were unjust.

Where I erred was in the final stages of the deliberation of the review of the governor's pardon with his chief of staff. At a meeting with Roberto Hernandez, Lalo Valdez, and others, in his office, the governor's chief of staff suggested that Chacon do some time first before being pardoned. I thought this outrageous and lost my cool. I stood up and vigorously argued against Chacon doing any prison time, as he had been convicted and sentenced unjustly and should not have to serve one day in jail. The pardon must be issued, I informed him, to prevent Chacon and Puente from serving any time at all. My actions were deemed threatening, and I found out later that I was no longer welcome in his office.

This was unfortunate as we were waiting for the governor to review recommendations from the Governor's Committee on Migratory Labor. Further, I had earlier been appointed to the Governor's Committee on Offender Rehabilitation and more recommendations were forthcoming after riots had broken out at Waupun State Prison. When the riots broke out in Waupun, I sent the governor a telegram recommending that he defuse tensions. I visited Waupun and other correctional facilities. At Waupun, I met with Latino prisoners and brought their concerns to the

Governor's Office. Lastly, I intervened when a Latina minor was incarcerated simply because she was pregnant and homeless and needed a temporary foster home rather than incarceration. Vel Phillips advocated for their release and the Valdez family agreed to foster the child so that she could be released, as she was being incarcerated basically for being a homeless Latina youth.

Preventing me from having access to the governor would affect issues that went beyond our demand for pardons for Chacon and Puente. They included legislative initiatives: proposed statutory changes to migrant labor laws that we had been working on with Professor Brandeis for a decade, a bilingual act that had emerged in the desegregation of Milwaukee Public Schools, and later revisions to UW–Madison's budget to incorporate the student Chicano Advisory Committee's recommendation for a Chicano Studies department. The Wisconsin Latino community had no representatives in the state legislature and depended on support from Wisconsin's progressive, labor, religious, and student communities to appear at hearings in support of our legislative agenda during the Lucey administration.

Thankfully, my outburst did not negatively affect the outcome for Puente and Chacon. Governor Lucey granted Puente and Chacon conditional pardons on April 7, 1971. It was a tremendous victory for the Latino community. First of all, it prevented innocent people from being charged, convicted, and sentenced to prison for exercising their constitutional rights. Among our community, it reaffirmed our commitment to not leave anyone behind. Chacon was an essential member of our community, but Puente's arrest had also occurred while supporting our cause. Our movement was built on community support, so it was important to stand by anyone willing to participate.

At the time, I thought it was essential that we not fail to take advantage of our relationships with the Lucey administration. Earlier misunderstandings were partially my fault, and I had shut myself out of the Governor's Office by my perceived threat to his chief of staff. Further, when the governor responded positively to the establishment of a Hispanic desk at his office, we failed to agree on a candidate who would represent us. Perhaps it was unrealistic to expect that all of the emerging Latino community-based organizations and community leaders could agree on all policy and

Governor Patrick Lucey tours the Milwaukee barrios with local community leaders from
UMOS, El Centro Hispano, and the Social Development Commission's Concentrated
Employment Program.

political appointments that impacted our community. In fact, in retro-
spect, it was a sign of political maturity to have diversity of opinion. Nevertheless, relationships deteriorated between the governor's cabinet and
staff members and some of us in the Latino community. Dissatisfaction
grew about the future role of the Governor's Committee on Migratory
Labor, its leadership, its recommendations, and in particular, its more
effective advocacy for the enforcement of migrant housing codes and labor
standards by the Department of Industry, Labor, and Human Relations.
By early August 1972, organizers had started discussions and meetings
about marching to Madison in protest.

24

SPLIT DECISION

I had resigned my position as director of UMOS in 1971 as part of my pledge to stay for only two funding periods. I had only taken the job when I saw that our demands had led to threat of resignation by all five non-Latino administrators unless they were given guarantees to their positions in December of 1968. After initially stating that I had no personal interest in UMOS, I publicly stated to fellow Chicano community leaders that I would stay only to protect UMOS from defunding. Now UMOS was again fully funded, with a network of supportive initiatives both public and private. Besides the collaboration with local employment and training programs through SDC's CEP project, we now collaborated with El Centro Hispano in referrals to MATC's vocational programs and later with UW–Milwaukee's SSOI postsecondary initiatives. I supported Salvador Sanchez, a former Obreros Unidos organizer, to succeed me at UMOS. I genuinely felt that as it related to migrant issues, Salvador and the team in place would provide strong leadership, along with an administration that included Beverly Seekamp in accounting, Alejandro Nieri in education, and Beba Medina as the Milwaukee-area coordinator anchoring the program. Additionally, Irene Santos provided effective leadership as the Racine/Kenosha-area coordinator, and the other migrant regions were led by young, energetic activists. Attorney Ness Flores with his thoughtful and deliberate manner provided excellent in-house assistance when our request for a full-time attorney was granted. By this point, Salvador and I had also hired Lupe Martinez, who would eventually succeed Salvador and lead UMOS for forty-five years. The team had demonstrated its ability to

249

lead. Salvador had to be given the opportunity to represent Wisconsin migrants and to develop strategies with this core group and its corresponding supporting Latino community-based organizations.

In the two OEO Migrant Division funding cycles during which I led UMOS, not only did I succeed in reinstating funding for UMOS, but I was able to obtain additional funds to expand the operations to other areas. The volunteers at UMOS established a migrant self-help housing program in southeastern Wisconsin and founded an economic development project by coordinating community-based organizations to pool their pension, health, and hospitalization outlays and to negotiate as a group for better benefits at lower costs. Projected savings in turn would be reinvested in community development projects.

UMOS funded the creation of Wisconsin's Southeastern Housing program; created and trained an advisory board; and hired Arturo Gonzales to develop teams of former migrant workers into self-help groups that would work together to develop sufficient "sweat equity" to obtain local financing to build new homes. But in regard to savings garnered by effectively leveraging moneys in the economic development project, UMOS and El Centro were the basis for the initiative. Although Salvador, Arturo, and I followed each respective board's direction, we depended on each other for our survival. This was threatened when, at a community strategy meeting, I disagreed about whether we should carry out a march to protest Wisconsin agencies' lack of an effective response to our demands. I didn't think we could do it without negatively impacting our relationships with the Governor's Office and legislative leaders who were working on our legislative initiatives. Governor Lucey had earlier visited Milwaukee's Latino community and had set up a Migrant Task Force to recommend statutory and administrative changes. I did not want to risk undoing that work.

At the community meeting called to discuss the march, Salvador asked for anyone not supporting it to leave the room. I was extremely worried how we could carry out a march against bureaucratic inefficiencies and not challenge the Governor's Office and our friend Phillip Lerman, head of the Department of Industry, Labor, and Human Relations (DILHR; formerly the Industrial Commission). I knew that the great majority of those migrant advocates in the room, including LAUCR leadership, supported

Salvador and his recommendation to march. I could not support him, nor would I walk out. I stayed quiet.

One of the biggest challenges that migrant advocates faced was to get state agencies, in particular the DILHR, to enforce social and progressive legislation that had been on the books for years but had not been enforced, including those recommendations that Professor Brandeis and I had initiated a decade before. The other was to respond to recommendations to establish work orders, to enhance the migrant housing code, and to effectively enforce it. The enforcement phase of dealing with inadequate, unsanitary, overcrowded conditions could only occur if we gave the housing inspectors the power to shut down noncompliant labor camps. We wanted to deputize them. I wasn't sure that the march would get us any closer to effectuating this. I thought we had the support for the Governor's Committee on Migrant Labor to design a policy and to have the newly named Wisconsin Industry and Human Relations Commission, under Lerman's leadership, carry it out. We also wanted the legislature to pass a bill addressing migrant rights, and for hearings to be held in Milwaukee.

Most of the participants supported Salvador and his call to organize a march from Milwaukee to Madison to protest the lack of action on migrant issues that had been discussed since Governor Lucey had met with community leaders in Milwaukee's near south side and Riverwest areas. UMOS had proceeded in one of the important services for migrants that Obreros Unidos had developed: access to legal services to advocate for the enforcement of Wisconsin's progressive legislation and to advocate and defend migrant seasonal workers. UMOS helped found Legal Action of Wisconsin when the OEO National Office ordered UMOS be reorganized with local legal services and had excellent legal assistance in attorneys Ness Flores and John Ebbott.

My lack of support of the march to Madison had long-term consequences. It reshaped my role in the Latino community. I immediately informed the group that once the decision to march had been made, I would not oppose it. I thought at the time that what was best was for me not to be part of the planning process or to attend meetings. In fact, as the march began, I was out of town, on my way back from Texas.

The economic development corporation I led at this time targeted not only emerging Latino community-based organizations but other

UMOS protesters march from Milwaukee to the State Capitol in August 1972 to urge the legislature to do more to protect migrant seasonal farmworkers. UMOS Director Salvador Sanchez (wearing a hat and sunglasses) leads the march.

SDC-funded agencies as well. As part of the plan, we presented proposals to other national, OEO-funded migrant programs. We were invited to present our national economic development plan to the Indiana and Michigan state migrant boards of directors. My visit to Crystal City at the time of the march was for a previously scheduled presentation to federally funded agencies now led by Chicanos as a result of recent electoral victories. UMOS had been able to accumulate yearly cost savings from its programs and invest them in health insurance and pensions for more than one hundred employees. I traveled to Crystal City in 1972 to make a presentation on how organizations there could achieve similar financial success.

After visiting Crystal City that summer, I considered returning and joining the political counterrevolt that had begun with school walkouts and the formation of an independent third political party, La Raza Unida. La Raza Unida administered federally funded projects such as the ongoing urban renewal project and the housing authority initiative that was being led by Rodolfo Palomo, a former Obreros Unidos organizer during the 1968 summer. The Crystal City Council had been retaken by Chicanos, and Panchillo Rodriguez, another former Obreros Unidos organizer, was city manager, Palomo was urban renewal director, and my uncle Julian was Crystal City's municipal judge. But I could not just abandon Wisconsin.

With the present split from UMOS and the fact that my wife, Glorie, and I were divorcing, I considered choices other than remaining in Milwaukee, but I was extremely concerned about being so far removed from our son, Miguel. Glorie and I had agreed on our incompatibility, but I had made a bad situation worse by dating another woman, Viviana, who became pregnant before the divorce was finalized. Viviana's family was greatly offended by my behavior, and we exacerbated the situation by departing without their permission to Madison to have the baby. I took a job as an outreach worker with DILHR. Although I enjoyed working with Joe McLain and John Gauthier, both of whom I had known from Milwaukee's protests, it was not what I had anticipated doing. Nonetheless, I had no choice but to make a living and sustain my new family. Viviana and our infant daughter Gabriela soon returned to Milwaukee. I left for Wautoma, where I had not permanently lived for nearly ten years, when I first returned to the labor camps to organize the migrant education programs and later Obreros Unidos.

My departure from Milwaukee was solely my decision, because I did not want my disagreement with Salvador and other community leaders to be public. I had seen how the disagreement between Crystal City's political leaders Juan Cornejo and Moises Falcon had fractured the Chicano political coalition there and led to the Anglo minority taking advantage of the community fissure to return to power. I didn't want our personal disagreement to affect UMOS's direction and future funding.

My return to Wautoma was both timely and welcomed, but for the wrong reasons. Both of my parents were glad to have me, but my mother was not feeling well and needed medical attention. Local doctors at first thought she had an asthmatic condition or some form of bronchitis. I contacted a doctor and professor of medicine at UW–Madison's hospitals, whom I had met through Professor Brandeis and who had been helpful in bringing the first migrant health services to Waushara County in the

mid-1960s. He made arrangements to have a specialist see her. The long
and short of it was she needed a break from the restaurant. After toiling
over a poorly ventilated grill for nearly two decades, her lungs were dam-
aged. Although she had never smoked, her lungs exhibited the signs of
a miner or a lifelong smoker from inhaling the exhaust from the smok-
ing grill.

My brother Frank and his new bride, Barbara, had moved from the
Milwaukee area first to help the family with Brocks Motel, which my parents had acquired in 1967. Frank and Barbara later bought a small farm to
raise horses and provide horseback-riding lessons. Rodolfo, upon his return from Vietnam, had married Maria, sister of Salvador Sanchez, and
later taken over the restaurant, freeing my mother from the grill. She and
my father decided to manage Brocks Motel, which greatly helped my
mother's health.

Panchillo, my boyhood friend and fellow Obreros Unidos organizer
who had been recruited to become the first Chicano city manager of Crystal City, was interested in returning to Wisconsin. I informed him that I
was living in Wautoma and not in Milwaukee. He said he would join me in
Wautoma. From there we would plot our return not to Milwaukee but to
Madison. He applied for and was selected as Chicano minority recruiter
for UW–Madison. When he moved to Madison, on Doty Street, he lived
closer to the Wisconsin State Capitol than to the university, where we
would spend almost as much time. He rented a multibedroom apartment
so that when my parents closed the motel after deer-hunting season, I
could have a place to hang my hat. I moved to Madison as fall was ending
and proceeded to complete my application for admittance as a graduate
student in the Department of Political Science. I began my studies in
mid-academic year that January.

I could not have moved to Madison without Panchillo's assistance. I
also could not have sustained myself as a graduate student without his
paying the rent and household expenses.

25

LEGISLATIVE PROGRESS ON CAMPUS

Salvador Sanchez, as UMOS's director, had succeeded in carrying out the migrant march without rupturing the Latino relationship with Governor Lucey and especially Wisconsin's legislative leadership. He was right, and I was wrong. The march accelerated our legislative agenda. Now, we had to execute it! I was happy to be in Madison supporting it. I continued to have excellent relationships with Assemblyman Lloyd Barbee and Reverend Monroe Swan, who would later be elected state senator and hire my brother Carlos as his administrative assistant. They, in addition to support from Wisconsin Assembly speaker George Molinaro of Racine/Kenosha and later state Senator Carl Otte from Sheboygan, as well as other legislators that the Dane County Human Rights Council and labor lobbyists had introduced me to as early as 1966, made it possible to have a legislative agenda without having a single Latino representative in either of Wisconsin's legislative chambers.

The legislative agenda that emerged began with the decades-long attempt to enforce the state's progressive legislation that impacted more than fifteen thousand annual migrant workers. How does a community battle for decades? What sustains organized, multiyear efforts with few, if any, gains? Why do some organizations continue to battle after suffering defeat after defeat? After organizing migrant farmworkers for nearly five years, we never gained a contract in spite of the fact that we showed through marches, strikes, walkouts, and elections that the workers wanted to be represented by Obreros Unidos, the Wisconsin farmworkers union.

Migrant families in the first strike in 1966 endured because they were effectively organized for community. But the community succeeds in its efforts when its members are effectively led. Farmworkers' leadership was never about one person leading or making all of the substantive decisions. Since most of the actions undertaken impacted families, major decisions were always deliberated and undertaken by the collective action of families. The nature of the workforce was family based. When we organized in the labor camps, we organized entire families, not heads of households; that would have meant that most decisions would be carried out by men. Our attempts at organizing never wavered long after we left the labor camps after the 1968 Libby's summer walkouts and started organizing in urban areas. In the barrio, families were at the center of our organizing efforts, not in labor camps, but meeting in large halls of social service organizations that we had organized and now administered.

A decade-long process of hearings and written recommendations had developed respective parts of what would become the Wisconsin Migrant Labor Act of 1975. When Governor Lucey agreed to visit Latino neighborhoods in 1970, in spite of the fact that we faced formidable challenges in accommodating the resettlement of displaced migrant workers in Wisconsin urban areas, the written recommendations we handed him were primarily on migrant worker issues. Later, he ordered Phillip Lerman at DILHR to hold hearings in Milwaukee on proposed administrative law changes. The UMOS protest march to the capitol in 1972 helped speed the passage of the law.

Our other major legislative initiative, the Bilingual–Bicultural Education Act of 1976, was compelled by the US Supreme Court decision *Lau v. Nichols*, which ordered the San Francisco Unified School District to instruct the dominant Chinese-speaking students in their own language. Like the proposed Wisconsin Migrant Act, Wisconsin's bilingual education initiative had a decade-long history. It began in 1962 with a project funded by the Wisconsin Division of Children and Youth to provide child care and early education to Spanish-language-dominant migrant children. The Bilingual Education Act of 1968 was of limited assistance for the bilingual initiatives being undertaken both in the Wisconsin rural school districts and the Milwaukee Public School System (MPS), which was also being challenged by attorney Lloyd Barbee's desegregation lawsuit. The establishment of UW–Milwaukee's Spanish Speaking Outreach Institute in the 1970s, which established parameters for recruiting and academically assisting educational staff for both Latino community-based educational programs as well as Milwaukee Public Schools, proved crucial. As the legal aspect of the MPS desegregation lawsuit proceeded through courtrooms and boardrooms, school walkouts demanded a culturally relevant curriculum in the Walker's Point barrio, including recognition and celebration of fiesta patria holidays.

Following its reorganization, UMOS expanded educational curriculum to incorporate bilingual instruction under new educational offerings that broadened its already excellent instructional and academic staff. They laid the instructional foundations and trained personnel for the forthcoming MPS bilingual–bicultural programs that appeared as a result of the 1968 law but which began to be widespread after the Wisconsin Bilingual–Bicultural Education Act.

Most important was the establishment of the UW–Milwaukee SSOI in 1970 and the hiring of former Marquette professor Ricardo Fernandez as director and later Luis "Tony" Baez as his assistant. Besides establishing the outreach design, mission, and services in Milwaukee's Latino community, Fernandez and Baez began to issue reports and recommendations for both bilingual/bicultural education as well as the desegregation of MPS and other urban public educational systems. Their leadership in recommending the theoretical framework for bilingual education based on our community experience was crucial in creating an effective Wisconsin Bilingual–Bicultural Education Act. Attorneys Ness Flores and John Ebbott, who had begun working together in UMOS's funded legal services in the early 1970s and then helped establish Wisconsin's Legal Action, were key in providing the legal expertise and content for the Migrant Labor Act.

A turning point happened in 1974, when the Chicano Studies Advisory Board in the UW–Madison College of Letters and Sciences recommended a Chicano Studies department, and the administrators responded negatively. The UW Board of Regents was retreating from established goals for system-wide minority recruitment and retention. UW–Madison Chicano students initiated the legislative agenda that would begin with amending the UW–Madison budget to include fifty thousand dollars to initiate

Chicano Studies, support the Bilingual–Bicultural Education Act and Migrant Labor Act, and initiate the successful support of the Migrant Tuition Bill.

Although we had succeeded in amending the UW–Madison budget to include Chicano Studies, the College of Letters and Science had not requested the academic program and resisted implementing it. Chicano students and the greater Latino community faced a protracted battle to implement the state's legislative intent. At that time, I was broke, and my roommate Panchillo and I were behind on our rent. My involvement in UW's Latino student activities had led to my taking incompletes for my graduate courses, and I could not get my scholarship renewed until I finished my incomplete work. I had to get a job and took one with La Raza Unida Political Party in the county of Zavala, Texas. The county had just gotten a planning grant for an economic development initiative.

In Texas, I put a team together and organized a membership organization that would establish a board to plan and carry out investments for the Zavala County Economic Development Corporation. Every time I traveled, I made sure to visit Madison to meet with community and student leaders on the status of the UW–Madison response to Chicano Studies. After three years in Texas, I returned to Wisconsin and worked for a year with Ernesto

Students rally in the Great Hall at Memorial Union to establish a Chicano Studies department at the University of Wisconsin–Madison, circa 1975. WHI IMAGE ID 128566

Chacon and LAUCR. We collaborated on community initiatives, including after-school programs for MPS-enrolled Latino students and events for Fiesta Mexicana, after obtaining access to celebrate Mexican independence in the developing Summerfest grounds on the Lake Michigan lakefront. Most exciting, I helped Chacon by supporting LAUCR's newly formed office in Madison.

I could not immediately return to my graduate studies in the Department of Political Science due to my incompletes in two courses. I needed to complete those courses before I could request readmission to the department. I had to finish the courses during the final year of my leave of absence, which would expire after five years, or risk losing my status as a graduate student. Most importantly, I could not just move to Madison and crash in Panchillo's apartment, finish my work, and reapply for my scholarship and supporting financial aid. I had remarried, and I had a son in Milwaukee and a daughter in Berlin, Wisconsin, during this time. I was now applying for housing assistance and had made an application to UW–Madison's Eagle Heights family housing compound for graduate and professional married students. My wife, Imelda, helped type my papers.

I worked with LAUCR for the year before I was readmitted to the Department of Political Science and personally continued my efforts to implement the legislative mandate to create a Chicano Studies program. Two fellow LAUCR employees were crucial in reenergizing the community to support UW–Madison's Chicano students. Irma Guerra Morales organized resettled migrant families in the Lake Mills and Jefferson area, while Rosa Escamilla worked in Madison.

Irma later enrolled in UW–Madison's graduate program and Rosa in UW–Madison's Law School. Irma's enrollment brought Lutecia Gonzales, a UW–Madison Law School student and migrant law advocate, who added a crucial aspect to our student effort. All three were mothers and were wonderful assets as well as role models and mentors for our younger Chicana undergraduate students whom we were recruiting. Rosa, with student and community support, became the first Latina elected to Madison's city council. Following graduation, Lutecia would become an Equal Opportunity Office administrator, while Irma, along with Pedro Rodriguez and later Alfredo Luna, organized support for early community development initiatives in the Lake Mills and Jefferson areas.

At UW–Madison, we enjoyed an excellent relationship with other minority student groups, especially with the American Indian student organization Wunk Sheek. We would eventually be housed in the same building, with offices next to each other for several decades; the weekly Native American drum became part of both of our experiences. Chicano political manifestation, as well as social gatherings, often opened with this sound. Our dances were tied to this beat.

La Raza Unida's students also had access to the University Catholic Center's large basement meeting room with adjoining kitchen facilities, where we began to raise funds by selling tacos. Obreros Unidos had ten years earlier been successful in union fundraising activities that included taco sales in local city parks. We reached out to the Latino community and began to invite them to UW–Madison student organization La Raza Unida events. Our fiesta celebrations on campus were not exclusively student events. They were filled with recently resettled migrant families. We brought issues to the microphone that had to do with their interests, including equitable employment practices by local industries, protests against Immigration and Naturalization Service (INS) raids, and criticism of the Simpson–Mazzoli immigration bill that included employer sanctions for those who hired the undocumented.

We also sought support of Chicano students' demands for university minority enrollment and retention efforts in the Latino community. We continued our links to the Milwaukee community-based organizations and called them for statewide La Raza Unida events and student-organized area-wide meetings and cultural celebrations. The fiesta celebrations included dances, and scores of families joined us at the UW Memorial Union, where we sang and danced until closing time. La Raza Unida provided key support for Los Hermanos Avila, pre-Columbian danzas and drums that became part of all of our gatherings, social as well as political. Tony Castaneda founded Olmeca, a band that played Latin jazz fusion music that brought hundreds to Ricardo Gonzales's Cardinal Bar fundraisers, where we communicated our message, celebrated our heritage, and danced to our sounds.

Both UMOS's resettled migrants in the Dane County area and the City of Madison's newly established Organizacion Hispana Americana (OHA) joined La Raza Unida students' picket line on Bascom Hill. OHA families set up a soup kitchen and brought food for those on the picket line. LAUCR brought busloads of supporters from Milwaukee to the picket line on Bascom Hill throughout the spring of 1975. Most effective was the student/community strategy to lobby the Wisconsin legislature to respond to Chicano/Latino needs.

—‖—

What was unique about Wisconsin was that since there were no Latinos in the Wisconsin legislature at the time of the act, the mother of the acts was not a particular legislator but the migrant and former migrant worker community as a whole. We designed the Migrant Labor Act in the migrant fields and Latino educational community-based organizations in the barrios.

The Wisconsin legislature created a line item in its 1975 budget to fund the Chicano Studies program, but UW–Madison dragged its feet. The dean of the College of Letters and Sciences moved the Chicano Studies funds to the School of Education. In 1976 the Chicano Studies program focused on recruiting and retaining students but offered no Chicano academic courses as per its funding. It did not name a faculty adviser to guide it or to set up a representative advisory committee that met irregularly. The first faculty hired for the Chicano Studies program was denied tenure. For a time, the program was led by non-tenure track faculty and even graduate students, who could not offer academic courses as the Wisconsin legislature had intended.

Chicano campus organizing accelerated through the early 1980s, often moving beyond our university-based demands. The campus La Raza Unida organization by unanimous consent reorganized itself as Movimiento Educacional Chicano de Aztlan (MEChA) and began a series of daylong political workshops for community members and students to address a broad-based response to administration recalcitrance in establishing Chicano Studies academic courses on campus. Professor Prospero Saíz, chair of the Comparative Literature Department, was instrumental in organizing the workshops to deliberate on strategies that would guide us during this time. In the spring of 1982, a statewide meeting of Chicanos was called on campus in support of several MEChA-proposed resolutions for UW–Madison. Families from Racine/Kenosha, Milwaukee, Oshkosh, and Wautoma attended. They also received support from another campus organization,

MEChA members protest in opposition to President Reagan's Central American policies.

Students for Positive Change. The resolutions called for a more substantial Chicano Studies program, as well as opposition to President Ronald Reagan's intervention in Central America.

MEChA invited national Chicano organizations and leaders to join in its demand. In March 1982, the famed Chicano activist Reies Lopes Tijerina keynoted our statewide meeting. For the Cinco de Mayo celebration, MEChA was joined by Baldemar Velasquez, director of the Farmworkers Labor Organizing Committee. Jose Angel Gutierrez, La Raza Unida Political Party leader, frequently visited Wisconsin's resettled Tejanos who supported the third-party movement. MEChA students attended national Chicano movement meetings and made connections across the country. Locally, MEChA agreed to return in the 1983–84 academic year to the Chicano Advisory Committee format to discuss the status of the Chicano Studies academic courses only after it was agreed that we would select our own representatives.

When Professor Harland E. Sampson, associate dean of the School of Education, made available a list of names for Chicano Studies director, MEChA opposed the list of names. None of the faculty members for consideration were Chicano, nor did they have a previous meaningful interest in Chicano Studies. Most importantly, we demanded that Chicano Studies academic courses be offered by the College of Letters and Sciences, as intended in the original recommendations to establish a Chicano Studies Department, not in the present School of Education. When talks with the university failed, MEChA returned to the Wisconsin legislature as it had done in 1975.

We demanded that the Wisconsin legislature address Latino access to Wisconsin postsecondary institutions, including UW–Madison, as well as consideration of in-state tuition for children of migrants who had previously toiled in Wisconsin's seasonal harvest. While these students qualified for enrollment, they were charged out-of-state tuition. Mario Caballero, outreach worker for Legal Action of Wisconsin's Migrant Division, had advocated more effective enforcement of housing regulations and violations of minimum wage laws during the summer months. He took the lead in circulating MEChA's proposed Migrant Tuition Bill. Mario sought legislative sponsors, organized community support for respective hearings, and later lobbied for its passage. We focused on our legislative initiative with a phone call and letter-writing campaign and appeared before the Joint Finance Committee. We secured a vote of 11–3 to recommend Senate Bill 317 and send it to both reconvening Wisconsin legislative chambers in February 1984. It passed!

Mario Cabellero testifies before the legislature on the migrant tuition law.

—||—

We strengthened our links to the broader Latino community by first of all engaging and addressing community issues and supporting OHA and UMOS by volunteering to serve on their boards. We joined them in seeking equitable adequate housing and job opportunities in the Madison and Jefferson area. MEChA in its newspaper, *Portavoz*, protested Reagan's INS raids as well as the lack of implementation of the 1975 Office of Civil Rights Law Remedies. We also demanded the immediate implementation of the US Supreme Court's *Plyler v. Doe* decision, which ordered local school boards to provide children of undocumented families access to a free public education.

On campus, all Chicano student candidates to the Wisconsin Student Association as well as campus faculty, staff, and student bodies, including the Chicano Advisory Committee, were elected at Raza workshops. We enjoyed excellent relationships with other campus minority groups and later welcomed the campus LGBT's Ten Percent Society in our office at 710 University Avenue on top of the bar, The Store. MEChA joined Wunk Sheek in its demonstration in support of fishing and spearing rights in northern Wisconsin. Our protest of Reagan's retreat on bilingual education and access to education for children of undocumented immigrants was joined by other campus organizations and student leaders who also protested Reagan's Central American policies: the invasion of Grenada and support of the Contras and the right-wing subversion of the Nicaraguan democratically elected government.

The July 1983 program and rally against Reagan's Nicaraguan policies at UW–Madison's Stock Pavilion was sponsored by the Union for International Action and MEChA, who spoke of racist university policies. MEChA also appeared with Farm Labor Organizing Committee leaders, who joined other local labor leaders in addressing farmworkers, as well as UW–Madison's Teaching Assistants Association, the union representing graduate student workers. Luis Echevarria, a musician and Puerto Rican activist, performed. After the event, more than one thousand people participated in a candlelit march down State Street to the federal building, where speeches defended Central American people's legitimate right to self-determination and criticized Reagan's cutbacks of social programs.

MEChA students reformulated their message to reach a broader audience through publications. Juan Montoya founded and edited *Portavoz* throughout his graduate work, bringing to the community reprints from other Chicano publications, poems, and Mexican Revolution art. Glyphs from Aztec writings blazed across each page. In November 1983, *Portavoz's* last issue was published. The front page showed a picture, taken by William Lanier, of Chicano students marching up UW–Madison's Bascom Hill, site of the College of Letters and Science office in South Hall. On it, there were three headlines: "Raza Barrios Invaded," "Reagonomics and Granada," and the latest report of "Raza Political Workshops."

UW–Madison's MEChA students enhanced their message by publishing a series of publications under the *La Onda* banner. *La Onda's* initial publication, which replaced *Portavoz*, featured the return of Chicano students to the Wisconsin state legislature to support Chicano Studies at UW–Madison and to establish a Migrant Tuition Bill. Since MEChA's first lobbying efforts, the Wisconsin legislature had passed two Latino-focused bills, the Bilingual–Bicultural Education Act and the Migrant Labor Act. In December 1983, MEChA-initiated legislation, known as the Migrant Tuition Bill (SB 317), was in the final stages of being passed. Once again UW–Madison administrators observed the successful lobbying initiatives of Chicano students. Once the Migrant Tuition Bill passed in 1984, we continued to lobby Wisconsin legislators to address the UW Board of Regents' failure in meeting minority recruitment and retention goals and in implementing Chicano Studies at UW–Madison.

The Raza Political Workshops decided that *La Onda* publication for the 1984–85 academic year would be a special edition focusing exclusively on UW and the failure of the Board of Regents to address minority enrollment and the lack of minority faculty. The publication was revised to be used for legislative lobbying and in organizing Latino community support for MEChA students. The research was later updated for testimony before the Wisconsin Assembly Select Committee on the Future of Wisconsin's University System, chaired by Assemblyman Thomas Loftus. After MEChA testified at the January 14, 1986, hearing, heavily attended by UW system staff, UW–Madison's administration, and college heads, Wisconsin legislators asked UW representatives to respond, to repudiate our detailed research on UW system failures. None could and none did!

The following academic year, affirmative responses to MEChA's demands finally began to appear. Chicano Studies was transferred from UW–Madison's School of Education to the College of Letters and Sciences in 1988. In 1990, Dr. Richard Flores, assistant professor of anthropology, was hired as acting director. The following two years, Assistant Professor Ruben Donato, Educational Policy Studies; Assistant Professor Ben Marquez, Political Science; and Professor Ruben Medina, Spanish, joined Professor Prospero Saíz, who had earlier taught the first Chicano Studies courses at UW–Madison. Hired by the UW History Department, I designed and taught two Chicano Studies 300-level courses that drew more than one hundred students in the first several semesters. With the support of teaching assistants, we enhanced retention rates by encouraging students to take advantage of academic support math and writing labs.

As wonderful as this teaching experience was, I could not leave Milwaukee Area Technical College, where I had been teaching since receiving my UW–Madison graduate degree in political science from UW–Madison. Nevertheless, my short tenure showed positive student response to our multidisciplinary approach to Chicano Studies. This led to a Chicano Studies certificate in 1994 and with the hiring of Professor Dionne Espinosa, assistant professor of Women's Studies, one of the most innovative and exciting programs emerged at UW–Madison.

—||—

As a member of UW system Board of Regents in 2003, I continued to support Chicano and Latino students by first of all maintaining support for Minority Disadvantage Programs during biannual budget cutbacks. Later, I sponsored a resolution encouraging UW system chancellors to admit qualified undocumented Latino and Latina students to UW system universities.

I met with UW–Milwaukee and UW–Madison Chancellor's Offices to encourage their support for the resolution. Later at UW–Madison, at the request of MEChA, I met with the dean of the College of Letters and Sciences and Chicano Studies faculty to enhance programming, and with UW–Madison's provost to find comparable office space for MEChA after the Board of Regents displaced the group from their forty-year residence near Frances Street and University Avenue. MEChA agreed to move to 206 Bernard Court, where they continue to reside to this day.

With strong support from the Latino and Chicano communities, alumni and students, Chicano Studies changed its name to the Chican@/Latin@ Studies Program in 2005, and the UW–Madison graduate school approved a Chican@/Latin@ doctoral minor in 2007. With an affiliated faculty of more than two dozen members, the program was granted departmental status, a crucial step. The decades-long struggle to establish a Chicano Studies department that was first initiated in 1975 by UW–Madison Chicano students was now bearing fruit.

26

LEGACY OF THE
FARMWORKERS MOVEMENT

The Chicano Studies department at UW–Madison is the university's only known academic program created by students. Its success was based on immediate and continued support by the Chicano community. We organized support for Chicano Studies, as we had earlier organized families in Milwaukee's barrios as well as farmworkers in central Wisconsin fields.

Obreros Unidos organizers previously had successfully sustained an effort to organize migrant seasonal workers because it organized whole families residing in migrant labor camps throughout three Wisconsin counties, Waushara, Marquette, and Portage. By organizing families, the union brought women and youth into the fore of all decisions on union activity. Women not only challenged the overcrowded and unsanitary housing conditions, they also joined the men in demanding changes to poor wages and working conditions, in particular the lack of potable water and sanitary facilities in the field. As the movement grew, women challenged their second-class status, carryovers of Spanish and Mexican colonial practices that relegated them to a lower tier when in fact they were at the center of the effectiveness of the family base workforce.

The organizational initiatives in the labor camps during the farmworkers movement were replaced in the Milwaukee urban barrio by mass meetings that took place in the emerging Latino community-based organization centers: El Centro Hispano, UMOS, and the ample offices of the Concentrated Employment Program at Fifth and National. The efforts to organize resettled families in urban barrios was family based, just as they had been in the fields. The way we came together was the only way we knew how, a cooperative community approach in the tradition of the sociedad funeraria. It was through such organizations in my Texas hometown that I learned of organizing and mutual assistance, long before I knew of the need to come together to negotiate wages and working conditions, support the grape boycott, or push for better inclusion of and services for Mexican Americans in communities and on campus. The daily social and economic interactions that I experienced growing up in the Mexico Grande settlement that my grandparents helped found in 1906 were guided by a community that believed in those fundamental values. Those values carried me as I became part of a transnational movement, one that stretched from Wisconsin to California. Hearing of César Chávez's grape boycott and protest march in 1966 was the spark that led me to join the movement and organize our own march from Wautoma and to Madison to protest migrant wages, living quarters, and working conditions. Our five-year organizational efforts expanded over time to encompass the publication of a union newspaper that encouraged farmworkers to join the movement, provision of free legal services by volunteer attorneys, a gas cooperative for union members, and a migrant health center.

Obreros Unidos achieved a number of successes over the five years it operated, starting a statewide conversation about the living and working conditions of migrant workers that led to the Migrant Labor Act of 1975. Gaining official union recognition was a key turning point, confirming the rights of migrant workers to organize for collective bargaining. We gained a seat at the negotiating table. By the early 1970s, however, many of the jobs migrant workers had done had been automated, and the union had lost national and state funding support. Many former migrant workers who remained in the state moved to urban areas to find work, where they needed different kinds of assistance to access job training, education, housing, and other services.

As my brother Manuel and others continued to organize farm workers through the early 1970s, I had moved to Milwaukee to focus on the grape boycott and community organizing. While working parallel to and often in cooperation with the civil rights movement, the community focus of my heritage melded with newly learned direct action strategies. We demanded better within our community organizations such as UMOS while also demanding better from our state.

Through it all, education was a recurring theme in my life, as I spent time on college campuses as a student, an organizer, and eventually a faculty member, my own experiences informing my drive for better inclusion and opportunities for students. In 1961, when my brother Manuel and I enrolled at Oshkosh State College, now UW–Oshkosh, we were the only Chicanos on campus. Later, when I took classes at Stevens Point College, now UW–Stevens Point, I was again the only Chicano. In the fall of 1968 at UW–Milwaukee, out of a total student enrollment that exceeded 25,000 students, all the Latino students could sit around one table. This was typical of all UW system schools at the time. When I enrolled in UW–Madison's political science graduate program in 1973, I was the only Chicano in the department again. Even in our own community organizations, Mexican Americans struggled for representation due to their lack of advanced education. The Latinization of the major southside community service organizations could not be successful without better access to UW–Milwaukee's programs as most of the jobs required post-secondary education and all educational program staff required educational credits or college degrees. As more Mexican American families remained in Wisconsin in search of opportunities, subsequent generations found many doors closed to them due to lack of higher education.

The community experience of the multiyear effort to establish UW–Milwaukee's SSOI would serve us well in the decade-long struggle to establish Chicano Studies at UW–Madison. Even after years of organizing experience, the complex UW system presented new challenges to us. The campuses were each guided by a chancellor who loosely directed almost autonomous colleges and schools, which in turn were led by respective deans. Non-academic entities such as admissions, financial aid, academic support, and libraries were separately guided. Most interesting was the role of student input though through elected student governments, in particular in the expenditure of segregated funds. Two additional entities remained unknown to us: one, the recently established UW System's Board of Regents and two, the Wisconsin legislature. We learned as we went along.

Beginning in the 1973–74 academic year, UW–Madison Chicano students were the key to making the Wisconsin Idea a reality to the Latino community. When Chicano students returned home for Christmas or summer vacation, they were overwhelmed with invitations to return to their local community schools and encourage high school students to apply to UW–Madison or other UW campuses. MEChA students served as personal guides through the application process, assisting applicants in seeking financial aid and even hosting them in their private residences until their dormitory assignment came through.

Since the Mexican independence celebration on September 16 was the first major Mexican cultural and social event of the fall semester, new students were immediately initiated with mariachi music on Library Mall in the afternoon and more music and dance at the Memorial Union in the evening.

—||—

In spite of the fact that I graduated in 1985 with my master's degree in political science, because of the recession, I could not find a full-time job at Madison Area Technical College, where I had begun to teach part-time. This was a wonderful job but with insufficient pay, as I still qualified for food stamps to sustain my wife, two children, and another on the way. I applied for and was hired at Milwaukee Area Technical College in late 1986. During the first six months of my assignment in Milwaukee in 1987, because I didn't have a reliable vehicle, I took the Badger Bus for the round trip. I was never late or missed a class for the first six months.

I permanently moved to Milwaukee that fall where except for a slight interruption I taught for the next twenty years, but I never disassociated myself from UW–Madison. The core of the College of Letters and Science faculty members, led initially by comparative literature chairperson Prospero Saíz, generated a tremendous response from UW–Madison students, including recently recruited Chicanos. From 1997 to 1999, I was able to reconnect with Madison after being hired as a senior lecturer to develop and teach two 300-level courses in the history department. I adjusted my MATC schedule so I could have both Tuesday and Thursday afternoons off to spend with UW–Madison students.

Although I looked forward to teaching courses that reflected my political science studies, I agreed to initiate bilingual basic skills courses in Spanish and English at MATC for dominant Spanish-language adult students, including many young high school graduates who could qualify for the two-year associate's degree or vocational career of their choice. The effort grew into a program with additional bilingual programs, with both Hmong and Spanish faculty hired to serve the growing minority population at MATC. My weekends were also kept busy after MATC applied for and was selected to fulfill a citizenship requirement for the Immigration Reform Act that provided amnesty for undocumented immigrants who completed and passed a course in their application for US citizenship. I designed the curriculum that saw hundreds of students attend the weekend courses. Over the twenty years, I was active in the American Federation of Teachers/AFL-CIO's Local 212 and later served in several positions in its executive committee.

My moving to Milwaukee allowed me to continue to support UMOS as a board of directors member from 1988 to 1989 and to volunteer for Fiesta Mexicana. The celebration of September 16 that we had carried out with Milwaukee Public School walkouts in the early 1970s coincided with Latino community support of bilingual education, the hiring of bilingual teachers, and the demand of recognition of our culture and history.

After moving the festivities to the Summerfest grounds in 1977, the first several celebrations were quite challenging as we wanted to hold it as close to September 16 as possible. Fall weather along Lake Michigan is quite unpredictable and sometimes rainy and turbulent and quite chilly. When the opportunity arose in 1987, the celebration was moved to late August and reorganized into the Wisconsin Hispanic Scholarship Foundation celebrating Fiesta Mexicana and offering food, music, and culture over three days. Most significantly, the new organization was focused on raising funds to offer scholarships for Latino youth. Since its inception it has become the premier community effort in raising funds for Latino youth who want to pursue a college education, awarding more than $1.7 million to date. This is done through the dedication of nearly a thousand volunteers to administer the presale of tickets, man the gates from noon to closing, support the three main musical stages that perform concurrently, and man the multitude of cultural events and exhibitions that feature Mexican and other Latin American culture held throughout the Summerfest grounds. Before the pandemic, more than eighty thousand individuals attended the event.

Regarding Latino scholarship initiatives, two more should be mentioned. A decade ago, when UW–Milwaukee's Roberto Hernandez Center was celebrating its fortieth anniversary, a scholarship endowment fund was established for Latino students at UW–Milwaukee. A decade later, the endowment fund that was created now exceeds more than two hundred thousand dollars. It presently awards Roberto Hernandez Center emergency grants that total ten thousand dollars a year by granting twenty awards of five hundred dollars each annually. At UW–Madison's Chican@/Latin@ Studies Program, faculty established the Regent Salas Activist Award Scholarship in 2006 and awards scholarships of five hundred dollars yearly. Additionally, Emerita "Tess" Arenas and former chancellor John Wiley established the Somos Students and Faculty Development Award with yearly grants of fifteen hundred dollars to students and faculty.

These funds we developed by and for the Latino community principally because of the lack of access to established state and federal financial programs. To date, qualified Wisconsin high school graduates whose undocumented parents brought them to the United States as children were regarded as non-residents, making them out-of-state applicants required to pay higher tuition and preventing them from qualifying for federal assistance. When these students gained access to in-state tuition, it not only removed a financial hindrance but was an acknowledgment that those who had lived and worked in Wisconsin for many years were truly residents of this state.

—II—

While in Madison, we cultivated a core group of Latino undergraduates with students recruiting and supporting fellow students. In contrast, at UW–Milwaukee, the first one hundred undergrad students enrolled came from the network of the established barrio community-based organizations that had protested to demand the establishment of the Spanish Speaking Outreach Institute (now the Roberto Hernandez Center). We had opened UW–Milwaukee's doors ourselves; we had not waited for the chancellor to decide if he wanted us. While negotiations were ongoing with the Chancellor's Office, we began to enroll program staff, community board members, and most important opened the door to the whole family. These included new Spanish language-dominant adult learners who had obtained their GED or were enhancing their basic skills at barrio community agencies. Over the years, MATC and UW–Milwaukee facilitated the transfer of credits from the two-year associate's degree with UW–Madison's baccalaureate programs.

As a result of these efforts, the enrollment of Latino students has grown from a handful in 1968 to 13 percent, or 2,646, of UW–Milwaukee's enrolled students by 2022. In the spring of 2022, UW–Milwaukee's Roberto Hernandez Center celebrated graduating 512 bachelor's degree recipients with much more varied career interests than those fifty years ago. The College of Letters and Science continued to be one of the university's top five schools with 659 Latino enrolled students, while the School of Business had 354. And 14.8 percent of students at the School of Nursing, responding to the demands of the growing US health system, were Latino. About 80 percent of UW–Milwaukee graduates remain in Wisconsin, a virtual treasure for Latino community development. They leave school armed with an education, career prospects, and tools to contribute to the communities that fought to provide these opportunities. In many ways, they are fulfilling the broader goals of the farmworkers movement.

While many students attend college with an eye to the future, a significant number focus on their heritage as well. In 2020 UW–Madison's Chican@/Latin@ Studies Program, which covers the peoples and cultures of Mexican and Latin American origin, celebrated the graduation of 763 students with bachelor's degrees. Enrollees in the program complete coursework in a variety of academic disciplines while gaining a broad knowledge of diverse Latino and Latina populations. The top degrees received in 2020 were computer and information services, economics, and math for men, and general psychology, general biological sciences, and international public health for women.

The program is one of the most innovative and successful at UW–Madison. Among the many certificate programs on campus, it was number one in the offering of more than one hundred certificates. While UW graduates contribute to our state, UW–Madison's College of Letters and

Science grads are scholars that will have a national impact. With an extensive knowledge of the issues facing their communities, some of them may go on to continue the work of the organizers and activists before them. Their achievements and aspirations are a testament to Chicano students and the community that supported them.

ACKNOWLEDGMENTS

This book is dedicated to Mexican families, including my grandparents Teofilo and Maria, who in 1906 crossed the Rio Bravo from the Mexican border state of Coahuila to Texas when Anglo land-speculating colonizers found artesian water at the turn of the century. With few tools but mule-pulled plows, picks, and shovels, they constructed in the area's semiarid but fertile lands elaborate systems of earthen irrigation to spread this precious resource to tens of thousands of acres in south central Texas and convert it to a Winter Garden, as the four Texas counties became known.

These accounts were written:

In recognition of the resilience shown by the majority Mexican American settlers and their families who sustained their fundamental sense of community in spite of being systematically deprived by the Anglo land-speculating colonizers of access to civic government, public education for their children, and political participation due to poll taxes.

In appreciation of the founders who provided the second generation of our community in Crystal City, Texas, a viable means to sustain the segregated barrios through a dues-paying, self-help membership organization guided by maintaining the final resting place El Panteon Benito Juarez for their loved ones. Members maintained the fundamental values of benevolence and self-help and later built offices to meet and a plaza to celebrate the fiestas patrias, el Cinco de Mayo and el 16. With the support of the mutualistas, in the early 1960s, Mexican workers agreed to be represented by the Teamsters Union at the Del Monte canning company. Later, together, they organized a community-wide initiative to pay Texas poll taxes of $1.75 per voter and end the forty-year domination by the minority Anglos of Crystal City.

In recognition of the families who, in spite of suffering the dislocation of the Great Depression and having to journey near and far to feed their families, never lost their sense of community. This generation of Texas migrants, including my parents Manuel and Argentina Salas, were drawn to the fertile lands west of Wisconsin's Kettle Moraine for the cultivating of sugar beets and other vegetables for processing and canning. By the early 1960s, more than one hundred thousand migrant seasonal workers journeyed to the Great Lakes region, including more than fifteen thousand to Wisconsin. They converted the agricultural household economy to a national powerhouse, providing fresh and canned fruits and vegetables for the emerging industrial urban centers growing in the Midwest.

In gratitude for the unity of migrant seasonal workers who came together to found Obreros Unidos, a farmworkers union that would demand, first of all, the dignity of work that was absent in the experience of the fifteen thousand migrant workers who journeyed yearly to Wisconsin. They called themselves *Obreros* rather than *campesinos*, as many California migrants referred to themselves, or *trabajadores*, a common Spanish translation of workers. They were obreros and they produced *obras*. They cultivated, harvested, and produced something of value.

In dedication to Wisconsin migrant workers who initiated a five-year effort in August 1966 by organizing a march to protest the lack of enforcement of Wisconsin statutes and administrative codes. That fall they organized the first Wisconsin strike by migrant workers against a local potato processing plant and the following year organized Libby's five hundred cucumber harvesters. When the Wisconsin labor board ordered a union certification election, the farmworkers voted 405–8 in August 1967 in favor of the union. The following year, in the summer of 1968, the union organized walkouts in Libby's locations in three Wisconsin communities to force Libby's to negotiate, to no avail.

In recognition of how the Wisconsin farmworkers movement followed the precepts of their ancestors who established mutual aid societies along the Texas Borderland by establishing offices in Wisconsin for worker meetings, organizing free legal services for members, publishing a union newspaper *La Voz Mexicana*, and providing a gasoline coop for members. Obreros Unidos's strategy of organizing the whole family in migrant labor camps allowed women and youth to assume active roles and leadership positions in the union. Organizers later pursued the same organizational initiatives among Latino families in Milwaukee's Latino barrio.

In admiration of the transnational links between Wisconsin and the south Texas political revolt and California grape boycott. Obreros Unidos located offices at El Centro Hispano in the heart of Milwaukee's Latino community in Walker Point neighborhood. Union organizers supported migrants' claims of employment discrimination and lack of representation on the UMOS board, leading to coalitions of Latinos across all major educational, social service, and employment and training agencies serving the near south side of Milwaukee. Most significantly, the Latino coalition supported the intersection of the Wisconsin farmworkers movement with the Black civil rights movement, which had been demanding an open housing ordinance, desegregation of public schools, and an end to employment discrimination.

In recognition of how Milwaukee's Black civil rights leaders supported the California grape boycott and together with the Latino community coalesced to protest the Wisconsin legislature's dismantling of safety nets for the indigent. Minority communities supported the Welfare Mothers' March on Madison and occupation of the Wisconsin Assembly Chambers.

Most importantly, in acknowledgment of the courageous and resilient multiyear Latino community challenge of improving access to the University of Wisconsin–Milwaukee, the establishment of the Spanish Speaking Outreach Institute (Roberto Hernandez Center), and the decade-long struggle of Chican@ students to establish the Chican@/Latin@ Studies Program at UW–Madison that celebrated their lived reality and prepared them for careers and professions of their choice.

INDEX

Locators in *italics* indicate illustrations

ABOUT THE AUTHOR

PHOTO BY GARY PORTER

Jesus Salas is a third-generation Mexican American whose family and neighbors first came to Wisconsin in the early 1940s as migrant workers. He cofounded Obreros Unidos and organized numerous protests, including an eighty-mile march in 1966 from Wautoma to Madison to raise awareness of the conditions in which laborers lived and worked, and assisted with César Chávez's national grape boycott. In 1969 Salas became the first Latino CEO of United Migrant Opportunity Services. He also contributed to efforts create the Spanish Speaking Outreach Institute at UW–Milwaukee and the Chican@/Latin@ Studies Program at UW–Madison.

After receiving his bachelor's degree from UW–Milwaukee's School of Education in 1971 and master's degree in political science from UW–Madison in 1985, Salas taught bilingual courses at Milwaukee Area Technical College for two decades. He was also a lecturer at UW–Madison and UW–Milwaukee before being appointed to the University of Wisconsin System Board of Regents. Salas lives in Milwaukee, where he continues to be active in Latino community organizations.